Charismatic Renewal and Pentecostalism

Charismatic Renewal and Pentecostalism

The Renewal of the Nigerian Catholic Church

Isidore Iwejuo Nkwocha, CSSp

FOREWORD BY
Elochukwu Uzukwu, CSSp

WIPF & STOCK · Eugene, Oregon

CHARISMATIC RENEWAL AND PENTECOSTALISM
The Renewal of the Nigerian Catholic Church

Copyright © 2021 Isidore Iwejuo Nkwocha, CSSp. All rights reserved. Except for brief quotations in critical publications or reviews, no part of this book may be reproduced in any manner without prior written permission from the publisher. Write: Permissions, Wipf and Stock Publishers, 199 W. 8th Ave., Suite 3, Eugene, OR 97401.

Wipf & Stock
An Imprint of Wipf and Stock Publishers
199 W. 8th Ave., Suite 3
Eugene, OR 97401

www.wipfandstock.com

PAPERBACK ISBN: 978-1-6667-1438-8
HARDCOVER ISBN: 978-1-6667-1439-5
EBOOK ISBN: 978-1-6667-1440-1

09/17/21

This work is dedicated to Chukwu Okike Abiama the God of my ancestors and through him to my late parents Nwanna Celestine Nkwocha and Ahụrụchioke Celine Nkwocha and their children and descendants.

Contents

Foreword by Elochukwu Uzukwu | ix
Acknowledgement | xiii
Abbreviations | xiv

Introduction | 1

CHAPTER 1: Charismatic and Pentecostal Theology of the Holy Spirit | 11

CHAPTER 2: Charismatic and Pentecostal Ecclesiology | 53

CHAPTER 3: Charismatic and Pentecostal Theology of Worship | 87

CHAPTER 4: Charismatic Renewal and Pentecostalism within the Context of Nigerian Worldview | 127

CHAPTER 5: Charismatic Renewal and Pentecostalism: The Renewal of the Nigerian Catholic Church | 181

Conclusion and Recommendations | 218

Bibliography | 223

Foreword

PENTECOSTALISM IS THE FASTEST growing movement in African Christianity. This is the common opinion of scholars of Christianity in Africa. On the other hand, the Charismatic Renewal movement is admittedly the most popular way of encountering God-in-the-Spirit in Catholicism. The clerically controlled Catholic Church in Nigeria, and in Africa, is gradually welcoming this pattern of Catholicism that is lay-driven. Despite the claim made by some scholars that the influence of the charismatic renewal movement may be on the "decline" in African Catholicism, Ludovic Lado should know,[1] its popularity, its successful adaptation and adoption of Pentecostal worship patterns is not underestimated. Iwejuo Nkwocha carefully describes and defends the impact of the charismatic-Pentecostal patterns in Catholic communities. Indeed, in *Charismatic Renewal and Pentecostalism,* Nkwocha stresses, without equivocation, the "change" in the practice of Catholicism, in Nigeria, generated by the movement: the "Charismatic Renewal in the Nigerian Catholic church" is "an essential part of the changing face of the Catholic church in Nigeria." This assertion is convincingly argued with supporting evidence in this book. Pastors, adepts of the Pentecostal and charismatic movement, students, and scholars will benefit from the fruits of this research.

Nkwocha describes, for the benefit of the general reader, the many approaches to the study of the experience of the Holy Spirit active in the Churches. He does not tarry only on the doctrinal positions on the Holy

---

1. See his "The Catholic Charismatic Renewal as Ecumenical and intercultural experiment in Africa", in Stan Chu Ilo, ed. *Pentecostalism, Catholicism, and the spirit in the world*, Studies in World Catholicism (Eugene, Oregon: Cascade Books, 2019), 208; 192-210. See also Lado's earlier work, Ludovic Lado, *Catholic Pentecostalism and the paradoxes of Africanization : processes of localization in a Catholic Charismatic movement in Cameroon* (Leiden ; Boston: Brill, 2009).

Spirit as presented in mainline Catholic and Protestant manuals, distinct from the experiential model that dominates Pentecostalism and the Charismatic movement. Rather, he opens a broad window for the reader to delve into the pastorally attractive experiential and praxis-oriented patterns of life-in-the-Holy-Spirit. In this way, he successfully draws attention to the therapeutically effective impact of the Spirit in the lives of individual Christians. In the Nigerian Church life, the attraction of the praxis-dominated life in the Spirit is displayed in exuberant liturgy, person-focused pastoral ministry, the ubiquitous healing ministry, and in the mission of the church-community. Nigerian Catholics, Nigerian Christians, laity and clergy alike, participate in, to be renewed by, the Spirit in daily life.

Charismatic Renewal and Pentecostalism, in its broadest and daring scope, addresses a subject of salience to the worldwide expression of the Christian faith, and, of course, the faith of African Christians. It is the fruit of a painstaking and carefully researched PhD dissertation, successfully defended in Duquesne University, in 2019. Nkwocha ensures the worldwide Christian relevance of his work by attentiveness to the historical and theological pertinence of his argument. This book is deeply rooted in the sources of historical Christianity, the Bible, Patristic theology, history, and the contemporary experience of *Spirit* in world Christianity. Nkwocha's grasp of the literature is stunning. He uses the best resources in the historical study of the theology of the Holy Spirit and calls to the tribunal the most knowledgeable scholars in the comparative theological conversation on *Spirit* across the religions, and on the Holy Spirit in Christianity. He successfully provides a guideline for the student of Pentecostalism and Charismatic movement to evaluate and benefit from the historical, global and local developments. His attempt to connect the present experience of the Nigerian church to the historical and worldwide reach of Pentecostalism and Charismatic movement is noteworthy. Next, the claim he makes, and the effort to provide proofs, of the interconnection between the theology and praxes of Pentecostalism and the Charismatic movement with the *spirit-embedded* Nigerian indigenous religions, a claim that Pentecostalism and the Charismatic movements would reject, is critically and wisely presented.

The centrality of the gifts of the Holy Spirit in the Pentecostal and Charismatic practice is acknowledged and strongly stressed. What makes the contribution of Nkwocha very interesting, and, perhaps, more challenging pastorally and theologically, what possibly could make his work enduring in its effectiveness is the bold positioning of the key assumptions and methodology of Pentecostalism and Charismatic renewal at the heart of Catholic ecclesial renewal. The assumptions and methodology, he proposes, must be the cardinal drivers of the renewal, if not the full reform, of the church. Without idealizing the assumptions of Pentecostal and charismatic theology that must always be open to ongoing renewal, Nkwocha's book strongly suggests that the reform and renewal of the mainline Churches, precisely of the Catholic Church in Nigeria, must truly come from the margin. In other words, reform and renewal must come from the pattern of the praxis-oriented theologies of Pentecostalism and the Charismatic movement.

That the Churches emerged in the outpouring of the Holy Spirit at Pentecost, and that members are gifted with charisms of the Holy Spirit, all Pentecostals and Charismatic renewal movements and the mainline Churches agree. However, that the renewal of individual spiritual life, sought by the members of the charismatic movement, like their Pentecostal fellowship namesakes, should be positioned as the central theological, pastoral and missionary strategy is admittedly new. If embraced by the Nigerian church, the strategy will be novel; and grudgingly so. However, the fundamental claim and proposal of this book is that all churches, and particularly Catholic churches in Nigeria, will do well to learn from the margin, from the Pentecostal and Charismatic movement, the canons of renewing the church.

This bold project has come at a good time, at the right time. *Charismatic Renewal and Pentecostalism* that seeks for the *Renewal of the Nigerian Catholic Church*, is a treasure for pastors, students, researchers and the ordinary reader. The author tries to reduce the hesitation to renewal by stressing that, in the Nigerian church the praxis-oriented theology, liturgical performance, style of preaching, and mission focus of Pentecostalism and the charismatic movement are already well received. Many pastors already adopt this methodology. What remains is to normalize the method.

It is ironical that like the Catholic Church in many parts of Africa, despite the impact of the second Vatican Council, the Nigerian Catholic hierarchy, more often than not, only tolerates the charismatic renewal movement. It is still considered marginal to the task of building a relevant church. To bring to the center of pastoral performance the fundamental concerns of the movement, as Nkwocha suggests, could be the effective way of integrating, within the Nigerian Church, the "reform and renewal" initiated by the second Vatican Council. This is not an unusual or radical proposal. Rejoicing with the church in Italy, in 1998, at the fruits of the work of the Spirit in the life of the faithful, through the charismatic renewal, Pope (Saint) John Paul II connected the movement to the Vatican II Council. He declared, "The Catholic charismatic movement is one of the many fruits of the Second Vatican Council, which, like a new Pentecost, led to an extraordinary flourishing in the Church's life of groups and movements particularly sensitive to the action of the Spirit."[2]

Reading through this book helps one to advance in the knowledge and admiration of the amazing power and work of the Spirit, whose gifts become manifest in the individual life of Christians and in the Christian community. How can we not give thanks for the precious spiritual fruits that the *Renewal* has produced in the life of the Church and in the lives of so many people?

Elochukwu Uzukwu, C.S.Sp.
Professor of Theology, Duquesne University

---

2. https://www.vatican.va/content/john-paul-ii/en/speeches/1998/april/documents/hf_jp-ii_spe_19980404_spirito-santo.html [accessed September 11 2021]

Acknowledgement

I sincerely thank God the Father, who in Jesus Christ sustained me throughout this project through his empowering presence, the Holy Spirit. My heartfelt appreciation goes to professor Elochukwu Eugene Uzukwu, the human agent the Holy Spirit used to guide me through. His academic resilience, dedication, skills, and acumen made this work what it is today. Maureen O'Brien, PhD, and Bogdan Bucur, PhD, are great people. I thank them for the pains and time they took to read the work and made wonderful inputs. I'm indebted to the Rev. Gaea Thompson who patiently proofread the work, making sure that all grammatical errors were dictated and corrected. I honestly thank my Spiritan family for support and encouragement. Lastly, I'm grateful to Chizobam Tonia Nwachukwu. Her academic advice, moral support, and prayers were very helpful.

Abbreviations

AIC   African Initiated Church; also called African Independent Church; and even African Initiatives in Christianity (plural AICs)

ATR   African Traditional Religion

ITR   Igbo Traditional Religion

CSSp   Congregation of the Holy Spirit (Spiritans)

Introduction

Statement of the Problem and Scope of Study

THIS WORK IS USING charismatic and Pentecostal theology and praxes to argue for the renewal of the Nigerian Catholic Church. Pentecostalism started at the beginning of the twentieth century with its roots in the holiness movement and revivalism that took place in America during the nineteenth century. This beginning led to the formation of Pentecostal churches as we have them today.[1] The charismatic renewal started in the middle of the twentieth century. This is the time, Pentecostal doctrines spread into the mainline Protestant and Catholic Churches.

Unlike the Pentecostals who separated and formed Pentecostal churches, charismatics remained with their mainline churches. Pentecostals and charismatics believe in the doctrine of tongues. However, charismatics do not place as much emphasis on this doctrine as Pentecostals do. While Pentecostals see it as initial sign of Spirit Baptism, charismatics believe that one can receive the baptism and not speak in tongues. Recently, many Pentecostals as Anthony Thiselton pointed out, have come to accept the position of charismatics on this. According to him most of them even go as far as admitting that it may also be a "learned behavior."[2]

Despite these differences between Pentecostals and charismatics, they both believe that the Spirit Baptism which Jesus bestowed on his disciples "on the first Pentecost Day is meant to be bestowed on all Christians."[3] They also believe that the charismatic manifestations that were present after Pentecost as Luke/Acts narrated are meant to continue and "to be experienced

---

1. Walsh, *Key to Charismatic Renewal*, 5.
2. Thiselton, *Holy Spirit*, 489.
3. Walsh, *Key to Charismatic Renewal*, 5.

and used by every Christian."[4] In practice, they both lay emphasis on private and group prayer, on "faith in the Lordship of Jesus, and the attempt to live according to gospel maxims."[5]

It is these aspects of the theology which charismatics and Pentecostals hold in common, which is more praxis-oriented and experiential, that bring charismatic renewal and Pentecostalism together in this work. Charismatics and Pentecostals according to Melissa Archer see worship as "a *felt* experience of being in the presence of God—an experience made possible by the Spirit."[6] Charismatics and Pentecostals like the mainline churches, therefore, believe that the Holy Spirit is the enabling Spirit who empowers the chosen people of God for the fulfilling of God's purpose. Still, like the mainline churches they believe that the giving and reception of the Holy Spirit has immediate and extended effects as was the case with the early Christians. Unlike the mainline churches however, they embark on a theology that is more praxis-oriented and experiential. This is evident in their style of prayer, preaching, healing, and lively and joyous expressive ways of worship.[7]

In fact, the attraction of charismatic renewal and Pentecostalism in Nigeria is traced to indigenous worldview of Nigerians and their character is derived from the mode of response Nigerians have given to Christianity at least since the nineteenth century.[8] No doubt, Nigerian political and social characters played a vital role in shaping their message and structures of meaning.[9] Charismatic and Pentecostal theology and praxes are, therefore, interpreted within the Nigerian context as an expansion and reinvention of indigenous religious experience of God, deities, spirits, and ancestors into the Christian life.[10]

However, the style of prayer, preaching, healing, and lively and joyous and expressive ways of worship of the charismatic and Pentecostal movements has been under constant attack and criticisms by some Nigerian theologians. The more conservative group, which is dominated by some Catholic theologians, is concerned that the traditional style of prayer, preaching, healing, and worship of the Catholic Church is gravely truncated and abused by members of the Catholic charismatic renewal. These theologians are, therefore, worried

4. Walsh, *Key to Charismatic Renewal*, 6.
5. Walsh, *Key to Charismatic Renewal*, 6.
6. Archer, "Worship," 115.
7. Achunike, *Influence*, 61.
8. Wariboko, *Nigerian Pentecostalism*, 18.
9. Wariboko, *Nigerian Pentecostalism*, 18.
10. Uzukwu, *God, Spirit and Human Wholeness*, 176.

that the Catholic Church is losing its orthodoxy. Some of them, therefore, see the Movements as a phenomenal disorder;[11] Christianity without memory[12] dressed in borrowed robes.[13]

Despite the attacks and criticisms, the Movements have continued to flourish. For instance, the style of prayer, preaching, healing, and worship of Catholic charismatic renewal of Nigeria has continued to influence Catholic liturgy in Nigeria especially in parishes controlled by priests who are members of the renewal.

Anthropologist Devaka Premawardhana in his ethnographic study of Pentecostalism among the Makhuwa people of northern Mozambique avers that Pentecostalism in this part of the world is not flourishing as people move in and out as in circular migration. He attributes this failure partly to the fact that Makhuwa people see Pentecostalism as one potential path among many like urban migration and other Makhuwa people's ways of life characterized by circular mobility in their search for abundant life.[14] This is an interesting and revealing study. For, it shows that no matter how flourishing and explosive Pentecostalism may appear, it doesn't succeed in entirely capturing the daily workings of real-life experiences. As interesting and revealing as Premawardhana's study is, it is beyond the scope of this work to focus on this religious fluidity and circular mobility in the case of Pentecostalism and charismatic renewal in Nigeria. Rather, this work recognizes charismatic renewal in the Nigerian Catholic Church as an essential part of the changing face of the Catholic Church in Nigeria. It maintains that the Holy Spirit is a *sine qua non* in the life of the church and in all Christian life and experience; and that the experiential and praxis-oriented theology of the charismatic renewal and Pentecostalism cannot be ignored when it comes to the realization of the potentials of a Spirit-animated church.

This work is, therefore, using charismatic and Pentecostal theology and praxes to argue for the renewal of the Nigerian Catholic Church. It avers that the praxis-oriented and experiential theology of charismatics and Pentecostals, which characterize them as Spirit-filled groups and churches are enabling the Nigerian Catholic Church to realize the potentials of a Spirit-driven church. It upholds that the Nigeria Catholic Church through the Nigerian Catholic charismatic renewal, which is an indispensable part of the changing face of the Catholic Church in Nigeria, has wittingly or unwittingly begun the renewal of her pneumatological,

---

11. Allam, "Pentecostalism," 97.
12. Akinwole, "Christianity without Memory," 111.
13. Ayegboyin, "Dressed in Borrowed Robes," 70.
14. Premawardhana, *Faith in Flux*, 1–173.

ecclesiological, and liturgical doctrines and practices[15] in accord with those of a truly Spirit-animated church.

Though there are many ethnic groups in Nigeria with nuances in culture, this study does not focus on any specific ethnic group. Rather, it considers Nigeria as sharing in the broader West African religiosity. In this broader sense, charismatic renewal and Pentecostalism are seen within the context of Nigerian worldview as a Nigerian religion that flows from Nigerian roots and addresses Nigerian issues and realities.

The study is limited to four areas of interest: (1) The charismatic and Pentecostal theology of the Holy Spirit, (2) charismatic and Pentecostal ecclesiology, (3) charismatic and Pentecostal theology of worship, and (4) charismatic renewal and Pentecostalism within the context of Nigerian worldview. These are used as dialogue partners in the final chapter, charismatic renewal and Pentecostalism: the renewal of the Nigerian Catholic Church, to argue for the renewal of the Nigerian Catholic Church's pneumatology, ecclesiology, and liturgy.

The work avers that the charismatic and Pentecostal experiential encounter and praxis-oriented theology particularly within the Nigerian context is enabling the Nigerian Catholic Church to realize the potentials of a Spirit-directed church. This, however, does not mean that their theology and praxis are perfect and beyond renewal.

In studying the areas, attention is paid only to what is relevant to the topic of this project. A catalogue of quality academic materials is provided in the bibliography for readers who are interested in reading in much detail the areas studied.

Contribution and Methodology

Numerous of scholarly works on charismatic renewal and Pentecostalism abound. Some of them dwell either on their phenomenological, sociological, and theological or religious dimensions, while others focus on their anthropological or historiographic trends. Some works have these dimensions combined. However, few works exist that focus on their ecclesiological dimension. Fewer still use charismatic and Pentecostal theology as foundation for the renewal of the church. This work's use of charismatic and Pentecostal theology and praxes to argue for the renewal of the Nigerian Catholic Church's pneumatological, ecclesiological, and liturgical beliefs and praxes

---

15. Praxis or practice is not used here in the broad sense that Gerben Heitink uses it in his *Practical Theology: History, Theory, Action Domains*. Rather, it is used in its simple sense as the opposite of theory.

is, therefore, its most unique contribution to pneumatology, ecclesiology, worship, and to systematic theology in general.

It is Stephen B. Bevans's synthetic model methodology that will be used in this work. In his models of contextual theology, he identifies six models of contextual theology. The models include the "anthropological" model, which places precise accent on listening to culture; the "translation" model, which emphasizes the message of the Gospel and the conservation of church tradition; and the "'praxis' model which sees as a primary *locus theologicus* the phenomena of social change, particularly the change by a struggle for justice."[16] Others are the "synthetic" model which tries to mediate the above three by engagement of an "analogical imagination"; the "semiotic" model which uses semiotic cultural analysis to listen to a culture; and the "transcendental" model which, as a meta-model, lays emphasis "not on theological content but on subjective authenticity within theological activity."[17]

The synthetic model, as its name indicates, synthesizes the insights of the anthropological, the translation, and the praxis models while remaining open to the "thought, values and philosophies of other contexts."[18] The goal of the synthetic model according to Bevans is to achieve "genuine dialogue or conversation between various positions which are true in themselves, but which become falsified if understood in isolation or taken too far alone."[19] This being the case, the synthetic model could be understood in Hegelian sense of the dialectic and could even be referred to be dialectical in nature. The synthetic model takes into cognizance the fact that a particular context or culture consists of rudiments or elements that are unique to it and the elements that it shares with others. For the synthetic model, it is not just cultural uniqueness that makes up cultural identity. Hence, it maintains that to develop a cultural identity one must emphasize what is unique to a culture while at the same time "drawing on what is common to cultures and contexts."[20] The fundamental procedure of this model of contextual theology can be pictured as multi-directional which allows for dialectic and dialogue.

No fieldwork is employed in this book—only the library and, occasionally, web materials are used.

---

16. Bevans, "Models of Contextual Theology," 186.
17. Bevans, "Models of Contextual Theology," 186.
18. Bevans, "Models of Contextual Theology," 194.
19. Bevans, "Models of Contextual Theology," 194.
20. Bevans, "Models of Contextual Theology," 194.

Chapter Synopsis

In the first three chapters, the charismatic and Pentecostal pneumatology, ecclesiology, and liturgy are synthesized respectively, bringing out their uniqueness and relating them to the pneumatology, ecclesiology, and liturgy of especially the mainline churches and the early Christians where applicable. These chapters also portray how this uniqueness plays out in the context of the Nigerian charismatic and Pentecostal pneumatological, ecclesiological, and liturgical doctrines and practices as preparation to use them as dialogue partners in the final chapter. The first four chapters are used in dialogue in the final chapter to argue for the renewal of the Nigerian Catholic Church's pneumatological, ecclesiological, and liturgical doctrines and practices.

Chapter 1, Charismatic and Pentecostal Theology of the Holy Spirit shows that the Pneumatology of Charismatics and Pentecostals is heavily influenced by Luke/Acts narrative of how witness to Jesus was borne by the early Christians. According to this narrative, the Holy Spirit animates the church, the individual members of the church, and is in fact, the principal figure in the mission of witnessing to Jesus. Charismatics and Pentecostals follow this principle. This is evident in the emphasis they lay on Spirit Baptism.

While not denying the importance of the other Persons of the Trinity, Pentecostals attach much importance to the Holy Spirit particularly to "his experiential and empowering dimensions."[21] They believe it is the Holy Spirit, who empowers believers, establishes Christian communities, transforms and guides believers, and inspires charismata in the church.[22] Indeed, the charismatic and Pentecostal experiential and praxis-oriented theology offers charismatics and Pentecostals the opportunity to understand and express the marvels of God in their own language as led by the Holy Spirit. They demonstrate this in their style of prayer, preaching, healing, and lively and joyous and expressive ways of worship in the understanding that the Holy Spirit is the soul of the church. The Nigerian charismatics and Pentecostals live out this experiential and praxis-oriented pneumatology as evident in the transferring of the roles of deities, spirits, and ancestors to God's empowering presence, the Holy Spirit, thereby placing the Holy Spirit at the vanguard of their theology. This contrasts in praxis with the pneumatology of the Catholic Church which Congar accuses of often misinterpreting the

---

21. Warrington, *Pentecostal Theology*, 46.
22. Warrington, *Pentecostal Theology*, 56–95.

signs of the times and remaining "attached to formal practices and to fixed structures of power."[23]

In fact, the teachings on the Holy Spirit in the New Testament Scriptures and through the centuries show that there is not much difference, if any, between these teachings which of course are the teachings of the mainline churches and the charismatic and Pentecostal theological and doctrinal understanding of the Holy Spirit. The fundamental difference is on the charismatic and Pentecostal emphasis on experiential encounter of the Holy Spirit. This experiential and praxis-oriented pneumatology of charismatics and Pentecostals influences their ecclesiological beliefs and practices.

Chapter 2, The Charismatic and Pentecostal Ecclesiology, demonstrates this. It avers that the charismatic and Pentecostal ecclesiology, like their pneumatology, is experiential and praxis-oriented. Having experience of God's immediate presence, being able to reflect God's nature "in areas such as unity and mission"; being transformed by God and being used "in the transformation of others" are features that underscore Pentecostal ecclesiology.[24]

The emphatic statement of the author of Luke/Acts in Acts 1:8, "You shall receive power when the Holy Spirit has come upon you, and you shall be my witnesses in Jerusalem, and all Judea and Samaria, and to the ends of the earth," is a crucial statement for the audience and readers of this author just as it is for charismatics and Pentecostals. It shows that "the good news or gospel concerns not only what God has done in Jesus but also what He has done in the spirit."[25] For Luke/Acts, the Spirit of God that inspired and moved the prophets of Israel is visibly active in a prophetic way at the commencement of the story of Jesus (Luke 1:15, 35, 41, 67, 80; 2:25–27) and at the start of the church (Acts 1:8, 16; 2:4, 17). Charismatics and Pentecostals believe that this same Spirit should be conspicuously active in a prophetic way in their witnessing.

Brown avers that "the distinguishing feature of Lukan ecclesiology is the overshadowing presence of *the Spirit*."[26] It is this same overshadowing presence of the Holy Spirit that is the uniqueness of the charismatic and Pentecostal ecclesiology. Brown points out that the interest of Luke is not in the characters or the men in his story as such, "but in them as vehicles of the spirit, bearing witness to Christ in Jerusalem, Judea, Samaria, and to the ends

---

23. Congar, *I Believe*, 57.
24. Warrington, *Pentecostal Theology*, 132.
25. Brown, *Churches the Apostles Left Behind*, 63.
26. Brown, *Churches the Apostles Left Behind*, 65.

of the earth."[27] For Luke, the principal actor is the Holy Spirit. Charismatics and Pentecostals have no single doubt about this. They believe that the Bible describes the church as the community of the Holy Spirit.[28]

The charismatic and Pentecostal ecclesiology differs from the ecclesiology of the mainline churches, particularly the Catholic Church, in the sense that while the ecclesiology of the mainline churches is Christocentric, the experiential and praxis-oriented nature of the charismatic and Pentecostal ecclesiology makes it pneumatocentric. This pneumatocentric ecclesiology is played out in a palpable way among the Nigerian charismatics and Pentecostals as they truly demonstrate in praxis that they are groups and churches led and animated by God's empowering presence, through the Holy Spirit, to be a redeemed, sanctified, healed, and redeeming, sanctifying, and healing presence of God among God's people through the power of the Holy Spirit.

Chapter 3, Charismatic and Pentecostal Theology of Worship reveals that the uniqueness of the charismatic and Pentecostal worship is centered on the fact that charismatics and Pentecostals understand worship as "a *felt* experience of being in the presence of God—an experience made possible by the Spirit."[29] This understanding of worship is evident in their style of prayer, preaching, healing, and lively and joyous expressive ways of worship.

Jacqueline Grey avers that early Pentecostal perceptions of worship stress an affective engagement with the Spirit.[30] The early Pentecostals according to her critiqued and abandoned formal liturgies which they perceived as empty worship in preference to what they see as spontaneous "and therefore (supposedly) sincere expressions of worship."[31] Contemporary Pentecostals she avers hold the same view of worship with their predecessors, as what matters to them in worship is "the need for personal and dynamic encounter with God—to enter the throne room and meet with the Holy Spirit."[32] In worship therefore, charismatics and Pentecostals allow themselves to be led by the Holy Spirit into the "throne room" where they encounter God.

Charismatics' and Pentecostals' style of worship involves pressing prayer, regular testimonies, excessive praise, manifestations of hope of answered prayers, and the reenactment of the Christian foundation story. The

27. Brown, *Churches the Apostles Left Behind*, 66.
28. Williams, *Renewal Theology*, 39–84.
29. Archer, "Worship," 115.
30. Grey, "Book of Isaiah," 37.
31. Grey, "Book of Isaiah," 37.
32. Grey, "Book of Isaiah," 38.

charismatic and Pentecostal worship is an encounter and a communion with the Spirit and with God's people through which the worshipers are led into God's glory, the fullness of which is to be realized eschatologically.[33]

The charismatic and Pentecostal experiential and praxis-oriented liturgy plays out in a concrete manner among the Nigerian charismatics and Pentecostals as evident in their spontaneous, joyful, Spirit-oriented, and lively expressions of worship; and in their appropriation of the Nigerian traditional religious expressions which makes their liturgical religious gestures to be homegrown. This contrasts with the liturgy of the Catholic Church which is fixed and priest-oriented.

Chapter 4, Charismatic Renewal and Pentecostalism within the Context of Nigerian Worldview, synthesizes the religious worldview of the African people, exposing its uniqueness, and what the charismatic and Pentecostal religious worldview, particularly, within the African context shares with the African traditional religious worldview. It shows that charismatic renewal and Pentecostalism are interpreted within the context of African worldview as an African religion that flows from African roots and addresses African issues and realities. Its experiential and praxis-oriented theology of encounter is interpreted to harmonize with the African religious experience of God, deities, spirits, and ancestors.

Although the Hebrew Scriptures and African traditional religious approaches to divinities take different trajectories, divinities as God's functionaries and intermediaries between humans and the Supreme Being, and as manifestations of God, is likened to what Benjamin D. Sommer refers to as the "Bodies of God" in the world of Ancient Israel.

The style of prayer, preaching, healing, and lively and joyous and expressive ways of worship of the charismatic renewal and Pentecostalism of Nigeria resonates with the Nigerian style of worship which emanates from the Nigerian worldview. In this way, charismatic renewal and Pentecostalism within the Nigerian context reflect continuity with the Nigerian traditional religious worldview, which makes them attractive to the Nigerian people. On the other hand, the mainline churches, particularly the Catholic Church, have continued to show in practice that they are alien to the Nigerian people. The charismatic and Pentecostal theology and praxis within the Nigerian context, therefore, enables the Nigerian Catholic Church to actualize the potentials of a Spirit-led church to be relevant in Nigerian Christianity by a renewal of her pneumatology, ecclesiology, and liturgy.

The final chapter, Charismatic Renewal and Pentecostalism: The Renewal of the Nigerian Catholic Church, uses the work of Wolfgang Vondey

---

33. Alexander, "'Singing Heavenly Music,'" 220.

Beyond Pentecostalism: The Crisis of Global Christianity and the Renewal of the Theological Agenda as a template to lay out the argument that charismatic renewal and Pentecostalism are Spirit-animated groups and churches that fall outside what is considered central to the dominant worldview, hence, belonging to the margins of Christianity the home of renewal. Being the home of renewal, the chapter avers that the experiential and praxis-oriented pneumatology, ecclesiology, and liturgy of charismatics and Pentecostals, particularly within the Nigerian context, are inspiring and enabling the Nigerian Catholic Church to realize the potentials of a Spirit-directed church. This is made possible by the experiential and praxis-oriented pneumatology, ecclesiology, and liturgy of the Catholic charismatic renewal in the Nigerian Catholic Church which, no doubt, is an essential part of the changing face of the Catholic Church in Nigeria.

The work recognizes that some aspects of the charismatic and Pentecostal theology and praxis especially within the Nigerian environment need renewal. Emphasis is laid on the heightened dualism and "paranoid" preoccupation with demonic forces that have led to a wrongful demonization of Nigerian and indeed, West African deities and ancestors; and the heightened and exaggerated prophetic visions and messages that are causing irreparable hatred and division in many families in Nigeria and beyond.

Despite this inadequacy, the work maintains that more than anything else, charismatic renewal and Pentecostalism, particularly, within the Nigerian context are enabling the Catholic Church in Nigeria to realize the potentials of a Spirit-driven church. Such realization, consequently, implies a renewal of her pneumatology, ecclesiology, and liturgy in line with those of a Spirit-filled church. The work is finally concluded with some recommendations to the Nigerian Catholic Church with the hope that if well-taken, it would greatly help her to realize the potentials of a Spirit-animated, Spirit-directed, and Spirit-filled church.

CHAPTER 1

Charismatic and Pentecostal Theology of the Holy Spirit

CHARISMATIC AND PENTECOSTAL THEOLOGY in general is praxis-oriented and experiential. According to Warrington, "Pentecostals have always emphasized experiential Christianity rather than doctrinal confession. Rather than describe or explain doctrines in the mode of systematic or dogmatic theologians associated with the seminary and scholar, they typically explore them in the biblical narrative and by the testimony of those affected by them."[1]

In their theology, charismatics and Pentecostals pay less attention to the speculative interpretations of their doctrinal beliefs. Rather than spend time thinking theologically, they prefer to live out their theology practically unlike their non-charismatic and Pentecostal counterparts. Warrington captures it in these words: "Pentecostals (traditionally) do not think theologically so much as live out their theology practically."[2] In other words, while Pentecostal theology does not neglect the detailing of Pentecostal beliefs and doctrines, it places more emphasis on discovering these beliefs and doctrines in the milieu of praxis.

Charismatic and Pentecostal theology is therefore a theology of encounter where charismatics and Pentecostals encounter God, the Bible, and the community in a lively and experiential manner. It is not a surprise then that Alan Anderson sees Pentecostalism in the Western world in its early stages as an "ecumenical movement of people claiming a common experience rather than a common doctrine."[3] Walter J. Hollenweger

---

1. Warrington, *Pentecostal Theology*, 15–16.
2. Warrington, *Pentecostal Theology*, 16.
3. Anderson, *Introduction to Pentecostalism*, 60.

expresses in the same vein that "What unites the Pentecostal churches is not a doctrine but a religious experience."[4]

In fact, what is fundamental and at the heart of charismatic renewal and Pentecostalism is not a set of doctrines or rules to be proved and defended against all odds, but "a personal, experiential encounter of the Spirit of God."[5] The members expect "a radical experience of the Spirit, and, in particular, as it relates to their identity as children of God, their perception of God, their worship and service, their mission and evangelism, their reading and application of the Bible and their relationships with other believers."[6]

The experiential knowledge of God both through a rational recognition of his being and via an emotional or expressive appreciation of his character is the goal of charismatics and Pentecostals, which practically differentiates them from other Christian traditions.[7] If other Christian faith traditions perceive revelation as something meant to affect only the mind, charismatics and Pentecostals see it as something intended to affect the mind as well as the emotions. They therefore explore theology not only in a rationalistic context "but also with a readiness to encounter the divine and be impacted by one's discoveries in a way that will enlighten the mind but also transform the life."[8] They believe that these kinds of encounters have antecedents in the Bible. Hence, where an absence of creedal confession and formal ceremony have sometimes appeared in charismatic and Pentecostal spirituality, "there is the presence of experience, often spontaneous, emotional, heartfelt, intensely personal and life-transforming."[9]

For these experiential encounters to take place, charismatics and Pentecostals sometimes allow fluidity in their praxis and thought "as they seek to locate a biblical framework that is sufficiently flexible for their spirituality, a spirituality that is, by definition, dynamic since it is pneumatic."[10] One would have thought that charismatics and Pentecostals would have been perturbed by incomprehensible divine acts experienced and consequently engaged themselves with searching out some theological explanations. But the fact is that they are not unnerved by this.[11] This portrays the height to which charismatics and Pentecostals hold experiential

---

4. Hollenweger, "From Azusa Street," 7.
5. Warrington, *Pentecostal Theology*, 20.
6. Warrington, *Pentecostal Theology*, 20–21.
7. Warrington, *Pentecostal Theology*, 21.
8. Warrington, *Pentecostal Theology*, 21.
9. Warrington, *Pentecostal Theology*, 22.
10. Warrington, *Pentecostal Theology*, 23.
11. Anderson, "Pentecostals Believe," 55–56.

encounter. In fact, "Pentecostals are prepared to accept the dangers of pragmatism rather than miss the opportunity of observing and experiencing a new work of the Spirit."[12]

The theological intellectual knowledge and understanding of God which other Christian faith traditions focus on, is no doubt a noble and necessary act. But for charismatics and Pentecostals, knowing God is synonymous with experiencing God. "They are much more prepared to believe that God is dynamic, not static; complex, even mystifying, but one who desires to be encountered."[13] Charismatics and Pentecostals believe in life-transforming potentials of experiential encounters with God. Because of this, they value experience-based encounters with God more than intellectual knowledge of God. Indeed, they believe that "one experience with God can be more life changing than an encyclopedic knowledge of God."[14] For charismatics and Pentecostals, the Holy Spirit is fundamental in achieving experiential encounter with God, the Bible, and the community. Indeed, a renowned Pentecostal theologian Gordon Fee, describes the Holy Spirit as "the *sine qua non* of all Christian life and experience."[15] Warrington listed some tenets which charismatics and Pentecostals hold about the Holy Spirit of which most are also held by non-charismatics and non-Pentecostals.[16] Here is a summary of some of them. Charismatics and Pentecostals believe that the Holy Spirit is the third person of the Blessed Trinity. He is identified as a separate person in the Godhead. The relational knowledge of God the Father and God the Son is made known to Christians through his indwelling. It is also through his indwelling that Christians are transformed into God's own likeness. Although the Holy Spirit was functional in the lives of the Old Testament people and in the lives of believers before Pentecost, charismatics and Pentecostals see the advent of the Holy Spirit at Pentecost as an enormously significant event.

They believe that "the ministry of the spirit on behalf of and through believers is much more comprehensive after Pentecost than before."[17] For them, the worship of Jesus and belief in him are only possible through the inspiration and guidance of the Holy Spirit. They therefore believe that the Holy Spirit "is a personal, immediate, dynamic and perfect guide. He speaks

---

12. Warrington, *Pentecostal Theology*, 23.
13. Warrington, *Pentecostal Theology*, 25.
14. Warrington, *Pentecostal Theology*, 26.
15. Fee, *Listening to the Spirit*, 37.
16. Warrington, *Pentecostal Theology*, 46–48.
17. Warrington, *Pentecostal Theology*, 47.

and so must be listened to."[18] They believe in the involvement of the Holy Spirit in the salvation of believers, his commitment to set them apart; to affirm them; to proactively transform them ethically and spiritually; to inspire and to empower them, as well as to energize them; to create faith, to motivate sanctification; and to inspire prayer. The Holy Spirit is for charismatics and Pentecostals the source of all charismatic gifts. It is he who inspires and initiates evangelism, preaching, prophecy, and so on. He establishes the church as a body and animates it.[19]

The primacy of an experiential encounter with God over an intellectual knowledge of him, which charismatics and Pentecostals place on their theology in general, applies to their pneumatology in particular. They pay more attention to experiential encounters with the Holy Spirit than to doctrinal definitions and explanations about the Holy Spirit. Veli-Matti Kärkkäinen articulates it well. He says: "Rather than reflecting on the doctrine of the Holy Spirit, they have relied on the supernatural dynamics of the Spirit."[20] The fact that the Holy Spirit is to be encountered experientially is of fundamental importance to charismatics and Pentecostals. It is no surprise then, that Anderson prefers to define Pentecostalism "as a movement concerned primarily with the *experience* of the working of the Holy Spirit."[21] Indeed, for charismatics and Pentecostals the Holy Spirit is more than a creedal belief. Fee seemed to have recognized this and consequently identified the Holy Spirit as "God's empowering presence."[22]

Many if not most charismatics and Pentecostals have had this kind of experiential encounter with the Holy Spirit at one time or another during times of prayer or worship. The encounter, most of the time, results in people falling to the ground in a swoon and manifesting all kinds of behaviors and strange sounds.[23] Charismatics and Pentecostals believe that the experience often leads those concerned closer to God. This phenomenon is what they have come to identify as "Baptism in the Holy Spirit," and to understand their pneumatology, as far as this work is concerned, is to examine how they see this phenomenon.

This chapter, therefore, focuses on charismatic and Pentecostal theology of the Holy Spirit from the point of view of baptism in the Holy Spirit. It explores baptism in the Holy Spirit as empowerment for mission;

18. Warrington, *Pentecostal Theology*, 47.
19. Warrington, *Pentecostal Theology*, 48.
20. Kärkkäinen, "'Truth on Fire,'" 37.
21. Anderson, *Introduction to Pentecostalism*, 14.
22. Fee, *Listening to the Spirit*, 29.
23. Warrington, *Pentecostal Theology*, 49–50.

and the relationship between baptism in the Holy Spirit and the gift of tongues as initial evidence as well as the relationship between baptism in the Holy Spirit and conversion initiation. Where applicable, it will show how this plays out in the lives of the Nigerian charismatics and Pentecostals. The chapter will proceed to consider other views of the Holy Spirit in the New Testament specifically, in the synoptic Gospels, in Acts, and in the Johannine writings as well as key themes in Paul. Using Anthony Thiselton's work, *The Holy Spirit: In Biblical Teaching, Through the Centuries, and Today* it will explore the teachings on the Holy Spirit through the centuries. It will focus specifically on the Apostolic Fathers and the early Christian apologists, and on the ante and post-Nicene Fathers as well as on the medieval period. The study is not going into any details in each of these teachings. It will focus only on what is relevant to this work, the sole aim of which is to exude if there is any fundamental difference between these teachings and those of charismatics and Pentecostals.

Baptism in the Holy Spirit

The pneumatology of charismatics and Pentecostals is heavily influenced by Luke/Acts narrative of how witness to Jesus was borne by the early Christians. The story of Luke/Acts reveals that the event of the Pentecost in Acts chapter 2 marks the beginning of the church. According to this narrative, the Holy Spirit animates the church, the individual members of the church, and is in fact the principal figure in the mission of witnessing to Jesus. Charismatics and Pentecostals follow this principle. They believe that all Christians are meant to be baptized with the same Spirit baptism with which Jesus baptized his disciples on the day of Pentecost. Charismatics and Pentecostals also believe that the charismatic manifestations that were present after Pentecost as Luke/Acts narrated are meant to continue and to be experienced and used by every Christian. It is their belief that the reception of the baptism in the Holy Spirit with its charismatic manifestations is meant to empower believers for mission the same way it empowered the apostles and the early disciples in Luke/Acts narrative.

Baptism in the Holy Spirit and Empowerment for Mission

Charismatics and Pentecostals have a missiological understanding of baptism in the Holy Spirit.[24] They believe that the charismatic experience of

24. Cheung, "Understanding of Spirit-Baptism," 116.

the Holy Spirit or the reception of the baptism in the Holy Spirit empowers believers for mission. Whatever the conundrum for this may be, they anchor their belief and understanding on Lukan narrative "in which the promise foretold by John the Baptist and Jesus can be seen to be fulfilled in the early churches in Acts (Matt. 3. 11 pars.; Acts 1.8; 2.4–13; 10.44–48)."[25] Although James D. G. Dunn does not believe and accept that there is a dichotomy or a separation between the charismatic Spirit and the soteriological Spirit as will be seen later, he agrees that the Spirit for Luke on whom charismatics and Pentecostals anchored their understanding of baptism in the Holy Spirit "is indeed pre-eminently the Spirit of prophecy, the Spirit that inspires speech and witness."[26]

One of the strong proponents of this missiological understanding of baptism in the Holy Spirit is a Pentecostal scholar, Robert P. Menzies. Menzies draws a conclusion from a great redactic work he did on the development of early Christian pneumatology, with special reference to Luke/Acts, that the reception of the Spirit in Acts is for empowerment for mission. He argues "that Luke, influenced by the dominant Jewish perception, consistently portrays the gift of the Spirit as a prophetic endowment which enables its recipient to participate effectively in the mission of God."[27] He insists that early rabbinic tradition as well as the ancient exegetical traditions found in the Targums identifies the Spirit as the fount of prophetic inspiration. He draws a conclusion based on these sources "that the Jews of the pre-Christian era generally regarded the gift of the Spirit as a *donum superadditum* granted to various individuals so that they might fulfill a divinely appointed task."[28] He consequently avers "that Luke not only has a special interest in the Holy Spirit, but also that his understanding of the Spirit is inextricably related to prophetic phenomena."[29]

For example, Lukan allusion to the prophecy of Joel in his Pentecost narrative prompted Menzies to come to the judgement that the goal of the prophetic gift of the Spirit Luke mentioned in Luke 24:49 and Acts 1:8 is to arm the disciples with power for the missiological work ahead.[30] To him, the reception of the Holy Spirit by the Ephesians conveyed the same character as the one received by the Samaritans, Paul, Cornelius and his household, and the disciples of Jesus in Jerusalem on Pentecost day. The sole purpose of this

25. Cheung, "Understanding of Spirit-Baptism," 116.
26. Dunn, "Baptism in the Spirit," 8.
27. Menzies, *Empowered for Witness*, 45.
28. Menzies, *Empowered for Witness*, 102.
29. Menzies, *Empowered for Witness*, 110.
30. Menzies, *Empowered for Witness*, 187.

reception, according to him, is to empower the recipients to effectively carry out the mission of bearing witness to the resurrected Christ.[31] Menzies maintains his position and his missiological understanding of baptism in the Holy Spirit years later, in his article, "Acts 2.17–21: A Paradigm for Pentecost and Mission." In this work he maintains that "a careful analysis of Acts 2.17–21 reveals that Luke has carefully crafted this quotation in order to stress the missiological implications of the Pentecostal outpouring of the Spirit for his church (and by extension, ours)."[32] He argues that Luke, by incorporating the quotation from Joel into his Pentecost narrative in Acts 2.17–21, provided the early church as well as our church a model or a paradigm for mission.[33] He insists that the Spirit-inspired ministries of Peter, John, Stephen, and Paul which Luke presented in Acts should not be glossed over without underscoring the fact that he presented these ministries "because he sees them as models of missionary praxis that his church (and, indeed, our churches, situated as we are in these 'last days') should emulate."[34]

Roger Stronstad is another Pentecostal scholar who has a missiological understanding of baptism in the Holy Spirit. From his redaction of Luke/Acts he avers that the reception of the Holy Spirit by the disciples at Pentecost was meant to empower them and inaugurate them for the mission of witnessing to Jesus just as Jesus' earthly ministry was inaugurated by the Holy Spirit.[35] His argument is that, "since the gift of the Spirit to Jesus inaugurates and empowers his mission, then, whatever meaning Spirit baptism might have in other contexts, it has the same primary charismatic meaning for the mission of the disciples as the anointing by the Spirit had for the charismatic mission of Jesus."[36] Stronstad sees the missionary activities of Philip, Peter, and Paul as narrated by Luke as evidence that the Holy Spirit initiates and guides every missionary drive. In the same vein, he interprets the reception of the Holy Spirit by the Samaritans, Saul, Cornelius, and Ephesians through the lens of the Pentecost narrative; and consequently, sees the reception of the Holy Spirit or baptism in the Holy Spirit as having a missiological understanding.[37] Judging from the narratives of the missionary activities of these disciples, Stronstad concludes that every believer, either concurrently or subsequently, receives the charismatic gift of the Spirit. For the charismatic pneumatology

---

31. Menzies, *Empowered for Witness*, 225.
32. Menzies, "Acts 2.17–21," 202.
33. Menzies, "Acts 2.17–21," 202.
34. Menzies, "Acts 2.17–21," 211.
35. Stronstad, *Charismatic Theology*, 59.
36. Stronstad, *Charismatic Theology*, 58.
37. Stronstad, *Charismatic Theology*, 86.

of Luke "is no less valid for disciples in the twenty-first century than it was for the disciples in the first century."[38]

Frank Macchia agrees with Stronstad and Menzies that the Spirit in Acts is the charismatic Spirit that empowers believers for witness. He argues that baptism in the Holy Spirit "is an empowering calling and gifting for a living witness to Jesus that is the birthright of every Christian as a bearer of the Spirit."[39] However, he disagrees, as will be seen later, that baptism in the Holy Spirit as an experience of charismatic power and enrichment should "be separated from regeneration/sanctification and Christian initiation."[40]

James B. Shelton, like other charismatics and Pentecostals, views Lukan pneumatology as portraying the function of the Holy Spirit to be primarily that of witness. He avows that the Pentecost experience is primarily considered by Luke as "an experience of empowering for mission."[41] He consequently portrays a missiological understanding of baptism in the Holy Spirit. In other words, the function of the Holy Spirit in Luke/Acts is to equip believers with charismatic gifts to witness to the resurrected Christ. Pentecostals in general insist that baptism in the Holy Spirit, as far as Luke/Acts is concerned, is solely for witness or mission and should be separated from sanctification and regeneration. Ernst M. Conradie puts it succinctly, "In Pentecostal discourse Spirit baptism is primarily understood as an experience of empowerment for Christian service and mission that is distinct from conversion, initiation through water baptism, regeneration and sanctification."[42]

However, non-Pentecostals, including some Pentecostal scholars, maintain that although baptism in the Holy Spirit has primarily a missiological understanding in Lukan pneumatology, it cannot and should not be separated from sanctification and regeneration.

Baptism in the Holy Spirit and Conversion Initiation

Pentecostals assert baptism in the Holy Spirit is and should be subsequent to conversion-initiation. "They support their doctrine by the events recorded in Acts 2.1–42 (Pentecost event); 8.14–24 (Samaria event); 10.1–48 (Cornelius event); and 19.1-7 (Ephesus event). All these events, according to the classical Pentecostal view, clearly show that Spirit-baptism should be subsequent

38. Stronstad, *Charismatic Theology*, 14.
39. Macchia, *Baptized in the Spirit*, 79.
40. Macchia, *Baptized in the Spirit*, 84.
41. Shelton, *Mighty in Word & Deed*, 127.
42. Conradie, "Ecumenical Perspectives," 68.

to conversion as all the people mentioned here were already converts before they 'received' the Spirit."[43] For Cheung, it is doubtful if there should always be a time gap between conversion-initiation or regeneration and baptism in the Holy Spirit, or whether it is merely a rational subsequence.[44]

Robert Menzies seems to be the most prominent Pentecostal scholar who views baptism in the Holy Spirit as distinct from and subsequent to conversion initiation. He maintains that "Classical Pentecostals have long affirmed a baptism in the Holy Spirit (Acts 1.5; 2.4) 'distinct from and subsequent to' conversion."[45] His position on this, and those of other proponents of this view, flows "from the conviction that the Spirit came upon the disciples at Pentecost (Acts 2), not as the source of new covenant existence, but rather as the source of power for effective witness."[46] The missiological understanding of baptism in the Holy Spirit that Pentecostals have led to this doctrine of subsequence. Without this doctrine, Pentecostalism according to Menzies, loses its "sense of expectation and effectiveness in mission."[47] He maintains that Luke's pneumatology, as already indicated, views the gifts of the Spirit in exclusively prophetic terms which makes it impossible to relate Pentecostal gift with conversion or salvation.

To Menzies, Luke's pneumatology arms Pentecostals to forcefully argue "that the Spirit came upon the disciples at Pentecost, not as the source of new covenant existence, but rather as the source of power for effective witness."[48] Being missiological in character, Pentecostal gifts or baptism in the Holy Spirit in Luke/Acts, according to Menzies, "must be distinguished from the gift of the Spirit which Paul associates with conversion-initiation."[49] He maintains this view in articles he wrote in reply to James Dunn[50] and Max Turner[51] who, as will be seen shortly, insist that the missiological meaning of baptism in the Holy Spirit cannot and should not be separated from its soteriological understanding. The same view runs all through in an article[52] he wrote much later which has been referred above. He clarifies his position in this issue in his response to Turner. While he acknowledges that the

---

43. Cheung, "Understanding of Spirit-Baptism," 116.
44. Cheung, "Understanding of Spirit-Baptism," 119.
45. Menzies, *Empowered for Witness*, 230.
46. Menzies, *Empowered for Witness*, 232.
47. Menzies, *Empowered for Witness*, 236.
48. Menzies, *Empowered for Witness*, 238.
49. Menzies, *Empowered for Witness*, 238.
50. Menzies, "Luke and the Spirit," 115–38.
51. Menzies, "Spirit of Prophecy," 49–74.
52. Menzies, "Acts 2.17-21," 200–218.

Spirit in Luke's pneumatology "does indeed occasionally impact the ethical or moral life of the church (e.g. Acts 5.1-11)," he maintains that this is not the primary focus of Luke's pneumatology.[53] According to him, the gift of the Spirit in Luke/Acts "is never presented as the source of moral transformation for its recipients" but as "a prophetic enabling which empowers one for participation in the mission of God."[54] Menzies clarifies that when he refers to the Spirit in Luke/Acts as exclusively prophetic, or exclusively missiological, he means that "the Spirit in Luke-Acts is never presented as a soteriological agent."[55] He therefore accuses Dunn, Turner, and every other scholar who attributes a soteriological understanding to baptism in the Holy Spirit as reading Luke through the lens of Paul or other New Testament writers who attribute a soteriological function to the gift of the Spirit.[56]

Stronstad, as indicated already, is another Pentecostal scholar who maintains that the gift of the Spirit in Luke/Acts has fundamentally a missiological function. He consequently insists that baptism in the Holy Spirit is subsequent to conversion-initiation. He argues that the activity of the Holy Spirit in Lukan pneumatology is characterized by the Old Testament heritage and is therefore, "always Charismatic in both purpose and result."[57] He argues that only "those who resist the evidence can continue to interpret the gift of the Holy Spirit in Luke-Acts to be an initiation-conversion experience."[58]

As can be deduced from the arguments and responses of Menzies and Stronstad, non-Pentecostals and some Pentecostal scholars are non-proponents of this view. Dunn, for instance, agrees that the gift of the Holy Spirit in Luke/Acts has primarily a missiological function. He, however, disagrees that baptism in the Holy Spirit is subsequent to conversion-initiation. He avers that baptism in the Holy Spirit was for the writers of the New Testament part of the process of becoming a Christian.[59] Others that form part of this process are "effective proclamation of the Gospel, belief in (εἰς) Jesus as Lord, and water-baptism in the name of the Lord Jesus."[60] According to him baptism in or gift of the Spirit is for the writers of the New Testament "the chief element in conversion-initiation so that" one cannot be truly called a

---

53. Menzies, "Spirit of Prophecy," 52.
54. Menzies, "Spirit of Prophecy," 52.
55. Menzies, "Spirit of Prophecy," 53.
56. Menzies, "Spirit of Prophecy," 55.
57. Stronstad, *Charismatic Theology*, 96.
58. Stronstad, *Charismatic Theology*, 96.
59. Dunn, *Baptism in the Holy Spirit*, 4.
60. Dunn, *Baptism in the Holy Spirit*, 4.

Christian if one does not receive the Spirit in this way.[61] For the New Testament writers "the reception of the Spirit was a very definite and dramatic *experience*, the decisive and climactic experience in conversion-initiation, to which the Christian was usually recalled when reminded of the beginning of his Christian faith and experience."[62]

For Dunn, "the Pentecostal's belief in the dynamic and experiential nature of Spirit-baptism is well founded" in the writings of the New Testament authors; however, "his separation of it from conversion-initiation is wholly unjustified."[63] He reaffirms this position in an article he wrote in response to Pentecostal scholarship on Luke/Acts. He maintains "that according to Lukan theology, the gift of the Spirit is the most fundamental *sine qua non* in the making of a Christian."[64] The same Spirit that initiates one into the body of Christ, is the same Spirit that commissions and empowers one for witness and ministry.[65]

Max Turner's redaction of the Jewish traditions on the function of the Spirit makes him to conclude that the Spirit in Luke, John, and Paul most commonly inspires charismatic revelation, guidance, and wisdom. Sometimes, the Spirit also inspires invasive prophetic speech and charismatic praise.[66] As the Spirit of prophecy, Turner maintains that "the Spirit *simultaneously* provides the 'life' of the saved community and its empowering for service and mission."[67] He rejects the view that baptism in the Holy Spirit is subsequent to conversion-initiation. According to him, "the classical Pentecostal two-stage view of Spirit-reception needs to be replaced by a more broadly Charismatic one-stage conversion-initiation paradigm."[68] He avers that "the norm is a conversion-initiation pattern in which conversional repentance/faith is crystallized in baptism, and the Spirit is received in connection with the whole process."[69]

In his great exegesis of the Pauline epistles that talk about the Holy Spirit, Gordon D. Fee maintains that the Holy Spirit in the letters of Paul has fundamentally a soteriological function. According to him, by referring to the Holy Spirit as the "seal" and "down payment," Paul presents the Holy

---

61. Dunn, *Baptism in the Holy Spirit*, 4.
62. Dunn, *Baptism in the Holy Spirit*, 4.
63. Dunn, *Baptism in the Holy Spirit*, 4.
64. Dunn, "Baptism in the Spirit," 25.
65. Dunn, "Baptism in the Spirit," 26.
66. Turner, *Holy Spirit*, 8–14.
67. Turner, *Holy Spirit*, xii.
68. Turner, *Holy Spirit*, xii.
69. Turner, *Holy Spirit*, 45.

Spirit "as the fulfillment of the 'promise' that includes Gentiles among the people of God."[70] For Paul and for the later church, it is the Holy Spirit and not baptism that "is the 'seal' of ownership, the primary evidence that one belongs to the new people of God."[71] In this sense, baptism in the Holy Spirit does not refer to any subsequent reception of the Spirit distinct from conversion-initiation. For "the Spirit is the sine qua non of Christian existence."[72] In Pauline pneumatology, the soteriological dimension of baptism in the Holy Spirit is not separated from its missiological dimension. According to Fee, what Peter said explicitly about the Holy Spirit on Pentecost somehow was assumed and implied by Paul. He insists that if Paul, "does not expressly associate the soteriological dimension of the spirit with Old Testament texts, that is because such an understanding is assumed in the new covenant, which is evidenced by the *life-giving Spirit.*"[73]

For Fee, when Paul uses the language of "both signs and wonders and deeds of power," he uses it "to cover the broad range of miracles that attended his ministry through the power of the Holy Spirit."[74] Again, this shows that although the gift of the Holy Spirit in Pauline pneumatology has essentially a soteriological understanding, it is not devoid of missiological implications. And the two are not separated from each other. Hence, baptism in the Holy Spirit in Pauline pneumatology is not distinct from and subsequent to conversion-initiation. Indeed, "for Paul and his churches the spirit is not only the absolute key to the understanding of Christian life—from beginning to end—but above all else the Spirit was experienced, and experienced in ways that were essentially powerful and visible."[75]

Frank Macchia employs the concept of the kingdom of God in expanding the boundaries of baptism in the Holy Spirit. According to him, many Pentecostals now have the tendency "to accent the gift of the Spirit given in regeneration and to view the Pentecostal experience of Spirit baptism as empowerment for witness as a 'release' of an already-indwelling Spirit in life."[76] He sees this approach as a more helpful trend. He argues that Pentecostal assumption that Pentecostal experience will be lost if baptism in the Holy Spirit is not separated from conversion-initiation, has been called to question by the "growing body of Third Wave churches that

---

70. Fee, *God's Empowering Presence*, 669.
71. Fee, *God's Empowering Presence*, 670.
72. Fee, *God's Empowering Presence*, 670.
73. Fee, *God's Empowering Presence*, 915.
74. Fee, *God's Empowering Presence*, 356.
75. Fee, *God's Empowering Presence*, 894–95.
76. Macchia, *Baptized in the Spirit*, 77.

advocate something close to Pentecostal spirituality without the doctrine of Spirit baptism as distinct from conversion."[77] For Macchia, the work of the Holy Spirit is to inaugurate the kingdom of God in holiness and power. He, therefore, insists that baptism in the Holy Spirit "cannot be separated from regeneration/sanctification and Christian initiation."[78] Pentecostal experience or baptism in the Holy Spirit according to him "is both sanctifying and empowering, for it arises from the Spirit of the kingdom, the Spirit of God as love."[79] Within the framework of the kingdom of God, baptism in the Holy Spirit cannot be separated from conversion-initiation. "Yet, the sanctifying work of the Spirit needs to be released in life through powerful experiences of renewal and Charismatic enrichment that propel us toward vibrant praise, healing reconciliations, enriched *koinonia*, and enhanced gifting for empowered service."[80]

Through a concise but great study of the Holy Spirit in the biblical teaching, through the centuries, and today, Anthony Thiselton comes to the conclusion that no orthodox Christian, Pentecostal, or exponent of renewal would ordinarily wish to challenge the trinitarian framework of every experience of the Holy Spirit.[81] From this conclusion, Thiselton implicitly avers that baptism in the Holy Spirit is not and cannot be distinct from and subsequent to conversion-initiation. He maintains that "just as the Holy Spirit unites Christians throughout the world" so does the Holy Spirit ensure "*continuity of faith throughout the ages.*"[82] In fact, he argues that Acts 1:4-5, "you will be baptized with the Holy Spirit," is "addressed to *all* Christians, as they enter the New Age of world history *together.*"[83] By implication, he means that the gift of the Holy Spirit or baptism in the Holy Spirit is not distinct from and subsequent to conversion-initiation reserved only for few Christians.

Simon Chan maintains that the doctrine of subsequence cannot be sustained theologically without first expanding the meaning of baptism in the Holy Spirit beyond the enduement of power. He argues that "the comprehensive integration of Pauline pneumatology makes it imperative that the soteriological dimension, which Paul develops most fully, be made a central

---

77. Macchia, *Baptized in the Spirit*, 78.
78. Macchia, *Baptized in the Spirit*, 84.
79. Macchia, *Baptized in the Spirit*, 84.
80. Macchia, *Baptized in the Spirit*, 145.
81. Thiselton, *Holy Spirit*, 483.
82. Thiselton, *Holy Spirit*, 484.
83. Thiselton, *Holy Spirit*, 491.

issue to any discussion of Spirit-baptism."⁸⁴ He proposes seeing baptism in the Holy Spirit "as a distinct reality within the conversion-initiation complex, rather than simply as a more intense form of conversion experience."⁸⁵ He therefore, prefers a sacramental view of baptism in the Holy Spirit and projects the sacrament of holy communion as a locus under which classical Pentecostals can locate Spirit-baptism.⁸⁶

Pentecostals who hold the doctrine of subsequence see glossolalia or speaking in tongues as the initial evidence of baptism in the Holy Spirit.

Baptism in the Holy Spirit and the Gift of Tongues

For most Pentecostals, glossolalia is the initial evidence that one has been baptized in the Spirit. They claim that this is normative based on the Pentecost event. Marius Nel argues that "Because the Christians of the first church and first century spoke in tongues as the Spirit gave them utterance, twenty-first century Christians should expect to encounter the Spirit in the same way and receive the same spiritual gifts (χαριμάτων)."⁸⁷

Menzies, like many other Pentecostals strongly hold that glossolalia is the initial evidence of baptism in the Holy Spirit. According to him, "Luke consciously crafted his narrative in order to highlight the normative character of evidential tongues."⁸⁸ To him, the intrinsically demonstrative character of tongues uniquely qualifies it to be the initial physical evidence of baptism in the Holy Spirit. Judging from the Pentecost experience, Menzies concludes that "the manifestation of tongues-speech marks the speaker as a member of the end-time prophetic community."⁸⁹ He acknowledges that Pentecostal gift is not glossolalia, but that glossolalia is the initial evidence that Pentecostal gift has taken place. He says, "when one receives the Pentecostal gift, one should expect to manifest tongues, and this manifestation of tongues is a uniquely demonstrative sign (evidence) that one has received the gift."⁹⁰ He maintains this view in his later article. According to him, "speaking in tongues highlights, embodies, and validates the unique way that Pentecostals read the book of Acts. Acts is not simply a historical document; rather, Acts presents a model for the life of the contemporary

---

84. Chan, "Evidential Glossolalia," 204.
85. Chan, "Evidential Glossolalia," 207.
86. Chan, "Evidential Glossolalia," 210–11.
87. Nel, "Critical Evaluation," 302.
88. Menzies, *Empowered for Witness*, 246.
89. Menzies, *Empowered for Witness*, 251.
90. Menzies, *Empowered for Witness*, 255.

church."[91] He insists that speaking in tongues is a strong positive evidence that the reception of Pentecostal gift has occurred.[92]

Reading Luke's narratives, where people who received the gift of the Holy Spirit spoke in tongues after receiving it, inspired Stronstad to conclude too that glossolalia is the initial evidence of baptism in the Holy Spirit. He insists that by portraying those evidences, "Luke compels his readers to observe a pattern: being baptized in the Spirit is signified by speaking in tongues, and speaking in tongues signifies that 'being baptized in the Spirit' has taken place."[93] Kärkkäinen affirms this doctrine of initial evidence. However, he rightly maintains that it is held not by all Pentecostals, but by a large majority of them. Theologically, he sees it as an external sign that baptism in the Holy Spirit has occurred. According to him, "the initial evidence doctrine functions 'sacramentally': it is an external confirmation of the inner grace received from God's Spirit."[94]

Taking a clue from Joseph Roswell Flower who "noted that he was baptized in the Spirit months before he actually spoke in tongues," Frank Macchia sees the initial-evidence doctrine as a sacramental "sign" rather than a scientific "evidence."[95] He avers that the "important point to the doctrine of tongues as the initial sign of Spirit baptism is that there is a depth of experience in the Spirit, the consequence of which will quite naturally be speaking in tongues, and that the experience itself does not come to full biblical expression and signification without tongues."[96]

For Chan, it is difficult if not impossible for Pentecostals to theologically establish tongues as the initial evidence of baptism in the Holy Spirit, just as it is difficult to establish the doctrine of subsequence without expanding the meaning of baptism in the Holy Spirit beyond enduement of power. He avers that "as long as baptism in the Spirit is narrowly defined as the enduement of power, it is difficult to see how glossolalia could be theologically related to it as its initial evidence."[97]

While a large majority of Pentecostals hold the doctrine of initial evidence, charismatics believe that one can receive the Spirit baptism and not speak in tongues. In fact, many Pentecostal scholars do not subscribe to glossolalia as initial evidence of baptism in the Holy Spirit. Fee, for

---

91. Menzies, "Role of Glossolalia," 49.
92. Menzies, "Role of Glossolalia," 66–67.
93. Stronstad, *Charismatic Theology*, 77.
94. Kärkkäinen, "Pneumatologies in Systematic Theology," 229.
95. Macchia, "Groans Too Deep for Words," 157.
96. Macchia, "Groans Too Deep for Words," 157–58.
97. Chan, "Evidential Glossolalia," 196.

example, maintains that glossolalia or gift of tongues in Pauline pneumatology is understood as Spirit-inspired utterance, basically unintelligible to the speaker and the hearers, directed principally toward God.[98] It is a gift for private prayer; and the "regulations for its community use in 1 Cor 14:27–28 make it clear that the speaker is not in 'ecstasy' or 'out of control.'"[99] The fact that baptism in the Holy Spirit in Pauline pneumatology has essentially a soteriological function that is inseparable from its missiological function as Fee demonstrated, shows that glossolalia is neither for Paul nor for Fee the initial evidence of baptism in the Holy Spirit, distinct from and subsequent to conversion-initiation.

Turner corroborates this view. According to him, "both Luke and Paul regarded glossolalia as invasive charismatic praise in languages unknown to the speaker."[100] Focusing specifically on Luke, he maintains that "Luke sees tongues as a distinctive (but not universal) sign of the messianic outpouring of the 'Spirit of prophecy' which restores and transforms Israel."[101] Implicitly, Turner argues here that glossolalia is not and cannot be the initial evidence of baptism in the Holy Spirit. This is evident in the fact that Turner rejects the separation of baptism in the Holy Spirit from conversion-initiation as indicated above.

Thiselton apparently doesn't seem to be comfortable with the doctrine of initial evidence. According to him, a "number of Pentecostals, including Veli-Matti Kärkkäinen, admit that often too much has been made of tongues, and are openly embarrassed that some still regard tongues as 'initial evidence' of baptism in the Spirit."[102] He insists that most of them even go as far as admitting that it may also be a 'learned behavior' even if it is a gift of the Holy Spirit.[103]

So far, we have focused on the intellectual doctrinal debate of the charismatic and Pentecostal pneumatology based on baptism in the Holy Spirit. Intellectual theological debate of whether the Holy Spirit has a missiological or soteriological function or both, or whether glossolalia is the initial evidence of baptism in the Holy Spirit, is not the reason this work is averring for the renewal of the Nigerian Catholic Church through charismatic and Pentecostal theology and praxis. After all, Cheung sees the Catholic view of baptism in the Holy Spirit which preserves "the integrity and oneness

---

98. Fee, *God's Empowering Presence*, 889.
99. Fee, *God's Empowering Presence*, 889.
100. Turner, *Holy Spirit*, 233.
101. Turner, *Holy Spirit*, 233.
102. Thiselton, *Holy Spirit*, 488.
103. Thiselton, *Holy Spirit*, 490.

of the Spirit while still being able to account for the various possibilities of spiritual experience in Christian life," as the most comprehensive and theologically sound concept of Spirit-baptism.[104]

Charismatics and Pentecostals understand theology as an experiential encounter with God which plays out in their missiological, ecclesiological, and liturgical praxes. This is the reason this work is using charismatic and Pentecostal theology and praxis to argue for the renewal of the Nigerian Catholic Church. What does a pneumatology that is understood as an experiential encounter with the Holy Spirit mean in relation to baptism in the Holy Spirit? To explore this, is the focus of the next section.

Baptism in the Holy Spirit and Pneumatology of Experiential Encounter

Baptism in the Holy Spirit, however it is understood theologically, whether as having a missiological or soteriological function or both, is not a major concern of this work. What is fundamental to this work is that the charismatic and Pentecostal pneumatology, which is exemplified in baptism in the Holy Spirit, is a theology of experiential encounter with the Triune God through the power of the Holy Spirit. The Holy Spirit empowers believers to experience and encounter "the God who loves and cares for the daily needs of his people."[105] Because God loves and cares for his people, God becomes, in Jesus, the Savior and Redeemer of his people.

The Holy Spirit empowers believers not only to believe in God as the Savior but more importantly, to experience and encounter God as the Savior and to be witnesses of God's saving act. But what does experiencing and encountering God as the Savior and witnessing to God mean for a charismatic and Pentecostal to whom pneumatology means experiential encounter with the Holy Spirit? To answer this, it is important to note that charismatic and Pentecostal pneumatology demonstrates a holistic worldview in which the physical and material aspects of human life are as important as the spiritual aspect. In fact, as Wonsuk Ma points out, a "bowl of rice and healing of terminal diseases in a poverty-stricken society are as important as the matter of sin and salvation."[106]

Charismatic and Pentecostal pneumatology portrays a concept of salvation that is integral. Charismatics and Pentecostals from the Western world and in fact, Christians from the Western world in general may find

---

104. Cheung, "Understanding of Spirit-Baptism," 121–22.
105. Ma, "'When the Poor,'" 31.
106. Ma, "'When the Poor,'" 31.

it difficult to assimilate this due to their dualistic worldview. However, in "the 'majority world,' if the most powerful and loving God cannot heal a person, he is not as useful as the ancestor spirits many have been relying on for such needs."[107] People expect to experience and encounter in practice, the saving act of their loving and caring God here in earthly existence while waiting for the fullness of it in the afterlife. The charismatic and Pentecostal pneumatology comes to view here, as the Holy Spirit "comes in with 'signs and wonders.'"[108]

Charismatic and Pentecostal pneumatology in praxis rejects any separation between the soteriological and missiological functions of the Holy Spirit the same way it abhors any dualistic concept of salvation. Ma narrated a story about Badol a young Philippino who lived in Papasok, a village of the Kankana-ey tribe. Badol lost two of his young children on the same day and another two after a period of time despite the sacrifices he offered to his ancestral spirits. The experience led to his conversion to Christianity after being preached to by a Pentecostal Christian worker. Immediately after his conversion, he became himself a witness to the Gospel and a means of salvation to his people as God performed many signs and wonders through him by the power of the Holy Spirit. The story has it that Badol had ten more children with his wife and none of them died.[109]

To Ma, "Badol believed that the Holy Spirit came not only to save him from darkness, but also to empower him so that he could share the gospel with effectiveness."[110] Badol's story shows that charismatic and Pentecostal pneumatology indeed demonstrates a holistic soteriology. In this case, a believer is saved as many times as possible in this earthly existence before he or she is finally saved in the eschaton. Badol's worldview is similar to that of the Nigerian charismatics and Pentecostals. Hence, attention is now turned to how charismatic and Pentecostal pneumatology of experiential encounter exemplified in baptism in the Holy Spirit plays out in Nigerian charismatic renewal and Pentecostalism.

Baptism in the Holy Spirit and the Nigerian Charismatics and Pentecostals

The Nigerian worldview, like the worldview of most sub-Saharan African countries, is devoid of the polarity that characterizes the Graeco-Christian

---

107. Ma, "'When the Poor,'" 31.
108. Ma, "'When the Poor,'" 31.
109. Ma, "'When the Poor,'" 31–32.
110. Ma, "'When the Poor,'" 32.

worldview. In other words, one cannot clearly distinguish or separate the visible from the invisible, the body from the soul or the material from the spiritual, the temporal from the non-temporal, or the sacred from the profane.[111] At the center of this cosmic image are human beings, which positions human life as the most vital stake. Human beings, therefore, rely on the succor of benevolent spirits to gladly live their life in full in this present life and to improve it onto ancestorhood contrary to the evil and threatening designs of malevolent forces.[112]

To comprehend soteriology in the traditional Nigerian worldview, one needs to grasp the concept of sin within the same cosmological milieu. Sin is seen in traditional Nigerian society "as the violation of God's 'laws' for social order and human interaction."[113] In this worldview, the consequence of sin is suffered by the victim as well as the community he or she belongs to. In fact, as Kofi A. Opoku avers, the "prominent position of the supernatural in the moral order in West African (Nigerian) societies is borne out by the fact that breaches of the moral law are considered to be offences against the gods, the ancestors and God, not so much against the individual."[114] Nigerian worldview portrays a serious belief in the activities of spiritual beings in human affairs. People, therefore, "live under the influence of these powers and dread attacks of malevolent forces in the form of diseases, death or other mishaps."[115]

Salvation for the Nigerian, therefore, includes deliverance from one's enemies and whatever threatens one's wellbeing in life or can ruin one's wellbeing in the afterlife. As Daniel Darko said, quoting John Mbiti, these include but are not limited to "sickness, witchcraft, sorcery, magic, barrenness, failure, troublesome spirits, danger, misfortune, calamity and death."[116] Intercessions, sacrifices and libations are often made to the Supreme Being through intermediary spiritual beings for protection and deliverance from these enemies and threats. The sacrifice of Jesus and the shedding of his innocent blood is, therefore, seen within the prism of Nigerian sacrificial system as an atonement for sin—sin understood from the perspective of the Nigerian worldview. The sacrifice means nothing to the Nigerian if its salvific efficacy is not practically experienced, in which case, one is saved from one's enemies and all that threatens one's existence in this life and in eschaton. For

111. Ikenga-Metuh, *Comparative Studies*, 51.
112. Ejizu, "Liminality in the Contemporary," 13.
113. Darko, "What Does It Mean," 46.
114. Opoku, *West African*, 156.
115. Darko, "What Does It Mean," 48.
116. Darko, "What Does It Mean," 51.

the Nigerian, "faith in a God who cannot guarantee deliverance and protection from diabolic forces is fragile and dangerous."[117]

It is not strange that the charismatic and Pentecostal pneumatology, which is experiential and praxis-oriented, as typified in baptism in the Holy Spirit, appeals to the Nigerian society. In fact, salvation in charismatic and Pentecostal discourse is holistic as it is in the Nigerian worldview. "It encompasses" according to Nimi Wariboko, "the body, soul, and spirit and is simultaneously about the well-being in the here and now and in the afterlife."[118] It is essentially in this sense that "a demonstration of God's power through his Spirit will often convince Africans (Nigerians) that God is indeed more powerful than the surrounding evil forces and therefore worthy of worship, faith and service."[119]

Nigerian charismatics and Pentecostals, according to Christopher Ejizu, emphasize the "need for the empowerment by the Holy Spirit to enable a person to overcome malevolent spiritual forces."[120] He maintains that "the fundamental outlook and response of most of their charismatic leaders and exorcists to sickness, other forms of suffering and existential problems hardly deny their indigenous cosmological roots."[121]

The experiential and praxis-oriented theology of charismatics and Pentecostals, particularly their pneumatology, resonates well with the Nigerian worldview. Nigerian charismatics and Pentecostals cash in on this. They believe, according to Ayuk Ayuk, that every "spirit filled person is accompanied with signs and wonders and there is nothing as convincing as the manifestation of God's power in the lives of people. When people are healed or set free from demon possession, others are made to see the reality of God in their lives."[122]

For Nigerians, the pneumatology of charismatics and Pentecostals that is experiential and praxis-oriented is "sheer gain," to use Aylward Shorter's expression, "an 'extra' for which he has opted. It is an overlay on his original religious culture."[123] It is not a surprise that "many people flock to prayer houses and pentecostal rallies to ask for such favors as promotions in their jobs, success in examination and business ventures as well as personal safety and security against sorcery, ill-will, or threats of evil

---

117. Darko, "What Does It Mean," 51.
118. Wariboko, *Nigerian Pentecostalism*, 35.
119. Anderson, "Pentecostal Pneumatology," 73.
120. Ejizu, "Cosmological Perspectives," 170.
121. Ejizu, "Cosmological Perspectives," 171.
122. Ayuk, "Portrait of a Nigerian Pentecostal," 129.
123. Shorter, *African Christian Theology*, 10.

forces."¹²⁴ Ayuk Ayuk sees this as one thing Pentecostals brought back to life in the Nigerian churches. According to him, "Many persons used to flock to faith healers or witch doctors to get healing, but today they go to churches because the power of the Holy Spirit has been restored in full force."¹²⁵ It is no surprise that charismatic renewal and Pentecostalism are the most rapid growing religious movements and churches respectively in Nigeria today. As Ayuk says, people "go to churches where they see the power of God moving. A spiritually dead church does not allow the (S)pirit of God to manifest itself. It believes in God but does not believe in His power to move mountains if there is a need to do so."¹²⁶

The mainline churches in Nigeria were unable to provide their members with the salvation they needed and desired due to their non-experiential and non-praxis-oriented theology. They "were operating from the mindset of the West" according to Ayuk, "so they could not reach the Nigerian properly." It is no surprise that they were losing their members to Pentecostal churches. Ayuk argues that charismatic movements started in mainline churches in Nigeria when these churches "could not afford to continue losing their members due to the fact that they were not able to provide for them the needed remedy to their problems."¹²⁷ He believes that the Holy Spirit was neglected, and its experiential power denied by the mainline churches in Nigeria until the advent of Pentecostal and charismatic movements.¹²⁸

Nigerian charismatics and Pentecostals believe in the holistic concept of salvation as noted earlier. This conviction makes them to be "vigorously involved in the political life of Nigeria. They pray for the country and are involved in some government activities."¹²⁹ Politicians frequently patronize their prayer centers not only to ask for prayers but also to canvas for the votes of this large population.

Indeed, political instability, bad governance, nepotism, and the militarization of the Nigerian society have combined to create susceptibility, insecurity, and hopelessness. In situations like this, Nigerian charismatics and Pentecostals believe that the first task of Christianity according to Ogbu Kalu "is to save people from hopelessness by creating new empowering tools of hope and new sources of security, not by repeating old excuses

124. Ejizu, "Cosmological Perspectives," 169.
125. Ayuk, "Portrait of a Nigerian Pentecostal," 130.
126. Ayuk, "Portrait of a Nigerian Pentecostal," 129.
127. Ayuk, "Pentecostal Transformation," 191.
128. Ayuk, "Pentecostal Transformation," 189.
129. Ayuk, "Portrait of a Nigerian Pentecostal," 131.

about the redemptive qualities (of) being Christlike."[130] They therefore, encourage people "to fight back, to refuse to accept defeat, want, failure, pessimism, or negativity."[131]

Nigerian charismatics and Pentecostals don't believe in crossless Christianity, but they refuse to idolize suffering. Their experiential and praxis-oriented theology encourages them to attack every sociopolitical and moral structures they consider needing change.[132] Nigerians believe that poverty dehumanizes a person and the person's community. It is a 'disease' that needs to be healed. Its presence or absence is attributed "to both supernatural and human agency" as exuded in the Igbo proverb, "*onyekwe, chi yakwe*" (when one affirms, the personal god will affirm).[133]

Nigerian charismatics and Pentecostals know this very well as it resonates with their experiential and praxis-oriented theology. So, they embark on prosperity preaching in which they "provide the power of Jesus as the *agyenkwa* who rescues."[134] *Agyenkwa* according to Mercy Amba Oduyoye means "the one who rescues, who holds your life in safety, takes you out of a life-denying situation and places you in a life affirming one. The Rescuer plucks you from a dehumanizing ambience and places you in a position where you can grow toward authentic humanity. The *Agyenkwa* gives you back your life in all its fullness."[135]

Within the Nigerian cosmic milieu, which is devoid of the polarity between the natural and the supernatural, "lack of physical health is often understood to be symptomatic of a lack of spiritual, emotional or moral health; it is physically and spiritually harmful to the society and to the individual concerned."[136] Healing in Nigerian context is therefore, understood as the restoration of life; a liberation from all that dehumanizes.

In the words of Kalu, quoting Jacques Matthey's summary of a consultation organized by the World Council of Churches in Accra, Ghana, "to experience healing is not just to experience freedom from sickness and illness, or problems and suffering. Healing is a sign of what the Old Testament calls 'shalom' (peace, salvation) as the establishment or restoration of right and reconciled relationships, now and at the end of time."[137]

---

130. Kalu, *African Pentecostalism*, 213.
131. Kalu, *African Pentecostalism*, 214.
132. Kalu, *African Pentecostalism*, 213–20.
133. Kalu, *African Pentecostalism*, 262.
134. Kalu, *African Pentecostalism*, 263.
135. Oduyoye, *Hearing and Knowing*, 98.
136. Magesa, *Anatomy of Inculturation*, 81.
137. Kalu, *African Pentecostalism*, 265.

Nigerian charismatics and Pentecostals know this very well. In their context, signs and wonders or miracles must be seen "as divine-human mediating activity and as a way of producing specific, particular goods" as there is no dichotomy between the invisible and visible realms.[138] It is no surprise that they have centers scattered in almost all parts of the country for healing and deliverance ministries.

Irrespective of what people might think of the extremes and malfeasance of some of the wealth-and-health gospel preachers, Nimi Wariboko maintains that Nigerian charismatic and Pentecostal preachers who indulge in health and prosperity preaching craft a theology of hope to deal with the existential problems of the people. According to him, these "preachers are responding to the felt, practical needs of the people amid the collapse of Nigeria's economy, education facilities, and the health-care delivery system, just to mention a few."[139]

Having experienced and encountered the saving power of God through his Holy Spirit, Nigerian charismatics and Pentecostals feel obligated to witness to the saving power both at home and abroad. For instance, the Redeemed Christian Church of God (RCCG) alone has almost seven thousand parishes in Nigeria[140] and has missionaries in fifty nations of the world[141] as of 2004. For the Nigerian charismatics and Pentecostals, therefore, the soteriological function of the Holy Spirit is inseparable from its missiological function the same way the Nigerian worldview does not permit polarity between the supernatural and the natural. Because the Nigerian charismatics and Pentecostals have a holistic concept of salvation which is devoid of the Greco-Christian polarity, they get involved in social and health services together with the spiritual services they offer to the people.[142]

The Nigerian context exudes the fact that the distinctiveness of Pentecostalism is not necessarily its fivefold gospel; neither is it its doctrine of subsequence nor initial evidence as some Pentecostals maintain. Charismatic renewal and Pentecostalism, particularly in Nigeria, will lose their stronghold without their experiential encounter and praxis-oriented theology. It is this experiential encounter and praxis-oriented theology that is the main thrust this work is arguing for the renewal of the Nigerian Catholic Church using the charismatic and Pentecostal theology and praxis.

---

138. Wariboko, *Nigerian Pentecostalism*, 196.
139. Wariboko, *Nigerian Pentecostalism*, 35.
140. Adeboye, "'Arrowhead,'" 41.
141. Adeboye, "'Arrowhead,'" 46.
142. Adeboye, "'Arrowhead,'" 43–44.

The charismatic and Pentecostal experiential and praxis-oriented pneumatology opens the door for flexibility in doctrinal and liturgical praxes. The case of the Nigerian charismatic renewal and Pentecostalism is not different. How this plays out in the ecclesiology and liturgy of charismatics and Pentecostals will be the focus of the next two chapters respectively. For now, it suffices to ask that apart from being experiential and praxis-oriented, is there any major difference between the pneumatology of charismatics and Pentecostals and that of other Christians? To decipher this, attention will be turned in the next two major sections to the Holy Spirit in the teachings of the New Testament and through the centuries respectively.

The Holy Spirit in the New Testament Teaching

There is no intention of doing a comprehensive study of the New Testament teaching on the Holy Spirit here. Only a brief review is needed, which will be focusing on the synoptic Gospels, Acts of the Apostles, and on the Johannine writings. Some key themes in Paul on the Holy Spirit will also be examined. The aim of this as indicated earlier is to decrypt if the pneumatology of charismatics and Pentecostals is different from those of other Christians apart from the fact that it is experiential and praxis-oriented. Anthony Thiselton's *The Holy Spirit: In Biblical Teaching, through the Centuries, and Today* will be our source.

The Holy Spirit in the Synoptic Gospels

The synoptic Gospels according to Thiselton agree "that Jesus' baptism and temptations, as well as his ministry up to the cross, *occurred in the power of the Holy Spirit.*"[143] Mark reports the involvement of the Holy Spirit in the baptism of Jesus in these words: "As he was coming out of the water, he saw . . . the Spirit descending like a dove on him" (Mark 1:10). While Matthew 3:16 has a close parallel with Mark, Luke says: "I baptize you with water. . . . He shall baptize you with the Holy Spirit and fire" (Luke 3:16). Thiselton views the temptation of Jesus as a Messianic temptation originally initiated by the Holy Spirit as a test of Jesus' Messianic vocation.[144] In Mark's version, "the Spirit immediately drove him (Jesus) out into the wilderness. He remained in the wilderness for forty days, tempted by Satan" (Mark 1:12–13). Matthew's version reads: "Then Jesus was led up by the Spirit into

---

143. Thiselton, *Holy Spirit*, 33.
144. Thiselton, *Holy Spirit*, 34.

the wilderness to be tempted by the devil. He fasted forty days and forty nights" (Matt 4:1–2). For Luke, "Jesus full of the Holy Spirit, returned from Jordan, and was led by the Spirit in the wilderness, where for forty days he was tempted by the devil" (Luke 4:1–2).

Thiselton notes that Matthew is slightly more explicit than Mark as regards the activity of Jesus in the power of the Holy Spirit while Luke is clearly more explicit and emphatic than the other two. For instance, in addressing the allegation of Jesus casting out demons by the power of Beelzebul, the Marcan Jesus said, "whoever blasphemes against the Holy Spirit can never have forgiveness" (Mark 3:29). The Matthean Jesus said, "if it is by the spirit of God that I cast out demons, then the kingdom of God has come to you" (Matt 12:29). Luke's explicitness can be seen in the appropriation of Isaiah's statement by the Lukan Jesus: "the spirit of the Lord is upon me, because he has anointed me to bring good news to the poor. He has sent me to proclaim release to the captives, the recovery of sight to the blind, . . . to proclaim the year of the Lord's favor" (Luke 4:18–19). The Holy Spirit was instrumental in the conception and birth of Jesus according to Matthew and Luke (Matt 1:18; Luke 1:35).

The synoptic Gospel writers, especially Luke, appeal to the agency of the Holy Spirit in every event surrounding the Messianic vocation of Jesus. For instance, Elizabeth was "filled with the Holy Spirit" (Luke 1:41) to give birth to John the Baptist. The Holy Spirit revealed to Simeon that he would not see death before he had seen the Lord's Messiah and guided him to the temple to see Jesus (Luke 2:25–27). According to Thiselton, Turner describes this "appeal to the agency of the Holy Spirit as a 'metaphorical way of referring to the inception of a specific new activity.'"[145] Thiselton agrees with Smeaton that the "visible descent of the Holy Spirit, not only for the sake of the Jews and of the Baptist, but for a testimony to Christ himself (Matt 3:16), took place while Jesus (in Luke) was praying to the Father, probably with a view to attend the Spirit . . . (Luke 3:21)."[146]

Thiselton points out that to C. K. Barrett and J. E. Fison, there are relatively few references to the Holy Spirit in the synoptic Gospels before the resurrection and glorification of Jesus. He believes there is truth to this claim as it is supported by the temptation narratives and by some other references to the activities of the Holy Spirit in relation to Jesus' Messianic vocation. According to him, the actions "are initiated by the Holy Spirit, but in each case the more spectacular 'self-glorifying' way is renounced, in favor

---

145. Thiselton, *Holy Spirit*, 35.
146. Thiselton, *Holy Spirit*, 35.

of the hard path of the will of God and *kenōsis*, or self-emptying."[147] He also agrees there is truth in claims of James D. G. Dunn and Max Turner "that Jesus is seen through his exorcisms and deeds of power, as the Bearer of the Spirit and as what they call a 'charismatic' figure."[148]

Thiselton is of the opinion that the Holy Spirit is inseparable from the activities of the Father and the Son if we read the synoptic Gospels retrospectively through the lens of Christian tradition in the Church Fathers.[149] In the synoptic Gospels it is wrong to blaspheme or speak against the Holy Spirit (Mark 3:28–30; Matt 12:31–32 and Luke 12:10). The Holy Spirit guides believers in moments of crisis (Mark 3:12; Matt 10:19–20; Luke 12:12; see Luke 21:14–15). The Holy Spirit is connected to exorcisms and to the arrival of God's kingdom (Matt 12:28). The Father gives the Holy Spirit as a gift to those who ask (Luke 11:13). Believers in Jesus Christ are to be baptized in the name of the Father, the Son, and the Holy Spirit (Matt 28:19).

The Holy Spirit in Acts

According to Thiselton, the "Acts of the Apostles is structured around the mission and outreach of the Apostolic Church, and recounts the expansion of the gospel from Jerusalem to Rome."[150] Hence, the church from the beginning exists only by the reception of "the creative life of the Holy Spirit (Acts 1:8; 2:1-36)."[151] From then, the Holy Spirit directs subsequent events in the life of the church. The encounter between Philip and the Ethiopian on the road from Jerusalem to Gaza (Acts 8:29, 39) is a good example. The Holy Spirit was "poured out" upon the apostles and other Christians (Acts 2:1). "All of them were filled with the Holy Spirit, and began to speak with other languages, as the Spirit gave them ability" (Acts 2:4).

Thiselton agrees with Dunn whom he quotes as saying: "the Epoch and significance of Pentecost raises the whole course of salvation-history to a new plane. . . . In one sense, therefore, *Pentecost can never be repeated*—the new age is here, and cannot be ushered in again. But *in another sense . . . the experience of Pentecost can and must be repeated* in the experience of all who would become Christians."[152] For Thiselton therefore, Pentecost "initiated the birth and era of the Church"; its missionary context "is fulfilled

---

147. Thiselton, *Holy Spirit*, 39.
148. Thiselton, *Holy Spirit*, 39.
149. Thiselton, *Holy Spirit*, 42.
150. Thiselton, *Holy Spirit*, 49.
151. Thiselton, *Holy Spirit*, 51.
152. Thiselton, *Holy Spirit*, 55.

by the commissioning and empowering of the Church."[153] Thiselton avers that "*as a church* they (the Apostles and other Christians) experienced a *communal initiatory baptism with the Holy Spirit*; but *as individuals*, whatever experiences they had, or were yet to have, Luke agrees with Paul that 'baptism with the Holy Spirit' applies to 'becoming a Christian,' not to some subsequent experience."[154]

According to Thiselton, Frederick Dale Bruner "describes Pentecost as a unique *communal* 'baptism with the Holy Spirit,' which fulfills the promise made in Luke 24:49 and Acts 1:4 and 2:33 of these "free gifts" from God.[155] Thiselton reminds those who aver that Pentecost was decisive for all Christians to take note of "the fact that Luke recounts subsequent outpourings of the Holy Spirit, accompanied by phenomena like those of Pentecost, on at least three important occasions: in Samaria (Acts 8:17), on Cornelius the Roman centurion (10:44–46), and on some of the Ephesians (19:6–7)."[156]

For Thiselton, the Holy Spirit in Acts has a soteriological as well as missiological function. According to him, the "Holy Spirit in Acts brings about each new step in the Church's mission."[157] For example, the Holy Spirit instructed Peter to embark on the mission to the Gentile territory despite his resistance (Acts 10:14). The Holy Spirit initiated the decision of the Antioch community to take on the evangelization of Asia Minor (Acts 13:1-3). The Holy Spirit did not only initiate the mission, the Holy Spirit also directed them occasionally on where they should not go (Acts 16:6–7).

Thiselton believes that the reading of Acts shows that the Holy Spirit does not inspire people only through extraordinary means but also "through ordinary process of *reflection* and *reason*."[158] This is evidenced in "Paul's epistles and his sermon at Thessalonica (Acts 17:1–9), which includes 'arguing' and 'persuasion'(Acts 17:2, 4) but also implies a dualism of divine action" for both are inspired by the Holy Spirit.[159] When compared with the Acts narratives, Thiselton maintains that "Mark Cartledge's description of 'Third Wave' Renewal Ministry as '*inviting*' the Holy Spirit to fall upon a congregation may perhaps seem surprising and a little inappropriate" for the Holy Spirit has already been poured on all flesh.[160]

153. Thiselton, *Holy Spirit*, 55.
154. Thiselton, *Holy Spirit*, 55.
155. Thiselton, *Holy Spirit*, 55–56.
156. Thiselton, *Holy Spirit*, 62.
157. Thiselton, *Holy Spirit*, 66.
158. Thiselton, *Holy Spirit*, 68.
159. Thiselton, *Holy Spirit*, 68.
160. Thiselton, *Holy Spirit*, 69.

The Holy Spirit in the Johannine Writings

Thiselton seems to agree with George Montague that "While Luke is interested in the charismatic explosion of the Spirit in tongues, prophecy, and healing, John is more interested in the relation of the Spirit to the power over sin, . . . founded on a word of Jesus and the gift of the Spirit."[161] He notes that for John, the Spirit is like the wind; he "blows where he wills" (John 3:8); the Holy Spirit is the Spirit of truth that guides believers into all truth (14:17; 15:26; 16:13). The leitmotif of the Spirit of truth as witness, which is very prominent in the Fourth Gospel, is picked up in 1 John 5:6. The Spirit in John gives life (6:63) and is the medium of rebirth (3:5). For John, "God is Spirit" (4:24) and as Thiselton says, quoting Sanders and Martin, the Spirit (*pneuma*) in Johannine writings "'is as personal as the Logos, and not just an impersonal force (cf. John 16:13),' where John uses *ekeinos*."[162]

In John, the Holy Spirit is likened to "flowing water" (17:37-39). The Holy Spirit is the Paraclete (John 14:15-18, 26; 15:26-27; 16:5-15). The Holy Spirit in John, according to Thiselton, bears witness to Christ (15:26) and does not speak of himself (16:13). He quotes Max Turner as saying: "The coming Spirit . . . mediates the presence of the Father and of the glorified Son to the disciple."[163] Thiselton avers that the Holy Spirit in John's view, as with Paul, is Christocentric.[164]

Key Themes in Paul

Anthony Thiselton identifies eight basic themes on the Holy Spirit in Pauline epistles. According to him, the work of the Holy Spirit is christocentric in Pauline letters.[165] This is evident, for example, in Paul's sayings that "No one can say 'Jesus is Lord' except by the Holy Spirit" (1 Cor 12:3); and "God has sent the Spirit of his Son into our hearts, crying, 'Abba! Father!'" (Gal 4:6). Thiselton notes that James D. G. Dunn, judging from Romans 8:9-11, 1 Corinthians 12:4-6, and other passages, maintains that "Paul's experience of Christ and the Spirit were one, and . . . Christ was experienced through the Spirit."[166]

---

161. Thiselton, *Holy Spirit*, 133.
162. Thiselton, *Holy Spirit*, 136.
163. Thiselton, *Holy Spirit*, 143.
164. Thiselton, *Holy Spirit*, 144.
165. Thiselton, *Holy Spirit*, 70.
166. Thiselton, *Holy Spirit*, 70.

Despite the fact that some Pentecostals and charismatics have been accused of being Spirit-centered, Thiselton insists that some of them who are thoughtful reject being Spirit-centered. For instance, Gordon Fee, a highly respected Pentecostal scholar, insists that the "Spirit is none other than the Spirit of Christ."[167] In the same vein, Thiselton quotes Frank Macchia as saying: "The Spirit . . . binds us to Christ through the proclaimed gospel."[168] Thiselton sees the gifts of the Holy Spirit as not being the ends in themselves, but as pointing "beyond themselves to Christ and to the common good of the Church."[169]

The second theme Thiselton detects in Pauline letters on the Holy Spirit is the fact that the Holy Spirit is not the prerequisite of some elite, but rather, "*every Christian* receives the Holy Spirit, whether or not the believer concerned 'deserves' the Spirit."[170] Thiselton alludes to passages like these to support his view: "Because you are children, God sent the Spirit of his son into our hearts, crying, 'Abba! Father!'" (Gal 4:6). "Anyone who does not have the Spirit of Christ does not belong to him" (Rom 8:9).[171]

The Holy Spirit, as in the Old Testament, "constitutes both a special gift given to *a chosen individual* to perform particular tasks, and a gift poured out either over the *community of all* God's people, or within the framework of God's purposes for the *whole community*."[172] This is the third main theme on the Holy Spirit in Paul according to Thiselton. While the Spirit allots his gifts "to each one individually, just as the Spirit chooses" (1 Cor 12:11), the gifts are "for the common good" (12:7).

The fourth theme emphasizes that Paul believes that the Holy Spirit has been active before Pentecost. However, "he shares pre-Pauline apostolic testimony (including Peter's) that the Holy Spirit is given in a fresh way after the "eschatological' turning point of the last days, ushered in by Christ's resurrection."[173] Thiselton sees Paul's statement that "God through the Holy Spirit raised Jesus from the dead" (Rom 8:11) as constituting "*a cosmic act*, which created *a new era*."[174] Quoting W. D. Davies, he avers that the "Pauline doctrine of the Spirit, then, is only fully comprehensible in the

---

167. Thiselton, *Holy Spirit*, 70.
168. Thiselton, *Holy Spirit*, 70.
169. Thiselton, *Holy Spirit*, 70.
170. Thiselton, *Holy Spirit*, 71.
171. Thiselton, *Holy Spirit*, 71.
172. Thiselton, *Holy Spirit*, 71.
173. Thiselton, *Holy Spirit*, 71.
174. Thiselton, *Holy Spirit*, 72.

light of Rabbinic expectations of the Age to Come as an Age of the Spirit and of the Community of the Spirit."[175]

The reception of the Holy Spirit necessitates that the preaching of the gospel be done with full conviction, for the preaching of the gospel is "more than human."[176] This is the fifth main point of Thiselton on the Holy Spirit in Pauline letters. He cites Paul in 1 Thessalonians 1:5 as saying: "The gospel came to you not in word only, but also in power and in the Holy Spirit and with full conviction." He also alludes to Paul's exhortation to the Thessalonians in 1 Thessalonians 5:19 which says: "Do not quench the Spirit."[177]

The sixth main point Thiselton notes is that "the Spirit is 'Holy' most of all in the sense that, in Gordon Fee's words, the Holy Spirit brings the *power and presence of God himself.*"[178] For Thiselton, this "entails an emphasis on the *otherness* or *transcendence* of God, and on the *more-than-natural* character of his action through the Holy Spirit."[179] Thiselton used "more-than-natural" here instead of "supernatural" to avoid the dualism that characterizes the word "supernatural" from the point of view of the Enlightenment.[180]

The seventh basic theme on the Holy Spirit in Paul which Thiselton identifies is the fact that the Holy Spirit has an eschatological dimension. According to him, the "Holy Spirit transforms us into our future destiny; into that which God destines us to become. In the present life Christians enjoy the 'firstfruits' of the Holy Spirit, or that of which more is to come (Rom 8:22-23)."[181] Paul refers to God's gift of the Holy Spirit to us "as the first installment" (2 Cor 1:22) and "as a guarantee" (2 Cor 5:5) of future things to come.

The Holy Spirit in Paul as in the Old Testament, has a prophetic and revelatory function.[182] This is Thiselton's final main point on the Holy Spirit in Paul. He notes that "Paul saw the Holy Spirit as also Inspirer of the Scriptures, and as having a clear revelatory function (1 Cor 2:6-16)."[183] The Christocentric character of the function of the Holy Spirit in Paul is the major difference between the prophetic and revelatory function of the

---

175. Thiselton, *Holy Spirit*, 72.
176. Thiselton, *Holy Spirit*, 72.
177. Thiselton, *Holy Spirit*, 72.
178. Thiselton, *Holy Spirit*, 72.
179. Thiselton, *Holy Spirit*, 72.
180. Thiselton, *Holy Spirit*, 72.
181. Thiselton, *Holy Spirit*, 73.
182. Thiselton, *Holy Spirit*, 74.
183. Thiselton, *Holy Spirit*, 74.

Holy Spirit in Pauline epistles and the Jewish writings. Although charismatics and Pentecostals are accused of being "Spirit centered," Thiselton notes that many "Pentecostals follow Gordon Fee, Frank Macchia, Amos Yong, and Veli-Matti Kärkkäinen in adopting a 'Christocentric' rather than 'Holiness Movement' approach."[184]

Despite the importance of the gifts of the Holy Spirit, Thiselton reminds believers that in Paul, the gifts are for the common good—the building up of the body of Christ—even though they might be given to individuals. More importantly, he notes that Paul ranks love higher than the gifts as "the lists of charismata move into Paul's major concern for love, not only in 1 Cor 12:31, which is well known, but also in Rom 12:8–10."[185] He recalls Paul wrapping up "his list of gifts through the exalted Christ with 'Let love be genuine; . . . love one another with mutual affection.'"[186] He also notes that Paul, in 1 Corinthians 8:1b, warns that "knowledge puffs up or inflates, whereas love builds up the community."[187] In fact, Thiselton reminds believers that the gifts of the Holy Spirit in Pauline letters, convey that all "things are possible for God, whether this is a sheer 'spontaneous' gift, or God's working through human skills, expertise, and training."[188] Thiselton warns that invoking "a Pentecostal or Renewal 'lens,'" which emphasizes the supernatural at the expense of the natural as if there is a dyad between the two when dealing with the Holy Spirit and his gifts in Paul, is to deny "justice to Paul's own experience, as he records it."[189]

Thiselton's use of "a Pentecostal or Renewal 'lens'" here would have been better qualified as not all Pentecostals or renewal members see a dichotomy between the supernatural and the natural. This is evident, for example, in the case of the Nigerian charismatics and Pentecostals as indicated above; and in the case of the Philippinos in the story referenced earlier, which Wonsuk Ma narrated about Badol. All the same, having seen what the New Testament writers teach about the Holy Spirit, we now turn attention to the Holy Spirit through the centuries.

---

184. Thiselton, *Holy Spirit*, 74.
185. Thiselton, *Holy Spirit*, 94.
186. Thiselton, *Holy Spirit*, 94.
187. Thiselton, *Holy Spirit*, 94.
188. Thiselton, *Holy Spirit*, 103.
189. Thiselton, *Holy Spirit*, 103.

The Holy Spirit through the Centuries

In this section as in the previous one, Anthony Thiselton's work, *The Holy Spirit: In Biblical Teaching, through the Centuries, and Today*, continues to be our source. The study in this section is limited to the Apostolic Fathers and early Christian apologists, the ante and post-Nicene Fathers, and the medieval period. There is no special reason for limiting it to these, except that they are judged to suffice to make the point needed here as far as this work is concerned.

The Apostolic Fathers and Early Christian Apologists

The Apostolic Fathers, according to Thiselton, "belong to the so-called 'tunnel' between the New Testament and the early apologists and Church Fathers."[190] He identifies two main themes on the Holy Spirit in their writings. According to him, the Apostolic Fathers believe that the Old and New Testaments are inspired by the Holy Spirit. For instance, 1 Clement 13:1 states, "Let us do what is written, for the Holy Spirit says, 'Let not the wise man boast himself in his wisdom.'" For Clement, Christ "was humble-minded, as the Holy Spirit spoke concerning him. For it says, 'Lord, who has believed our reports?'"[191] In 1 Clement 45:2 he says, "You have studied the holy Scriptures, which are true, and given by the Holy Spirit."

According to Thiselton, Ignatius "argues that the threefold ministry of Bishop, presbyter, and deacon . . . was established by the mind of Christ 'according to his own will by the Holy Spirit.'"[192] Thiselton maintains that Didache 7:1 and 3, which alludes to "Baptism in the threefold name of the Father, the Son, and the Holy Spirit," echoes Matthew 28:19, "either directly or from current practice."[193]

The Epistle of Barnabas 6:14 quotes Ezekiel 11:19; 36:26 and applies the text to "those whom the Spirit of the Lord foresaw." For Barnabas, "Moses spoke in the Spirit" (Barn. 10:2; Deut 4:1–5). He spoke in the Spirit about the doctrines he received concerning food (Barn. 10:9; Lev 11:29). "Moses received from the Lord the two tablets, written by the finger of the hand of the Lord in the Spirit" (Barn. 14:2; Exod 31:18). Thiselton believes

---

190. Thiselton, *Holy Spirit*, 163.
191. Thiselton, *Holy Spirit*, 164.
192. Thiselton, *Holy Spirit*, 164.
193. Thiselton, *Holy Spirit*, 164.

that it "is possible that Hermas thinks of the Holy Spirit as the Teacher and Sanctifier of believers (*Similitude* 25:2)."[194]

For the Apostolic Fathers, the Holy Spirit inspires prophets. The term "prophets" here includes preachers in some cases. For instance, 1 Clement 42:3–4 declares: "they went forth in the assurance of the Holy Spirit, preaching the good news that the kingdom of God is coming. They preached from district to district." Thiselton admits that Stanley Burgess "cites the passage in which 'the Holy Spirit was poured out in abundance on you all' in the past (1 Clement 2:2; cf. 1:1–3)."[195] Thiselton notes that Ignatius believes that he is inspired by the Holy Spirit. However, "it is not clear whether this is the Spirit of prophecy or the Spirit who equips believers for church office, perhaps at ordination," as he admonishes to give "'heed to the bishop and to the presbytery and deacons, as also 'God's own voice,' spoken by him."[196]

Thiselton records that the Spirit can induce "spiritual" or "charismatic" exegesis as in the case of Barnabas 10:2–3; 6:14 and 16:7–8. In the same vein, "The Shepherd of Hermas recounts the 'rapture' or seizing of Hermas when he is carried by the spirit through a wilderness, and the heavens opened (Vision 1:1:3 and 2:1:1)."[197] For Barnabas, it appears that "faith in Christ is not a human work, but one which the Holy Spirit initiates" (Barn. 19:7).[198] Barnabas also refers to the body as "the vessel of the Spirit" (Barn. 7:3; 11:9).[199] Thiselton warns based on the writings of the Apostolic Fathers not to generalize "concerning the relationship between the Charismatic experience and Church order." According to him, "we should avoid preconceived theories about charisma and order."[200]

The early Christian apologists spanned the early century from about 120 or 130 to 200 or 220 CE. For Aristides, the Holy Spirit is instrumental in the incarnation of Jesus for human salvation (Aristides, *Apol.* 15). Justin Martyr maintains that it is the Holy Spirit that instructs the human mind to see God at any time (Justin, *Dial.* 4). According to Thiselton, "Justin argues that Christ is preexistent 'filled with the powers of the Holy Spirit,' and 'became incarnate'" (*Dial.* 87).[201] After citing Acts 2:17 and Joel 2:28, which says, "I will pour out my Spirit on all flesh" (*Dial.* 87), Justin avows that it is now

---

194. Thiselton, *Holy Spirit*, 165.
195. Thiselton, *Holy Spirit*, 165.
196. Thiselton, *Holy Spirit*, 165.
197. Thiselton, *Holy Spirit*, 167.
198. Thiselton, *Holy Spirit*, 168.
199. Thiselton, *Holy Spirit*, 168.
200. Thiselton, *Holy Spirit*, 168.
201. Thiselton, *Holy Spirit*, 169.

"possible to see among us women and men who possess the gifts of the Spirit of God; as it was promised" (*Dial.* 88). Justin affirms that Christians worship the Holy Spirit along with the Father and the Son (1 *Apol.* 6). Athenagoras affirms the Trinity (*Emb.* 10:3) and maintains that the Spirit out-flows from God (*Emb.* 10), and unites God the Father, the Son, and the Spirit (*Emb.* 12).[202] For Theophilus, prophets and the evangelists are inspired by the Holy Spirit and carry the Holy Spirit in them (*Autol.* 2:9).

The Ante-Nicene Fathers

Irenaeus affirms the distinctness but inseparability of the Holy Spirit from God as well as his participation in the works of creation (*Haer.* 4; 4:20:3; Preface 4). Thiselton argues that the position of Irenaeus here, "makes it utterly clear that *the Holy Spirit is not creature*, a preexisting creation, and is distinct from the Son and inseparable from the Father."[203] Irenaeus also believes that the Holy Spirit anointed Christ for his incarnate ministry (*Haer.* 3:17:3; 3:18:3; 3:9:3; 18:3).

According to Thiselton, Irenaeus "endorses Paul's assertion that 'the Spirit . . . searches all things' (1 Cor 2:11)" and that "the Spirit gives 'diversities of gifts, differences of administrations, and diversities of operations' (1 Cor 12:4–6), not a conveyance of all knowledge (2:18:7)."[204] The reception of the Holy Spirit according to Irenaeus has an eschatological dimension. "We do now receive a certain portion of the Holy Spirit . . . , preparing us for incorruption, being little by little accustomed to receive and hear God; which the apostle terms 'an earnest,' that is, a part of the honor which has been promised by God" (*Haer.* 5:8:1). For Irenaeus, prophecy is inspired by the Holy Spirit. Thiselton refers to prophecy in Irenaeus's teaching as "not given by human beings, such as a magician, but by the 'Divinely bestowed power of prophesying when and where God pleases'" (1:13:14). He believes that the 'where and when' in this case "*should not exclude either Charismatic spontaneity or prepared, reflective preaching.*"[205]

For Clement of Alexandria, "faith with baptism is trained by the Holy Spirit" (*Instr.* 1:6) even though he does not accept that "all believers are 'spiritual' without qualification."[206] Thiselton notes that for Clement, "'the manifestation of the Spirit' entails qualities as 'the word of wisdom by the

---

202. Thiselton, *Holy Spirit*, 170–71.
203. Thiselton, *Holy Spirit*, 174.
204. Thiselton, *Holy Spirit*, 175.
205. Thiselton, *Holy Spirit*, 176.
206. Thiselton, *Holy Spirit*, 177.

Spirit, . . . faith through the Spirit, . . . healing, . . . miracles, . . . prophecy, . . . discernment of Spirits, . . . diversities of tongues, . . . interpretations of tongues . . . . All these works by the same Spirit . . . ' (1 Cor 12:7–11; *Miscellanies*, 4:21)."[207]

Tertullian, one of the ante-Nicene Fathers, was attracted to the immediacy of the Holy Spirit, and to prophecy. He believes according to Thiselton, that the "Spirit of God, who hovered over [the waters] from the beginning (Gen. 1:2), would continue to linger over the waters of the baptized" (Tertullian, *Bapt.* 4).[208] Thiselton notes that for Tertullian, the Holy Spirit "*is active in the conception, birth, and incarnation of Jesus Christ*, and is sent in place of Christ to guide the believers."[209] Tertullian believes that the Spirit proceeds from no other source than from Father through the Son."[210] According to Thiselton, Tertullian "encouraged the 'distribution of gifts' of the Spirit among the faithful" (1 Cor 12:4-12; *Bapt.* 20).[211]

Origen affirms that both Testaments of the Scripture are inspired by the Holy Spirit and that the Scripture teaches us what the Holy Spirit is (*Princ.* 1:3:1; 1:3:2; 2:7:1;). He "establishes in several ways," according to Thiselton, "the close relationship between the *Holy Spirit and Christ*."[212]

Origen maintains that there is no evidence in the Scripture that the Holy Spirit is "created" or "made" (1:3:3). According to him, baptism is "*not complete except by . . . the Trinity*" (1:3:2). The Holy Spirit for Origen is the medium of revelation (1:3:8) and sanctification of believers (1:3:8). The Holy Spirit is the giver of gifts (1:3:8) and works in collaboration with the other Persons of the Trinity (1:3:5). The Spirit is the giver of life (2:7:2). Thiselton notes that for Origen, like Paul, "the Spirit Himself makes special intercession with God with sighs too deep for words. . . . The Spirit intercedes for the saints according to the will of God (*On Prayer*, Preface 3)."[213] Thiselton avers that when Origen spots that the "Spirit of God is taken away from all who are unworthy" (*Princ.* 1:3:7), "he does not intend this to be understood in the way in which a minority of Pentecostals or some in the Renewal Movement might be tempted to use it." For "the Holy Spirit is a

---

207. Thiselton, *Holy Spirit*, 177.
208. Thiselton, *Holy Spirit*, 180.
209. Thiselton, *Holy Spirit*, 181.
210. Thiselton, *Holy Spirit*, 181.
211. Thiselton, *Holy Spirit*, 183.
212. Thiselton, *Holy Spirit*, 185.
213. Thiselton, *Holy Spirit*, 186.

power 'in which all are said to have a share, who have deserved to be sanctified by His grace' (1:1:3)."[214]

The Post-Nicene Fathers

In this section, the works of four post-Nicene Fathers on the Holy Spirit will be examined. Hilary of Poitiers and Ambrose of Milan will be representing the West while Athanasius of Alexandria and the Cappadocian Fathers will represent the East. There is no special reason for choosing them except that their views on the Holy Spirit are judged to suffice to make the point needed here. Thiselton's work mentioned earlier continues to be our source.

Thiselthon observes that "Hilary defended the deity *of the Holy Spirit* in the West, while Athanasius defended it in the East."[215] Hilary maintains that the Holy Spirit, the Spirit of truth, proceeds from the Father and is sent from the Father by the Son who "are one in nature, honor, (and) power" (*Trin.* 8:20). "If Father and Son are truly one, there is a sense in which it does not matter," if "we say, 'proceed from the Father and the Son,' or from the Father."[216] Hilary enumerates the gifts of the Holy Spirit listed in 1 Cor 12:4–10. However, he does not limit healing and prophecy to the realm of the 'supernatural,' as healing does not "exclude medical means," and prophecy means "'*our understanding of doctrine*' and being taught by God."[217]

The giving of the gifts is not solely the work of the Holy Spirit. "All three Persons of the Holy Trinity are involved," for there "is 'One Spirit' and 'One Divinity'" (8:32).[218] For Hilary, the Holy Spirit is not created (12:55); and "The Lord who was to send the Holy Spirit was himself born of the Holy Spirit" (*Syn.* 32:85). The Holy Spirit is the Spirit of God and is beyond what the human intellect can fully comprehend (*Trin.* 12:56).

Ambrose of Milan likens the moistening of the threshing floor in Gideon narrative as "a type of the Holy Spirit, poured out on the Gentiles" (On the Holy Spirit, 1:1:8).[219] Ambrose insists that the Holy Spirit is not created. For the "Spirit of God is the same as the Holy Spirit" (1:4:56). He avows that the prophets and the apostles received the one Holy Spirit. "For we have all drunk of one Spirit" (1:4:61). He asserts that God anointed Jesus with the Holy Spirit (1:9:101), demonstrating in this sense that the Holy Spirit is inseparable

---

214. Thiselton, *Holy Spirit*, 187.
215. Thiselton, *Holy Spirit*, 194.
216. Thiselton, *Holy Spirit*, 194.
217. Thiselton, *Holy Spirit*, 194.
218. Thiselton, *Holy Spirit*, 195.
219. Thiselton, *Holy Spirit*, 196.

"from the Father and Christ" (1:6:80). Thiselton observes that Ambrose "follows Basil in recognizing that the *Holy Spirit is to be worshiped and glorified, though not in isolation from the Father and the Son*."[220]

Ambrose maintains that the Holy Spirit is life and the giver of eternal life (*Spir.* 2:3:26-27). The Holy Spirit, he avers, is creator (2:5:32); and the "earth exists only with the 'operation of the Holy Spirit'" (2;5:35).[221] Ambrose alludes to the work of the Holy Spirit in the virginal conception of Jesus (2:5:38). He also avows that the Holy Spirit is eternal (2:6:51) and "the Author of the grace of the Spirit" (2:7:64). The Holy Spirit inspires believers to pray (2:10:102). No doubt, Ambrose agrees that the "Spirit glorifies the Son, as the Father glorifies Him, but the Son of God also glorifies the Spirit" (2:11:121).

The gifts of the Holy Spirit in 1 Corinthians 12:4-7 have trinitarian basis according to Ambrose as they come from the same Spirit, the same Lord, and the same God (2:12:138). In *The Christian Faith*, 2:6:48, Ambrose enumerates the gifts of the Holy Spirit in 1 Corinthians 12:8-11. Thiselton notes that Ambrose insists that the Father, the Son, and the Holy Spirit work together in all acts and are inseparable.[222] The sanctification of the believer is the work of all three Persons of the Trinity (*Spir.* 3:4:25-28). Ambrose avows that the Holy Spirit brings moral character (3:6:41-43), punishes the Antichrist (3:7:44), and is the sword of the Word (3:7:45). He maintains that the "Spirit of the Lord is the very Spirit of God" (3:9:54), and where "the Spirit is, there also is Christ" (3:9:55). For Ambrose, "God is worshiped in Spirit, for the Spirit is also worshiped" (3:11:81). He reiterates Paul's assertion that the Holy Spirit dwells in the church, which is God's temple (3:11:90; 1 Cor 3:16; 6:19). According to Thiselton, "Ambrose cites many passages from the New Testament to show that the Father, the Son, and the Holy Spirit *share together in every stage of salvation* (3:19:132-52)."[223]

Athanasius of Alexandria is among those post-Nicene Eastern Fathers who insist that the Holy Spirit is not created. He considers it evil and erroneous to call the Holy Spirit a "creature," for the Holy Spirit is the Spirit of God (*Ep. Serap.* 1:4). Thiselton observes that Athanasius insists that when "the Holy Spirit is given to us, . . . God is in us" (1:19).[224] He avows that the Holy Spirit is inseparable from Christ. For "Paul declared that the works he worked by the power of the Spirit were the works of Christ" (1:19). The

---

220. Thiselton, *Holy Spirit*, 198.
221. Thiselton, *Holy Spirit*, 198.
222. Thiselton, *Holy Spirit*, 199.
223. Thiselton, *Holy Spirit*, 201.
224. Thiselton, *Holy Spirit*, 212.

Spirit, for him, is a quickening Spirit and giver of life who raised Christ from the dead (1:23). He is "a well of water springing up into eternal life" (1:23). Athanasius maintains that the Holy Spirit anointed Jesus Christ for his work (1:23), and that he dwells in Christians, who are God's temples (1:24). He acknowledges the Holy Spirit as the image of the Son (1:24). For the "Spirit is 'proper to the Son and not alien from God,'" as he "'is from God himself'" (1:25).[225] Athanasius upholds that the "activity of the Triad is one" (1:31). Hence, the giving of the gifts enumerated in 1 Corinthians 12:1–11 is the activity of the Father, the Son, and the Holy Spirit as there "are diversities of gifts, but the same Spirit; . . . the same Lord; . . . the same God . . . " (1:30). Athanasius asserts that the Holy Spirit sanctifies and anoints believers (1:22-23). "He is the indwelling Spirit," (1:23-24) and the "Spirit in the Trinity and the faith of the Church" (1:28).[226]

Basil of Caesarea is one of the Cappadocian Fathers who, influenced by Athanasius, maintains that the Trinity is one in Being and should be given equal glory.[227] According to Thiselton, Basil asserts "that the Holy Spirit should be accorded the same honor and glory as the Father and the Son, *especially in the threefold Gloria*"; and that "the Spirit is *holy without qualification* and on that ground must be indivisibly one with God, who alone is holy without qualification."[228] Thiselton points out that Basil teaches that the "Spirit gives us the earnest of life, . . . having our fruit in holiness. . . . (T)he Spirit pours in quickening power, renewing our souls from the deadness of sin. . . . born again of water and the Spirit" (15:36).[229] For Basil, our restoration to paradise is through the Holy Spirit (15:37) just as prophecy and other gifts come through the Holy Spirit.[230] The Holy Spirit makes it possible to behold the face of God (16:38). The confession of Jesus as Lord is by the Holy Spirit who is also the source of Christian holiness (16:38). Basil avers that the Holy Spirit intercedes for believers (19:50). In harmony with Paul, he warns Christians not to grieve the Holy Spirit (19:20; Eph. 4:20).

Gregory of Nazianzus, like Basil, defended the divinity of the Holy Spirit (*Spir. Sanct.* 6, 7, 8). Alluding to Paul's assertion that the Holy Spirit intercedes for us (Rom 8:26) and prays with us (1 Cor 14:15), he declares, "Therefore to adore or pray to the Spirit seems to me to be simply Himself offering prayer or adoration to Himself" (*Spir. Sanct.* 12). He maintains

---

225. Thiselton, *Holy Spirit*, 212.
226. Thiselton, *Holy Spirit*, 213.
227. Thiselton, *Holy Spirit*, 214–15.
228. Thiselton, *Holy Spirit*, 215.
229. Thiselton, *Holy Spirit*, 216.
230. Thiselton, *Holy Spirit*, 216.

that the Holy Spirit "is glorified with One of coequal honor" (12). Gregory of Nazianzus avows that the "Spirit is called 'the Spirit of God, the Spirit of Christ, the Mind of Christ, the Spirit of the Lord . . . '" (*Spir. Sanct.* 29).[231] To him, the Holy Spirit is "sanctifying, not sanctified; measuring, not measured; sharing, not shared; filling, not filled; containing, not contained" (29). He persuades all "to worship the Father, Son, and Holy Spirit, the One Godhead and power" (33). He argues that the "Spirit shares with the Son . . . both the Creation and Resurrection . . . . He is the author of spiritual regeneration" (*Pent.*).[232]

Gregory of Nyssa together with Basil and Gregory of Nazianzus is popularly known as the Cappadocian Fathers. He too defends the divinity of the Holy Spirit. Referring to the trinitarian Godhead, he declares that we do not "learn that the Father does anything by Himself in which the Son does not work conjointly, or again that the Son has any special operation apart from the Holy Spirit. . . . Every operation . . . has its origin from the Father and proceeds through the Son, and is perfected in the Holy Spirit."[233] He further declares, "If we perceive that the activity of the Father and the Son and the Holy Spirit is one, . . . it is necessary to infer the unity of their nature" (*Trin.* 6). Gregory again states that the "Holy Spirit by the uncreatedness of His nature has contact with the Son and the Father, but is distinguished from them by His own tokens. . . . Joined to the Father by His uncreatedness, He is distinguished from Him again by not being 'Father'" (*Eun.* 1:22).[234]

The Medieval Period

In this section, the views of Gregory the Great and Thomas Aquinas on the Holy Spirit are examined. Anthony Thiselton's work, *The Holy Spirit: In Biblical Teaching, through the Centuries, and Today* continues to be our source.

Gregory has this to say about the Holy Spirit: "When the Lord was made flesh, he was anointed by this oil [i.e., the Holy Spirit] . . . since the Lord was made flesh by the Spirit's mediation, he was anointed with this oil at the very moment when he was created as a man . . . . His ointment is the aroma of the Holy Spirit, who . . . remains on him" (*Moral.* 14).[235] Gregory insists that the "Holy Spirit makes its [his] presence known to men not only in form of a dove, but also in the form of fire. The dove symbolizes

---

231. Thiselton, *Holy Spirit*, 219.
232. Thiselton, *Holy Spirit*, 219.
233. Thiselton, *Holy Spirit*, 219.
234. Thiselton, *Holy Spirit*, 220.
235. Thiselton, *Holy Spirit*, 223.

simplicity; the fire, zeal, . . . gentleness of spirit, . . . and the zeal of uprightness" (1:2:2).[236] Gregory argues that the "Holy Spirit from on high is imparted 'by the laying on of hands. There are men who undertake the care of souls, and yet they are afraid to lay snares of the flock of the Lord'" (*Moral.* 14).[237] For Gregory, "Christ was 'full of the Spirit of sevenfold grace,' as evidenced by Isa. 11:2 and Luke 4:18. In Luke we read, 'The Spirit is upon me, because he has anointed me to bring good news . . . .' In Isa. 11:2, 'The Spirit of the Lord shall rest upon him, the Spirit of wisdom and understanding, the Spirit of counsel and might, the Spirit of knowledge and the fear of the Lord.'"[238] This exudes that the "Spirit gives to the Church and to the Christian what he has given to Christ."[239] Thiselton argues that in "his work on Acts, Gregory refers to *various tongues as pointing to the universality of the Church*, and gives a cross-reference to the gifts of the Spirit in 1 Cor 12:8-10."[240] For Gregory, the Holy Spirit "proceeds *from the Father and the Son*" (*Hom. Gosp.* 26).[241]

The Holy Spirit as the Paraclete, the Advocate, "intervenes before the Father's justice on behalf of the wrongdoing of sinners; he who is one substance with the Father and the Son is said to plead earnestly on behalf of sinners . . . . Hence, Paul says: 'For the Spirit himself pleads for us with unutterable groaning' (Rom 8:26)" (*Forty Gospel Homilies*, Homily 30; p. 238 of the Cistercian translation).[242] For Gregory, the Holy Spirit is "coeternal with the Father and the Son" (Homily 30; Cistercian translation, p. 240). He asserts that the "Lord sends fire upon the earth when he enkindles the hearts of the materially-minded with the breath of the Holy Spirit . . . . The Spirit . . . *drives numbness and cold from every heart, fills and warms it to desire its own eternity*" (Homily 30).[243]

Thomas Aquinas avows that the name "[Holy Spirit] is genuinely a proper name for a person of the Trinity." For "'There are those who bear witness in heaven, the Father, the Word, and the Holy Spirit' (1 John 5:7)."[244] Aquinas concludes that the "*Holy Spirit is from the Father and Son,*

---

236. Thiselton, *Holy Spirit*, 223.
237. Thiselton, *Holy Spirit*, 223.
238. Thiselton, *Holy Spirit*, 223.
239. Thiselton, *Holy Spirit*, 223.
240. Thiselton, *Holy Spirit*, 223.
241. Thiselton, *Holy Spirit*, 223.
242. Thiselton, *Holy Spirit*, 224.
243. Thiselton, *Holy Spirit*, 224.
244. Thiselton, *Holy Spirit*, 244.

not made, not created, not begotten, but proceeding" (*ST* q. 36, art. 1, ad.).[245] For him, the Holy Spirit is love. "The name Love of God can be taken essentially and personally. If taken personally, it is the proper name of the Holy Spirit, as Word is the proper name of the Son" (*ST* q. 37, art. 1, ad.). Aquinas sees the Holy Spirit as the gift of God (*ST* Ia, q. 38, art. 2, ad.). Quoting Augustine's *On the Trinity*, 15:26, he asserts: "By the gift which is the Holy Spirit many particular gifts are portioned out to the members of Christ"; and none of these gifts of the Holy Spirit, according to him can "be called a gift of man, but the gift of God" (art. 2, ad. 3). For Aquinas, the "gifts of the Spirit include the sevenfold gifts given to Christ, and will endure even in heaven" (*ST* q. 68, art. 5–6).[246]

Thiselton notes that Paul's list of gifts of the Holy Spirit in 1 Corinthians 12:8–10 which hinges on "utterance of wisdom" and "utterance of knowledge" relates to Aquinas' grace of using words in part II, q. 177.[247] Aquinas "agrees that the word uttered needs to be confirmed 'by the working of miracles' (*ST* q. 178, art. 1). He quotes Mark 16:20, 'confirming the word with signs that followed'. But he adds a warning: 'some miracles are not true, but imaginary deeds; . . . they delude man' (art. 2)."[248] Aquinas also deliberates on the gift of "prophecy." According to him, "Prophetic revelation takes place in four forms, namely by the infusion of intelligible light, by the infusion of intelligible species, by . . . pictures of the imagination, and by the natural presentation of sensible images" (*ST* q. 173, art. 3). Aquinas's view here elicits two comments from Thiselton. According to him, it doesn't appear Aquinas is addressing "the question of *how we know*. Can we know whether what the imagination, or even analogy or pictures, may suggest appears to be *true*(?)" Secondly, he believes that Aquinas's view implies that he is commenting "on 1 Thess 5:19–20, namely, that *preaching* comes under the usual scope of *prophecy*, while 'prophecy' in the popular sense comes under '*exceptional*' examples."[249] Like Paul, Aquinas believes that the "spirit of the prophets is subject to the prophets" (art. 3, ad. 4). He also believes that genuine prophecy "comes 'not from oneself,' but from the Holy Spirit (Art. 4)."[250] Aquinas does not leave out "the grace of tongues" in his discussion (q. 176), which he believes is originally given for the preaching of faith everywhere (art. 1).[251] For

---

245. Thiselton, *Holy Spirit*, 244.
246. Thiselton, *Holy Spirit*, 245.
247. Thiselton, *Holy Spirit*, 245.
248. Thiselton, *Holy Spirit*, 246.
249. Thiselton, *Holy Spirit*, 246.
250. Thiselton, *Holy Spirit*, 246.
251. Thiselton, *Holy Spirit*, 246.

him, "the gift of prophecy surpasses the gift of tongues" (art. 2). In line with Augustine, Aquinas holds that the Holy Spirit "is the bond of love between God the Father and God the Son" (*ST* q. 24, art. 2).

This brief examination of the teachings on the Holy Spirit in the New Testament Scriptures and through the centuries has shown that there is not much difference, if at all any, between these teachings and the charismatic and Pentecostal theological and doctrinal understanding of the Holy Spirit. The major difference is that charismatics and Pentecostals strongly believe in the experiential encounter of the Holy Spirit. In the next two chapters, we shall examine how this theology of experiential encounter allows charismatics and Pentecostals flexibility in their ecclesiology and worship respectively.

CHAPTER 2

Charismatic and Pentecostal Ecclesiology

WRITING ABOUT THE WORD (*ekklēsia*) which the New Testament writers use to refer to the church, Gerhard Kittel and Gerhard Friedrich, in their edited work, *Theological Dictionary of the New Testament*, aver that there is no description of the church given in the New Testament. However, they maintain that "Paul gets to the heart of the matter with his understanding of it (parallel to that of Acts) as an assembly which is the assembly of God in Christ."[1] For them, Paul's epistles, particularly Colossians and Ephesians, unfold a more specific doctrine of the church as they present the church as the body of Christ, "with Christ himself as head (Col. 1:18, 24; Eph. 1:22; 5:23). There is a relation of coordination and subordination between it and Christ (Eph. 5:24–25, 29). The church is to be holy and without blemish (5:27). Through it, God's wisdom is to be made known (3:10)."[2] Kittel and Fredrich note that everything concerning Christ and the church is God's doing. They maintain that the imageries which Paul used to allude to the church, whether as the body of Christ or the spouse of Christ, "express the strict relation between Christ and the church, and thus serve a christological ecclesiology."[3]

Gordon Fee, a Pentecostal scholar referred to in chapter 1, like many other Pentecostals and charismatics, would no doubt agree that all that concerns Christ and the church is God's doing. However, he and other charismatics and Pentecostals would maintain that it is God's doing through God's empowering presence—the Holy Spirit. Hence, for him and his fellow Pentecostals, and charismatics, while the church is the body of Christ and Christ himself is her head, and while the church is betrothed to Christ as his

1. Kittel and Friedrich, *Theological Dictionary*, 353.
2. Kittel and Friedrich, *Theological Dictionary*, 353.
3. Kittel and Friedrich, *Theological Dictionary*, 353.

53

bride, the crucial role of the Holy Spirit in the church and in the lives of the individual members, makes them prefer a pneumatological ecclesiology to christological ecclesiology as will be seen in this chapter. Their pneumatological ecclesiology, however, is not completely devoid of Christology.

Returning to the word (*ekklēsia*), it comes from two Greek words, *ek*, "out," and *kaleō*, "call." Hence the New Testament writers present the church as the "assembly of the called";[4] a chosen race, a royal priesthood, a holy nation, God's own people, called to proclaim the mighty acts of him who called you out of darkness into his marvelous light (1 Pet 2:9). To proclaim the mighty acts of God is to worship God. Hence, the New Testament Greek lexicon defines (*ekklēsia*) or the church as "an assembly of Christians gathered for worship in a religious meeting."[5] Worship in this sense is understood from the charismatic and Pentecostal perspective as a deep and touched involvement of being in the presence of God made possible by God's empowering presence, the Holy Spirit.[6] Charismatics and Pentecostals hold on to this perception.

Franklin Segler and Randall Bradley had argued that the "forms of doctrine which the church embraces directly affect its understanding of worship."[7] This cannot be truer. However, it is important to add that the self-understanding of any church directly affects its forms of doctrine which consequently affect its liturgical understanding and praxis as will be seen in the next chapter. This chapter, however, focuses on a brief study of charismatic and Pentecostal ecclesiology.

This work does not pretend that there is no difference between the ecclesiology of charismatics and Pentecostals. In fact, it acknowledges that charismatics follow the ecclesiology of their mainline churches, which differs to some extent from Pentecostal ecclesiology. However, as noted in the introduction, this work is using the theology and praxis of charismatics and Pentecostals to argue for the renewal of the Nigerian Catholic Church based on charismatics and Pentecostals' belief on the role of the Holy Spirit in the church and in liturgy. More importantly, they are a source of renewal in how they go in praxis to live out their belief as evident in their style of worship, which will be the focus of the next chapter.

This chapter projects what Pentecostals theologically and doctrinally believe the church should be. It will also show that the major difference between the ecclesiology of the mainline churches, particularly the Catholic

---

4. Williams, *Renewal Theology*, 16.
5. "Ekklēsia," def. 1.d.1.
6. Archer, "Worship," 115.
7. Segler and Bradley, *Christian Worship*, 59.

Church and that of charismatics and Pentecostals, is that, like their theology in general, the ecclesiology of charismatics and Pentecostals is an ecclesiology of an encounter that is praxis-oriented and experiential. This makes their ecclesiology pneumatocentric unlike that of the mainline churches that is Christocentric. It should be noted here then that the use of the phrases "charismatic and Pentecostal ecclesiology" and "charismatic and Pentecostal theology of worship" in this chapter and the next are not to underestimate the difference between the two currents of theology. Rather, they are simply because this writer acknowledges the fact that both charismatics and Pentecostals believe and emphasize the role of the Holy Spirit in the church and in liturgy, and in praxis live out their belief as evident in their style of worship. The chapter will finally present a brief overview of how this manifests itself in the case of the Nigerian charismatic renewal and Pentecostalism.

Ecclesiology of Experiential Encounter

Pentecostal and charismatic emphasis on the role of the Holy Spirit in the church and in the life of individual members of the church essentially marks their ecclesiology as a pneumatological ecclesiology. That is, an ecclesiology of encounter, which is experiential and praxis-oriented. Their ecclesiology, no doubt, has trinitarian and christological perspectives in the sense that Christ's coming and the gift of the eschatological Spirit "marked the new way by which God's people are constituted. The community is now entered individually through faith in Christ and through the reception of the Spirit, signalled by baptism."[8]

In fact, Gordon Fee maintains that "The people of God as a community of believers owe their existence to their common, lavish experience of the Spirit."[9] For, both Jews and Gentiles, slaves and free who now make up the one body of Christ, were all alike "immersed in the same reality, Spirit, and *all* alike were caused to drink to the fill of the same reality, Spirit, so as to form one body in Christ."[10] Having been 'Created and formed *by* the Spirit," Fee argues that "the early communities thus became a fellowship *of* the Spirit."[11] Fee does not dispute the fact that for Paul, Christ is the center and not the Holy Spirit. However, he observes that the images especially the three major images—family, temple, and body which Paul used for the church, revealed the "centrality of the Spirit to Paul's view of the believing

8. Fee, *God's Empowering Presence*, 871.
9. Fee, *God's Empowering Presence*, 872.
10. Fee, *God's Empowering Presence*, 872.
11. Fee, *God's Empowering Presence*, 872.

community."¹² The image of the church as God's family, "which occurs explicitly only twice (Eph 2:19; 1 Tim 3:15; cf. 2 Cor 6:18), flows naturally out of Paul's reference to God as Father, believers as brothers and sisters, and the apostle as a household manager."¹³ Although Paul did not elaborate on this imagery per se, Fee insists that what

> is significant is the role of the Spirit, as both responsible for and evidence of believers becoming members of God's family. This is expressed most vividly in the parallel passages of Gal 4:6 and Rom 8:14–17. In the Romans passage in particular, the Spirit is actually identified as "the Spirit of adoption," which can only mean, "the Spirit, responsible for their adoption as God's children." The evidence of their being God's children is found in the Spirit's prompting them to cry "*Abba*, Father."¹⁴

Fee observes that Paul used the imagery of God's temple four times to refer to the church (1 Cor 3:16-17; 2 Cor 6:16; Eph 2:19-22; 1 Tim 3:15-16). According to him the "usage in 1 Corinthians 3 is especially instructive, both as to the role of the Spirit and as an image referring to the church as 'a gathered people' of God. . . . As a gathered community, they formed the one temple of the *living* God, God's alternative to Corinth; and what made them his alternative was the presence of the Spirit in their midst."¹⁵ In fact, Fee insists that as God's temple, indwelled by his Spirit, the family of God or God's children or people, "formed a powerful fellowship, evidenced by manifestations of the Spirit (1 Cor 12:7), including miracles (Gal 3:5) and prophetic utterances (1 Thes 5:19-20; 1 Cor 14:24-25; outsiders exclaim, 'surely God is *among you*')."¹⁶ By using the imagery of Christ's body to refer to the church, Paul conveys two crucial points: "the need for unity *and* for diversity in the believing community, both of which are the work of 'the one and the same Spirit' (1 Cor 12:11)."¹⁷ Fee argues that the "urgency of the appeal that begins with 4:1 and carries through the end is that they 'keep the unity that the Spirit has given them' (4:3)."¹⁸ To keep this unity, they must not "grieve the Holy Spirit (v.30), who has formed them into a body and whose continuing presence is intended to bring the body to full maturity. Hence the need to 'keep filled with the Spirit' (5:18), so as to ensure proper worship (vv. 19–20)

12. Fee, *God's Empowering Presence*, 873.
13. Fee, *God's Empowering Presence*, 873.
14. Fee, *God's Empowering Presence*, 873.
15. Fee, *God's Empowering Presence*, 874.
16. Fee, *God's Empowering Presence*, 876.
17. Fee, *God's Empowering Presence*, 874.
18. Fee, *God's Empowering Presence*, 875.

and proper relationships (5:21—6:9)."[19] According to Fee, the "Spirit who is responsible for their being *one body* is also the basis for the *many parts* necessary for the body to function at all."[20]

Fee observes that for Paul, "Christian life not only begins by means of the Spirit; the whole of Christian life is a matter of Spirit.... One must finish in the same way as one began, through the empowering and appropriating work of the Spirit. Thus the Spirit is as central to Paul's understanding of all of ongoing Christian life, including ethical life, as it is to conversion itself."[21] Fee avers that when Paul urged Christians to walk in/by the Spirit in Gal 5:13—6:10, he showed that "the Spirit is the key to ethical life."[22] The whole point of the argument according to Fee "has to do with the sufficiency of the Spirit, as we continue to live as Spirit people in the world where the perspective of the flesh is still the dominant force."[23] For Fee, the level of Paul's expectation on this matter of walking by the Spirit was high "because for him and his churches the Spirit was not simply believed in but was experienced in very tangible, visible ways."[24] In the same way, Pentecostals and charismatics do not simply believe in the Holy Spirit and in the role of the Holy Spirit in the church and in the lives of individual members of the church, they experience the Holy Spirit in very tangible and visible ways. This explains why their ecclesiology, while exhibiting trinitarian and christological trends, is essentially pneumatological.

It is no surprise that Clark H. Pinnock, an Evangelical Christian and an admirer and friend of charismatics and Pentecostals, while giving a keynote address at the 2005 annual meeting of the Society of Pentecostal Studies, notes what he feels the charismatic and Pentecostal ecclesiology should be, based on their theology and praxis. According to him, Pentecostal ecclesiology is a "power ecclesiology, in which believers are endued with power to serve as anointed witnesses to the kingdom of God. Pentecostals experience God as empowering and commissioning them for mission."[25] The church seen through the lens of the charismatic and Pentecostal theology and praxis, is not the kingdom but an anticipatory sign of the kingdom. Hence, she has no reason for self-exaltation. "She serves the reign of God as the anointed herald and witness ... In bearing witness, she experiences the

---

19. Fee, *God's Empowering Presence*, 875.
20. Fee, *God's Empowering Presence*, 875.
21. Fee, *God's Empowering Presence*, 876.
22. Fee, *God's Empowering Presence*, 879.
23. Fee, *God's Empowering Presence*, 880.
24. Fee, *God's Empowering Presence*, 880.
25. Pinnock, "Church in the Power," 151.

powers of the age to come and, by living together in community, witnesses to the character of God's reign."[26] For charismatics and Pentecostals, the church is a community called by God "to witness to the character of his reign and to serve as a medium through which God will express himself to the world" through signs and wonders.[27]

The charismatic and Pentecostal pneumatology of experiential encounter results in a fluidity of charismatic and Pentecostal ecclesiology. This is an ecclesiology in which charismatics and Pentecostals allow some flexibility in their understanding of the church so as to come up with some concepts of the church that fit into their theology of experiential encounter. Going by the ecclesiology charismatics and Pentecostals have been living out in praxis without bothering much about its intellectual development, Pinnock graciously proposes for them what he tags "power ecclesiology." This ecclesiology presents the church as an anointed herald of God's kingdom, a trinitarian society, a missional church, a fellowship in the Spirit, and a charismatic community.

The fluidity that gives rise to power ecclesiology, consequently, allows charismatics and Pentecostals to interpret the gospel primarily

> as healing and deliverance from bondage and death through the power of the risen Lord. It is also as a message, not communicated primarily in a rational way but as a word of power that mends broken lives and delivers from demonic powers—an interpretation that gives a sense of the present reality of the kingdom of God now not just in the great bye and bye.[28]

Interpreting the gospel in this way provides a new paradigm not only ecclesiologically but also soteriologically. For as Pinnock says, it amounts "to a new paradigm of salvation which lifts up a Jesus who ministered in the power of the Spirit and identified with the broken and the outcast—a paradigm where church is the presence in history of the crucified and resurrected Lord and is swept forward by the Spirit into ever-expanding possibilities."[29] In this kind of paradigm, all aspects of daily life are situated in the realm of the Spirit and "the risen Lord himself is here in the world manifesting divine power."[30] In this way, the charismatic and Pentecostal theology of experiential encounter offers charismatics and Pentecostals the flexibility of seeing the church as "the community that is called to be, on the finite level, the kind

---

26. Pinnock, "Church in the Power," 152.
27. Pinnock, "Church in the Power," 152.
28. Pinnock, "Church in the Power," 152–53.
29. Pinnock, "Church in the Power," 153.
30. Pinnock, "Church in the Power," 153.

of reality that God is in eternity."[31] In this ecclesiology, the church for charismatics and Pentecostals, becomes the medium of God's mission on earth; the chosen people of God "who will carry the gospel to the ends of the earth" accompanied by signs and wonders that will make the hearers to declare, "God is really among you!" (1 Cor 14:25).[32]

In fact, "power ecclesiology," proposed by Pinnock from the charismatic and Pentecostal theology of experiential encounter, portrays the church as a fellowship in the Spirit. Pinnock sees this as a new model of the church "where people gather not to hear a well-prepared lecture (the Protestant way) and not to witness a sacerdotal liturgy (the Catholic way) but to experience the presence of the living God."[33] According to him, it "is not so much a theory of church as it is an experience of the church now charismatically alive."[34] In this charismatic and Pentecostal model of church the outstanding "mark" is manifestations or indices of God's presence. In other words, the significant and defining thing is to have a living experience of the Spirit. It is the church understood to be "the community gathered to share in the fellowship of the Spirit."[35] In this church, God ceases to be a distant or detached figure but a reality that is encountered and experienced. Believers and participants in this model of church speak of Jesus and God not just as someone who is very real but as someone who can be trusted and counted on to help in daily struggles for life. Indeed, the poor and the broken in charismatic and Pentecostal churches according to Pinnock "discover that what they read in or heard from the gospel is happening now in their midst."[36]

There is no room for triumphalism in this ecclesiology as charismatics and Pentecostals believe there are situations the Spirit does not physically take believers out of but sustains and fortifies them in them and provides meaning to what could otherwise be destructive and damaging experiences. Pinnock believes this is part of the reasons "Paul could make such an impact on poor people who were struggling with the harsh realities of life, including slaves and the despised of his day."[37] Life in this model of the church is charismatic where all participate in the gifting. "The flow of manifestations constitutes the life and growth of the community. Any word or action that

---

31. Pinnock, "Church in the Power," 154.
32. Pinnock, "Church in the Power," 155.
33. Pinnock, "Church in the Power," 157.
34. Pinnock, "Church in the Power," 157.
35. Pinnock, "Church in the Power," 157.
36. Pinnock, "Church in the Power," 158.
37. Pinnock, "Church in the Power," 159.

manifests grace can be a means of grace to others. The community exists in a lively interplay of ministries that benefit the people."[38]

In response to Pinnock's proposal of Pentecostal power ecclesiology, Terry L. Cross avers that for many charismatics and Pentecostals, "the church is a gathering place for their meetings where the Spirit shows up."[39] According to him, how the Trinity operates amid charismatics and how the Triune God enters their experiences of life inform what they believe the church is and should be. Based on this assumption and in line with Pinnock's proposal of charismatic and Pentecostal power ecclesiology, which resonates with their theology of experiential encounter, Cross maintains that the church should be seen "as the people of God's immediate presence and power."[40] In this sense, the church becomes the sacrament of God's presence and power among his people; and the medium of the redemptive and salvific acts of the Triune God. In Cross's view, the church, from the perspective of charismatics and Pentecostals, "is the people of God who have been directly transformed and touched by God through the Spirit."[41] Having been touched and transformed, the church becomes reflective of God's transformative nature on earth.

This ecclesiology empowers charismatics and Pentecostals as a church "to enter the regions of this world that others have given up on and minister God's grace in physical and spiritual ways; . . . to walk in the power of God's Spirit so that demons flee and the Gospel is preached and the reign of God is advanced to the edges of the darkness in this world."[42] It is an ecclesiology in which the church "presents a God who is no longer a 'distant God' but one who engages and encounters people directly and immediately, transforming their lives forever."[43]

Frank Macchia seems to have a soft heart for Pinnock's proposed Pentecostal power ecclesiology. According to him, this ecclesiology encourages the gifted and interactive ministry of the whole people of God to resist clericalism or a juridical concept of the church.[44] He insists that spiritual gifts are held in high esteem in this ecclesiology as they "are the specific means by which the church becomes a graced community ever more faithful to its ministry and its mission as it becomes ever more faithful to Christ. Through

---

38. Pinnock, "Church in the Power," 160.
39. Cross, "Response to Clark-Pinnock's 'Church,'" 176.
40. Cross, "Response to Clark-Pinnock's 'Church,'" 177.
41. Cross, "Response to Clark-Pinnock's 'Church,'" 178.
42. Cross, "Response to Clark-Pinnock's 'Church,'" 179.
43. Cross, "Response to Clark-Pinnock's 'Church,'" 179.
44. Macchia, "Pinnock's Pneumatology," 171.

the cultivation of spiritual gifts, the church grows toward the 'full stature of Christ' in the world (Eph. 4.13)."[45]

Taking into cognizance the ontological concept of the charismatic and Pentecostal theology, which is in general a theology of encounter that is praxis-oriented and experiential, Peter Althouse articulates a Pentecostal ecclesiology that is trinitarian, missional, and eschatological in scope. According to him, "Pentecostal ecclesiology must start in the reflection of triune God, who constitutes the Church as a sent and sending community. In triune contemplation the Church lives out its mission as it participates in the missional life of God."[46] In a charismatic and Pentecostal ecclesiology which is trinitarian, missional, and eschatological in scope, Althouse maintains that "the Pentecostal themes of (S)pirit baptism, Pentecostal outpouring and Charismatic enablement become signs and instruments of God's mission to the world and all creation, in which the people of God are invited to participate."[47] For God, through the power of the Holy Spirit "enables the Church to be light and witness to the world in both Word and deed, so that we may participate in God's redemptive activity in conforming to the reign of the kingdom, a world without end."[48] Within the charismatic and Pentecostal ecclesiology, the church becomes a sent community by the Triune God not only to be the instrument of the coming kingdom of God, but also its foretaste and sacrament.

Althouse rightly argues that the "Father, Son and Spirit together send the Church into the world as a foretaste, sign and instrument of the coming reign of the kingdom."[49] In this ecclesiology, the "Spirit is the agent of the Church and its life giving mission, witnessing to the reign of God already here in the atoning work of Christ and activity of the Church, spreading into the world through the Church, as the vision of the eschatological kingdom transforms both the Church and the world."[50]

The mission of the church in a charismatic and Pentecostal ecclesiology that conveys the church as a sent community is, therefore, to bring "people, nations and the whole world into the eschatological reign, in which God gives priority to the poor, the sick, the downtrodden, and the widows."[51] In all this, charismatics and Pentecostals rightly affirm that the church is more the locus

---

45. Macchia, "Pinnock's Pneumatology," 172.
46. Althouse, "Towards a Pentecostal Ecclesiology," 231.
47. Althouse, "Ascension—Pentecost—Eschaton," 231.
48. Althouse, "Ascension—Pentecost—Eschaton," 231.
49. Althouse, "Ascension—Pentecost—Eschaton," 232.
50. Althouse, "Ascension—Pentecost—Eschaton," 233.
51. Althouse, "Ascension—Pentecost—Eschaton," 234.

of mission than its agent. For, it "is God who acts in the power of his Spirit, doing mighty works, creating signs of a new age, working sincerely in the hearts of men and women to draw them to Christ."[52]

Terry Cross believes that charismatics and Pentecostals see themselves as experiencing through the power of the Holy Spirit, precisely "that" which occurs in the Bible.[53] As a sent church, they believe that they are empowered by the same Spirit to bring others, especially the sick, the poor, the oppressed, and the abandoned to experience the same. When charismatics and Pentecostals talk of experience, they mean an encounter with God made possible through the power and agency of the Holy Spirit. Ecclesiology for charismatics and Pentecostals, in line with their theology in general, is praxis-oriented and experiential, being an ecclesiology of encounter. This, consequently, empowers them with "a radical openness to God's presence and power."[54]

In accord with their theology of experiential encounter, charismatics and Pentecostals see the church as the presence of the Triune God among his people. This presence is made possible by the power of the Holy Spirit who animates the church. For charismatics and Pentecostals, therefore, the church is God's doing, into which believers are baptized and nurtured. This is what Simon Chan means when he sees the church as Mother in his proposed Pentecostal ecclesiology.[55] Chan decries what he tags a "sociological concept of the church," which emanates from the Pentecostal concept of baptism in the Holy Spirit, which prioritizes a personal experience of the vivifying power of God's Spirit over the communal life of the church. Chan is justified in his worries when viewed from the perspective of the Western worldview which polarizes between the individual and the communal life the same way it polarizes between the natural and the supernatural. For Pentecostals in a cosmological milieu like that of Nigeria where there is no polarity between the individual and the community, this is not an issue. For, in such worldview, what affects the individual affects the community and what affects the community affects the individual. For people in such worldview, therefore, the church is truly the presence of the Triune God, the *Agyankwa* who has come to give them back their life in its holistic form and restore them to paradise. Charismatics and Pentecostals would emphasize that this presence is made possible through the power of the indwelling Spirit.

---

52. Althouse, "Ascension—Pentecost—Eschaton," 234.
53. Cross, "Divine-Human Encounter," 23.
54. Cross, "Divine-Human Encounter," 6.
55. Chan, "Mother Church," 178.

In an ecclesiology that sees the church as Mother, Chan insists that "To be baptized into Christ is to be incorporated into a Spirit-filled, Spirit-empowered entity."[56] This charismatic and Pentecostal ecclesiology reveals the all-embracing inclusiveness that characterizes the church in line with the character of the Triune God whose presence, the church is. It further brings to the fore the true significance of glossolalia according to the mind of Seymour, where speaking in diverse kinds of tongues is "a symbol of God's bringing together into one body people from every conceivable background."[57] Charismatics and Pentecostals are convinced that what this ecclesiology offers them in this life is only but a foretaste of the future kingdom. They believe that the "powers of the age to come are already in some measure present in signs and wonders"[58]—the fullness of which can only be in the eschaton.

In an ecclesiology where the church is the presence of the Triune God through the power of the Holy Spirit, "it is not only true to say that the Spirit constitutes the church, giving the church its unique identity as a Spirit-filled body, but it is also true that the church thus constituted gives the Spirit's distinctive character and role in the world as the church-located and church-shaped Spirit."[59] This is what some charismatic and Pentecostal scholars have called an ecclesiological pneumatology, and what Clark Pinnock tagged power ecclesiology, as noted earlier.

For Veli-Matti Kärkkäinen, Pentecostal ecclesiology has been more of a lived charismatic experience rather than discursive theology. And as a lived charismatic experience, he believes that it "naturally leans toward the charismatic structure of the church and free flow of the Spirit."[60] He argues that the church as a charismatic fellowship is, therefore, "a communion of participating, empowered believers."[61]

For charismatics and Pentecostals, the church is apostolic not necessarily in the sense of apostolic succession, but in the restoration of the apostolic signs of healing, miracles, prophecy, speaking in tongues, and so on. This is no surprise as charismatics and Pentecostals are "'doers' rather than 'thinkers' and instead of writing theological treatises, they went on living and experimenting the New Testament type of enthusiastic church life."[62]

56. Chan, "Mother Church," 180.
57. Chan, "Mother Church," 186.
58. Chan, "Mother Church," 195.
59. Chan, "Mother Church," 198.
60. Kärkkäinen, "Church as Charismatic Fellowship," 100.
61. Kärkkäinen, "Church as Charismatic Fellowship," 100.
62. Kärkkäinen, "Church as Charismatic Fellowship," 102.

According to Keith Warrington, Pentecostal theology is in general a theology of encounter which establishes it as "praxis-oriented and experiential."[63] Having experience of God's immediate presence, being able to reflect God's nature "in areas such as unity and mission," being transformed by God, and being used "in the transformation of others" are features that underscore Pentecostal ecclesiology.[64] In fact, this stems from the Pentecostal fivefold gospel. The Pentecostal fivefold gospel presents Jesus as the Savior, the Sanctifier, the Spirit Baptizer, the Healer, and the Coming King.[65]

Kenneth J. Archer alludes to Thomas's proposal of the character and fivefold ministry gifts of the church deduced from this fivefold gospel. Presenting Jesus as the Savior he shows the church as the Redeemed Community with "Water Baptism" as the ecclesiastical sacramental rule.[66] Archer would add apostles and the apostolic function to this. According to him the redeemed community retains the "apostolic authority, purity, and power" having been commissioned and sent by Christ in the power of the Holy Spirit to "carry forth the mission and message of God."[67] The apostolic character he avers is demonstrated, for example, "through the restoration of apostolic signs such as healing, miracles, prophecy, (and) speaking in tongues."[68] Presenting Jesus as the Sanctifier affirms the church as a Holy Community with "Footwashing" as the ecclesiastical mark, to which Archer adds teachers and the teaching function.[69] From the perspective of Jesus the Spirit Baptizer Thomas proposes that the church be seen as a "Charismatic Community"; the ecclesiastical sign of which is "Glossolalia."[70] It has already been noted that many Pentecostals are no longer eager to make glossolalia or tongues "'initial evidence' of baptism in the Spirit."[71] For Thomas, Jesus is the Healer; hence, he avers that the church is a "Healing Community"; and "praying for the sick with the laying on of hands and anointing with oil" is the ecclesiastical sign.[72] To this Archer adds pastors and the pastoral function.[73] The Gospels present

---

63. Warrington, *Pentecostal Theology*, 16.
64. Warrington, *Pentecostal Theology*, 132.
65. Archer, "Fivefold Gospel," 40.
66. Archer, "Fivefold Gospel," 40.
67. Archer, "Fivefold Gospel," 40–41.
68. Archer, "Fivefold Gospel," 41.
69. Archer, "Fivefold Gospel," 40.
70. Archer, "Fivefold Gospel," 40.
71. Thiselton, *Holy Spirit*, 489.
72. Archer, "Fivefold Gospel," 40.
73. Archer, "Fivefold Gospel," 40.

Jesus as the "Coming King."[74] Hence, Thomas sees the church as a "Missionary Community with the Lord's Supper serving as the ecclesiastical sign" to which Archer adds the "evangelists and the *evangelistic* function."[75] Archer argues that the "Fivefold gospel marks the character of the church, shapes its relational identity and directs its salvific path."[76]

Whether it is Paul's imageries of the church as God's family, God's temple, and Christ's body or the imageries of the church by Thomas and his cronies as a redeemed, sanctified, charismatic or empowered, healing, and eschatological or missionary community, the emphasis for charismatics and Pentecostals is the crucial role of the Holy Spirit in this church and in the lives of individual members of this church. The rest of this section is dedicated to each of these latter imageries of the church as revealed in the fivefold gospel with the aim to portray the centrality of the Spirit in each of them. It will treat them under the following subheadings:

- The Church as the Redeemed Community
- The Church as Sanctified Community
- The Church as a Charismatic or Empowered Community
- The Church as Healing Community
- The Church as Eschatological or Missionary Community

The Church as the Redeemed Community

Gordon Fee observes that "whatever else the Spirit meant in Paul's understanding, it meant at least that the desire for God's presence had been fulfilled by the coming of the Spirit."[77] He avers that "'salvation in Christ' not only begins by the Spirit, it is the ongoing work of the Spirit in every area and avenue of Christian life. We miss both Paul's own life in Christ and his understanding of salvation if we do not see the central role the Spirit plays at every juncture."[78] Charismatics and Pentecostals, as noted in chapter 1, hold a cosmological worldview different from the Graeco-Christian worldview which is characterized by polarity between the supernatural and the natural,

---

74. Archer, "Fivefold Gospel," 40.
75. Archer, "Fivefold Gospel," 40.
76. Archer, "Fivefold Gospel," 42.
77. Fee, *God's Empowering Presence*, 868.
78. Fee, *God's Empowering Presence*, 869.

the spiritual and the physical, the soul and body, and so on and so forth. Their worldview like the Nigerian worldview, is devoid of these polarities.

When charismatics and Pentecostals, therefore, acclaim Jesus as the Savior, they see him as one who saves not just their soul alone but their body as well. He does this through the power of his indwelling Spirit. In fact, "to confess that Jesus saves, as Pentecostals have insisted, and continue to insist in light of the fivefold Gospel which they proclaim, more than affirming that the salvation which Christ offers to all people is a 'salvation of disembodied souls,' is the affirmation that Jesus saves the whole human being within the historical reality in which they are found."[79] Such historical reality includes all kinds of "diverse social, political, economic, cultural, and religious factors which affect all human beings, whether they be believers or non-believers."[80] For charismatics and Pentecostals, the salvation or redemption that Christ brings in one's life through the power of the Holy Spirit completely liberates one from whatever dehumanizes one, and strengthens one to deal with situations that ordinarily would have been very devastating. Saved and redeemed in this manner, charismatics and Pentecostals see themselves as a saved or a redeemed community or church. Church for them becomes a redeemed community by the action of the Triune God made manifest by the power of the Holy Spirit. As the redeemed community, the church is empowered by the Holy Spirit to witness to the saving action of the Triune God and to proclaim to the world the reign of the God of life, and to affirm and defend life as a gift from God. In other words, a redeemed community or church is also a redeeming community or church.

The "Church as a redeeming community whose members know and enjoy the fullness of life which Christ offers and imparts, is called to affirm and defend life as a gift from God. This is the mission of salvation which has been entrusted to her. This is a holistic, integral salvation which liberates human beings from all oppressions."[81] For charismatics and Pentecostals, this mission is made possible by the empowerment of the Holy Spirit, which is God's empowering presence among his people.

Redemption or salvation for charismatics and Pentecostals is not a once-and-for-all event or experience in this life. It happens repeatedly until it reaches its final stage in the eschaton. Indeed, charismatics and Pentecostals believe that the redemption or the salvation they have here in this life, is only but a glimpse or a foretaste of what is to come in the

---

79. Rodriguez, "Redeeming Community," 69–70.
80. Rodriguez, "Redeeming Community," 70.
81. Rodriguez, "Redeeming Community," 70.

afterlife. Hence, when they say that the church is a redeemed community, they also know that the church is at the same time an unredeemed community always in need of redemption.[82] For charismatics and Pentecostals, the church is a redeemed community through the Spirit's presence. "Yet, it also finds itself in need of ongoing redemption, and is in fact trapped in certain facets of its life and practice. By overcoming these it becomes a redeeming presence within society and the world. It is at once redeemed, un-redeemed and a redeeming force."[83]

The fact that Jesus as well as his disciples had an option for the poor, the oppressed, the marginalized, those discriminated against, the sick, those possessed by evil spirits, the sinners, and so forth, as recorded in the Scriptures, validates charismatics' and Pentecostals' holistic concept of redemption.[84] In the same vein, the fact that Jesus's community of followers comprises mainly people from these categories of life gives credibility to this imagery, which these Pentecostals used to refer to the church as a redeemed, unredeemed, and redeeming community.

In fact, the church, according to Segler and Bradley, "is a redeemed fellowship (*koinonia*) of persons created by the Holy Spirit and united under the lordship of Jesus Christ."[85] The church must, therefore, see herself always as a "congregation of sinners" solely reliant on the grace of God, and constantly in need of renewal. She "must always be what the early church was after the ascension—a group of redeemed people, gathered together to pray and to wait for the coming of the Holy Spirit."[86]

The Church as Sanctified Community

For charismatics and Pentecostals who see Jesus as the sanctifier, the church is a holy or sanctified community. Pentecostals try to live this out in praxis by embarking on what they tag footwashing.[87] The ecclesiology of charismatics and Pentecostals is an ecclesiology of an experiential encounter. Hence, the church for charismatics and Pentecostals is not a sanctified community per se. Rather, charismatics and Pentecostals believe that the church is a sanctified community because the Triune God whom they encounter and experience as a church through the power of the Holy Spirit, is holy. In

82. De Koch, "Church," 55–62.
83. De Koch, "Church," 68.
84. Rodriguez, "Redeeming Community," 71–78.
85. Segler and Bradley, *Christian Worship*, 58.
86. Segler and Bradley, *Christian Worship*, 58.
87. Wenk, "Church as Sanctified Community,"130–32.

an encounter with the holy Triune God, the Father, in Jesus Christ, sanctifies the church through the power of the Holy Spirit. Daniele Castelo avers that charismatics and Pentecostals come to this self-understanding of the church as a sanctified community because of whom they come to know within a certain understanding of religious experience. According to him, charismatics and Pentecostals "are convinced that through their doxological experience they encounter the holy Triune God."[88] For Castelo, "Pentecostals believed that the God who was at work in revealing Godself on Mount Sinai and on Calvary was the same God who was working in the context of Pentecostal worship. In this regard, Pentecostals demonstrated to themselves to be a holy fellowship when they embodied and put in motion the implications of encountering this holy God."[89]

The charismatic and Pentecostal church as a community is holy to the extent that this church knows and experiences Jesus as the Lord and the Giver of life.[90] In fact, the charismatic and Pentecostal church is holy as far as she continues to encounter and experience through the power of the Holy Spirit the Holy God who comes to give people back their life by healing the sick, enriching the poor, liberating the oppressed and the marginalized, setting sinners free, and liberating people from whatever dehumanizes them. The Scriptures attest to Jesus's affinity and the formation of his community with people of these categories. He sanctifies this community through the indwelling of his Holy Spirit. The church is therefore holy not per se, but by whom she encounters and experiences; by the Holy Spirit who indwells her.

Frank Macchia avers that "The holiness of the church is dependent on Jesus' sanctification and our participation in it through consecration and empowered witness by the baptism in the Holy Spirit (John 17:17–19)."[91] It is the presence of the Holy Spirit and grace that make the holiness of the church secure. Hence, the holiness of the church transcends the personal holiness of her individual members.[92] Macchia warns that the fact that the holiness of the church is secured by the presence of the Holy Spirit and of grace does not mean that the holiness of the church should be taken for granted as if it is unrelated to the actions of the individual members of the church.[93] Based on the universal outpouring of the Holy Spirit, Macchia argues that "the category of 'saint' is not just an elite title for a chosen few but belongs to the

---

88. Castelo, "Improvisational Quality," 89.
89. Castelo, "Improvisational Quality," 92.
90. Castelo, "Improvisational Quality," 101.
91. Macchia, *Baptized in the Spirit*, 222.
92. Macchia, *Baptized in the Spirit*, 222.
93. Macchia, *Baptized in the Spirit*, 223.

entire church by virtue of being 'in Christ,' for all of the elect redeemed in Christ are sanctified by the Spirit (1 Peter 1:1–2)."[94]

Charismatics' and Pentecostals' concept of the church as a redeemed, unredeemed, redeeming, and sanctified community is seen through the lens of Paul Tillich's Spiritual Community as a community of faith and love; a holy community "participating through faith in the holiness of the Divine Life."[95] In this case, the church is holy despite not being holy. Her holiness according to Tillich is dependent on the New Being present in her.[96] Mathias Wenk corroborates this view. He maintains that for "Paul, Luke, and John, the presence of the Spirit in the Church is essential for its understanding as a holy community, a people belonging to God that reflects his character for this world."[97] Wenk argues that "Sin and immorality are clearly addressed by all New Testament authors. However, the Church's status as a holy community never is defined on the presence or absence of such issues but on the presence of the Spirit in its midst."[98] It is no surprise that charismatics and Pentecostals see the church also as an empowered community.

The Church as a Charismatic or Empowered Community

Frank Macchia proposes a charismatic and Pentecostal ecclesiology that is rooted in Spirit baptism. According to him, "*Spirit baptism gave rise to the global church and remains the very substance of the church's life in the Spirit, including its Charismatic life and mission.*"[99] The church in a Spirit-baptized ecclesiology has her being in the ecclesial and missionary Spirit, which makes her an empowered community. As an empowered community redeemed and sanctified by the holy Triune God, the church shares in the fellowship or *koinonia* that is the characteristics of the Triune God. For Macchia, "The Spirit in the koinonia and empowered mission of the church seeks to draw humanity into communion with God and to inspire a sighing for the day when all of creation becomes the temple of God's presence to the glory of God."[100] To draw humanity into communion with God implies bringing humanity to have an experiential encounter with the Triune God through the power of the Holy Spirit who indwells the

---

94. Macchia, *Baptized in the Spirit*, 223.
95. Tillich, *Systematic Theology*, 155.
96. Tillich, *Systematic Theology*, 167.
97. Wenk, "Church as Sanctified Community," 133.
98. Wenk, "Church as Sanctified Community," 134.
99. Macchia, *Baptized in the Spirit*, 155 (emphasis original).
100. Macchia, *Baptized in the Spirit*, 156.

church. Macchia avers that the church is now the natural upshot of Pentecostal outpouring of the Spirit in the world due to the importance of *koinonia* to God's reign in the world.[101] He maintains that the "church is not incidental to Spirit baptism but is rather its integral outcome. Also, Spirit baptism is not a *super-additum* but is essential to the life of the church. As a relational dynamic, Spirit baptism not only empowers and renews the people of God, it has birthed the people of God as the sign of grace in an increasingly graceless world."[102]

The encounter between God and God's people through the power of the Holy Spirit brings redemption, sanctification, and empowerment of God's people. In other words, charismatics and Pentecostals believe that the experiential encounter between God and God's people through the indwelling of the Holy Spirit produces a redeemed, sanctified, and empowered community as a church. It is no surprise that Macchia insists that the "Spirit embraces us or fills us with the divine presence in order to sanctify us and empower us to be living witnesses to Christ as the Son of God and the Spirit Baptizer. When God surrounds and fills us with the divine presence, it is so that we can give ourselves back to God in worship and witness."[103] Charismatics and Pentecostals believe that Jesus, as the Spirit baptizer, is anointed by the Spirit as the Scriptures attest to seek and to save the lost, on behalf of the Father. The church, therefore, as the Spirit-baptized or empowered community is to follow in the footsteps of the Spirit-baptizing God so that she "might in witness to Jesus seek the lost as well."[104]

The Church as Healing Community

Charismatics and Pentecostals acclaim Jesus as the Healer who has come to bring the Father's healing love and mercy through the power of the Holy Spirit to God's children. They believe that the church as a redeemed and redeeming community, is sanctified and empowered through the indwelling of the Holy Spirit to become a healing community through which God's healing presence will continue to abide with his people. It is no surprise that healing ministry is very prominent among charismatics and Pentecostals and is taken very seriously by them. Many scholars attribute the growth and expansion of charismatic renewal and Pentecostalism in the world to their healing and deliverance ministries. Allan Anderson for example, maintains

---

101. Macchia, *Baptized in the Spirit*, 156.
102. Macchia, *Baptized in the Spirit*, 156.
103. Macchia, *Baptized in the Spirit*, 159.
104. Macchia, *Baptized in the Spirit*, 160.

that "the main attraction of Pentecostalism in the Majority World is still the emphasis on healing and deliverance from evil. Preaching a message that promises solutions for present felt needs, the 'full gospel' of Pentecostal preachers is readily accepted."[105]

Kimberly E. Alexander rightly notes that "many Pentecostal and many charismatic groups today articulate a belief about healing that links it to the atoning work of Christ, situating it in the theological category of soteriology."[106] Alexander insists that "Pentecostals must endeavor to expand their view of the saving-healing work of Jesus the healer to include more holistic understandings. The healing ministry of Jesus is not separate from the work of social justice; it was and is, in fact, part and parcel of it."[107] This is true especially in the case of the Nigerian charismatic renewal and Pentecostalism as already noted in chapter 1 and will be highlighted later in this chapter. The cosmological milieu of charismatics and Pentecostals, like the Nigerian worldview, is devoid of the polarity between the soul and the body, the supernatural and the natural which characterizes the Greco-Christian worldview. Hence, it is no surprise that charismatics and Pentecostals link healing to the atonement work of Christ and see the church as a healing community that will continue through the indwelling of the Holy Spirit to make present this soteriological work of Christ. In this case, soteriology for charismatics and Pentecostals is very holistic as it encompasses physical, spiritual, mental, and psychological healing and healing from all that dehumanizes the human person. Charismatics and Pentecostals from the non-Western world, especially the Nigerian charismatics and Pentecostals, know this and demonstrate it in their pneumatology, ecclesiology, and liturgy.

Opoku Onyinah maintains that "The early church took Jesus' healing ministry seriously, and Christianity presented itself to the Mediterranean societies of the time as a healing community."[108] Onyinah admonishes that the church as a healing community must take into cognizance the holistic nature of healing which stretches to the social and political dimensions as a person is not separated from his or her community and society. He maintains that "Understanding of healing must correspond with an anthropology that is rooted in the biblical-theological tradition of the Church, which sees a human being as a multidimensional unity. Body, soul, and spirit and not separate entities but are interrelated and

---

105. Anderson, *Introduction to Pentecostalism*, 234.
106. Alexander, "Pentecostal Healing Community," 185.
107. Alexander, "Pentecostal Healing Community," 204.
108. Onyinah, "Pentecostal Healing Communities," 210.

interdependent."[109] The interconnectedness between the body, soul, and spirit and between the individual person and his or her community and society makes the physical, psychological, spiritual, social, and political dimensions of health imperative.[110]

In this case, healing for a physically challenged person, for example, "refers to experiences such as actions, attitudes, words, and processes which reflect something of God's empowering, renewing, reconciling, and liberating power that is working to reverse the negation of God's good creation."[111] This is where the charismatic and Pentecostal concepts of sickness and healing as a healing community become necessary. For, like the Nigerian traditional concepts of sickness and healing, the charismatic and Pentecostal concepts of sickness and healing "support the view that disharmony in relationships between individuals and families or society leads to alienation and brokenness, and physical disease."[112] The charismatic and Pentecostal churches as healing communities are empowered through the indwelling of the Holy Spirit to bring healing to such individuals and families or society. Such healings are seen to be within the confines of the atoning work of Christ. And "since God is sovereign whether healing takes place through prayers, caring, or medicine, God must be seen to be at work in all healing processes."[113]

The Church as Eschatological or Missionary Community

Charismatics and Pentecostals proclaimed that Jesus Christ saves, sanctifies, heals, and baptizes in the Holy Spirit. This proclamation, consequently, makes the charismatic and Pentecostal churches redeemed, sanctified, healed, and empowered communities or churches. But charismatics and Pentecostals also acclaim Jesus Christ as the coming King who comes in glory to fulfill his kingly reign. With this, the charismatic and Pentecostal churches are also seen as eschatological or missionary communities or churches that witness to the presence of the coming King. The eschatological dimension of the charismatic and Pentecostal churches has some implications on the charismatic and Pentecostal concepts of the church as a redeemed, sanctified, healed, and empowered community. For instance, the eschatological concept of the church implies that the church as a

109. Onyinah, "Pentecostal Healing Communities," 218.
110. Onyinah, "Pentecostal Healing Communities," 218.
111. Onyinah, "Pentecostal Healing Communities," 218–19.
112. Onyinah, "Pentecostal Healing Communities," 221.
113. Onyinah, "Pentecostal Healing Communities," 222.

redeemed community is also an unredeemed community. For, charismatics and Pentecostals believe that what they have now as a redeemed church is only but a glimpse or a foretaste of what it means to be a redeemed church, the fullness of which can only be realized in the eschaton. Until then, the redeemed church continues to deal with the paradox of being a redeemed and unredeemed church at the same time. More importantly, she continues to be the redeeming presence of the Triune God among God's people through the power of the indwelling Spirit. In the same vein, the sanctified church deals with her paradox of not being sanctified while at the same time remaining the sanctifying presence of the Triune God by the power of the Holy Spirit. In the eschatological milieu, the healed church does not lose sight of the fact that what she is now is a foretaste of what she will be in the eschaton while she continues her missionary mandate of being the healing presence of the Triune God through the power of the indwelling Spirit. It is no surprise that charismatics and Pentecostals as an empowered community or church insist that they are empowered by the Holy Spirit to witness to the reign of God's kingdom on earth. As Peter Althouse attests, "The gift of the Spirit promised in the ascension of Christ and fulfilled in the Spirit's descent, inaugurated the Church as the people of God under the eschatological reign of the Lord Jesus Christ (Acts 2.2–4)."[114]

The church which Paul identifies as the body of Christ is not the body of the historical Jesus but the body of the crucified and risen Christ. This, for charismatics and Pentecostals, makes the church "the eschatological community, who by the promise of the Spirit given at Pentecost lives in the tension of the already and not yet of the eschaton."[115] The eschatological dimension of the church, which charismatics and Pentecostals proclaim, humbles the church and saves the church from the danger of triumphalism. For "The church stands in profound ambiguity to the light of the risen Lord, representing the kingdom as a foretaste of Christ's full presence by his Spirit, but realizes his absence in the creaturely brokenness of a people who await the judgment of sin and the fullness of redemption."[116] Aware that biblical eschatology is proleptic in the sense that it is characterized by the already and not yet of the reign of God's kingdom, charismatics and Pentecostals as eschatological communities or churches, embark in praxis on those actions that allow the people of God to have here on earth the firstfruits, the down payment, and the foretaste of the kingdom. The people of God as the eschatological church "are empowered to go out and preach, teach, and do those

---

114. Althouse, "Ascension—Pentecost—Eschaton," 225.
115. Althouse, "Ascension—Pentecost—Eschaton," 227.
116. Althouse, "Ascension—Pentecost—Eschaton," 234.

things that Jesus preached, taught, and did, because the Spirit that enabled him now enables the Church."[117] In fact, since Christ is at God's right hand and is the head of the church, the church as an eschatological community "is a prophetic sign of the divine reordering of the world around the enthroned Christ and anticipation of the divine reordering of the cosmic order."[118] When viewed through the lens of Paul's metaphorical concept of 'seal,' "The Spirit of Pentecost is the guarantee of the eschatological consummation of that which has begun in Christ."[119] In other words, charismatics and Pentecostals know, as Peter Althouse says, quoting T. David Beck, that

> What we now savor of the Spirit's gracious activity is only a foretaste of the feast we will relish on that day. . . . As such, the present gift of the Holy Spirit is the guarantee that God would complete what he has begun. According to Rom 5.1–5, the hope of sharing God's glory survives because of the Holy Spirit. Precisely because God's love is already powerfully present and active in his Spirit, there is hope for something more, namely, the fulfillment of salvation, the completion and perfection of God's redemptive activity.[120]

The belief and the hope of all charismatics and Pentecostals is that "in the eschatological rotation God is drawing the Church, the world and the whole of creation into its eschatological goal: the glorification of God when God will be 'all in all' (1 Cor 15.28)."[121]

The eschatological dimension of the church generates cyphers and foretaste of the kingdom. It invites the church as an eschatological community, to take part in God's reign in humble and joyful service in appreciation for the redemptive work of God, and not to establish the reign of God by human efforts.[122] In other words, the church as an eschatological community, "is made the sign, foretaste, and instrument of Christ's eschatological reign by the mediation of the Spirit, but an instrument not of our own doing but of God's gracious activity through us."[123]

Using the charismatic and the Pentecostal metaphorical concept of the latter rain, Frank Macchia corroborates the charismatic and Pentecostal ecclesiology that views the church as an eschatological community.

---

117. Althouse, "Ascension—Pentecost—Eschaton," 237.
118. Althouse, "Ascension—Pentecost—Eschaton," 237.
119. Althouse, "Ascension—Pentecost—Eschaton," 238.
120. Althouse, "Ascension—Pentecost—Eschaton," 238.
121. Althouse, "Ascension—Pentecost—Eschaton," 242.
122. Althouse, "Ascension—Pentecost—Eschaton," 245.
123. Althouse, "Ascension—Pentecost—Eschaton," 247.

According to Macchia, the emphasis on the former and latter rain by charismatics and Pentecostals "indicates that the Church in Pentecostal preaching is the Church of the Spirit's outpouring on all flesh, which means that it is the Church dedicated to the eschatological fulfillment of God's kingdom or reign on earth."[124] For Macchia, the church's eschatological direction and fulfillment is found in what he tags the dogmatic framework of God's self-impartation through the giving of the Holy Spirit. Macchia does not speak of Spirit baptism in its limited form of a post-conversion experience of Spirit filling. Spirit baptism for him has an eschatological dimension. In other words, the church, for Macchia and for charismatics and Pentecostals is constituted by the outpouring of the Holy Spirit or the baptism in the Holy Spirit, "which grants the Church the down payment of the future inheritance of redemption (Eph. 1.13-14)."[125] Macchia argues that the kingdom of God as a pneumatological reality, "is not a place or the sum total of human moral strivings but is rather the dynamic presence of the Spirit through Christ to set the captives free and to involve them in God's liberating reign in the world: 'If I drive out demons by the Spirit of God, then the kingdom of God has come upon you' (Matt. 12.28)."[126]

The missiological and soteriological functions of the church as an eschatological community are defined by the eschatological outpouring of the Holy Spirit which constitutes the church through the indwelling of the Holy Spirit as the continuous presence of God's liberating reign in the world. Charismatic and Pentecostal churches as eschatological communities carry out their missiological and soteriological functions in cognizance of the ambiguities that characterize their ontology. In other words, while they make present the liberating reign of God in the world, they know they are not the kingdom.[127] While the charismatic and Pentecostal church is a redeemed and a redeeming community, she acknowledges she is an unredeemed community. While she enjoys her status as a sanctified and sanctifying community, she deals with the fact that she is unsanctified. While being a healed and a healing community, she grapples with her being an unhealed community. But the ambiguities of the charismatic and Pentecostal church does not deter her from effectively carrying out her missiological and soteriological functions. This may be viewed through the lens of Paul Tillich's paradox of the churches, which is based on the fact that "they participate, on the one hand, in the ambiguities of life in

---

124. Macchia, "Church of the Latter Rain," 249.
125. Macchia, "Church of the Latter Rain," 250.
126. Macchia, "Church of the Latter Rain," 251.
127. Macchia, "Church of the Latter Rain," 253–58.

general and of the religious life in particular and, on the other hand, in the unambiguous life of the Spiritual Community."[128] The charismatic and Pentecostal church as an unredeemed, unsanctified, and unhealed community subjects her "to the laws which determine the life of social groups with all their ambiguities,"[129] while being a redeemed and redeeming, sanctified and sanctifying, and a healed and healing community, points "to the presence of the unambiguous Spiritual Community."[130] According to Tillich, "the Spiritual Community as the dynamic essence of the churches makes them existing communities of faith and love in which the ambiguities of religion are not eliminated but conquered" from the beginning.[131] In the light of this, one could unequivocally say that the charismatic and Pentecostal churches are "existing communities of faith and love in which the ambiguities of religion are not eliminated but conquered."

Any church, including the Catholic Church in Nigeria, can rightly lay claim to all that is said about the charismatic and Pentecostal ecclesiology here. In fact, theologically and intellectually, there's little or no difference between the ecclesiology of charismatics and Pentecostals and that of other Christians. For instance, when Léon Joseph Cardinal Suenens, a cardinal of the Catholic Church, avers that the church is on one hand "modeled on civil, even military society" with "a descending hierarchy" and a uniformity that is erroneously "considered as an ideal," and on the other hand defined as "a mystical body of Christ,"[132] he brings to the fore the ambiguities that characterize the Catholic Church as do charismatic and Pentecostal churches.

Yves Congar maintains that the church was established in the world by Pentecost and that the Holy Spirit animates the church.[133] It is unlikely that any charismatic or Pentecostal will object to this. For this is part of what some Pentecostal scholars mean when they talk of power ecclesiology or pneuma ecclesia as noted above.

The New Testament writers, like charismatics and Pentecostals, present the church as the "assembly of the called";[134] a redeemed community and people whom God "called out of darkness into his marvelous light" (1 Pet 2:9). Peter, referring to this community, says, "You were redeemed from the empty way of life handed down to you by your forefathers . . . with the

---

128. Tillich, *Systematic Theology*, 165.
129. Tillich, *Systematic Theology*, 165.
130. Tillich, *Systematic Theology*, 166.
131. Tillich, *Systematic Theology*, 172.
132. Suenens, *New Pentecost?*, 15.
133. Congar, *I Believe*, 25
134. Williams, *Renewal Theology*, 16.

precious blood of Christ" (1 Pet 1:18–19). Paul puts it succinctly: "Our great God and Savior Jesus Christ . . . gave himself for us to redeem us from all iniquity and to purify for himself a people of his own" (Titus 2:13–14). Pope Paul VI corroborates this when he says: "Christ instituted this new covenant, namely the new covenant in his blood (see 1 Cor 11:25); he called a people together made up of Jews and Gentiles which would be one, not according to the flesh, but in the Spirit, and it would be the new people of God."[135] In line with this ecclesiology that sees the church as a redeemed community or people of God, Williams is right to maintain that "wherever the church assembles, it is a gathering of the redeemed people of God"[136] in communion with God and with one another. The estranged people whom Christ reconciled in his body through his death (Col 1:21), and called into one body (3:15), are now identified as the church, according to Raymond Brown, with Christ as its head (Col 1:18, 24; Eph 1:22–23; 5:23).

According to Brian Gleeson, Karl Rahner views Jesus as the primordial or original Sacrament of encounter with God. "He is the incarnate Son of God, the human face of God, the humanity of God, God's own body-language, God's liberating love made visible."[137] Though Jesus Christ is no longer humanly present in the world, "as sign of God and the Spirit of God" he "continues to be the sacrament of human encounter with God."[138] He does this, "through the community of the Church, as it exists now in time and space."[139]

The Council Fathers of Vatican II in *Sacrosanctum Concilium*, the Constitution on the Liturgy stress that "Christ is always present in his Church" (a.7). In other words, "the Risen Lord exists in history today in the Spirit-filled members of his Body and in their actions."[140] Put differently, the church as the community of Christ's followers is the sacrament of the risen Christ. As communities, they continue to show the existence of the risen Christ and of his love saving Spirit. *Sacrosanctum Concilium* is not the only Vatican II Council document that sees the church in this way. *Lumen Gentium* the Light of the Nations in article 8 defines the structure of the church as sacrament in these words: "The one mediator, Christ, established and constantly sustains here on earth his holy Church, the community of faith, hope and charity, as a visible structure through which he communicates truth

---

135. Paul VI, *Lumen Gentium*, 9.
136. Williams, *Renewal Theology*, 53.
137. Gleeson, "Church as Sacrament Revisited," 1.
138. Gleeson, "Church as Sacrament Revisited," 2.
139. Gleeson, "Church as Sacrament Revisited," 2.
140. Gleeson, "Church as Sacrament Revisited," 2.

and grace to everyone." As a community of committed disciples, animated by the Spirit of the risen Christ, the church is, in reality, more an event than a passive and inert institution or society. So, the more the disciples of Jesus "respond to the influence of Christ on the community and participate in its life, the more the Church becomes the Church. The more its members can demonstrate that they are becoming Spirit-filled, Christ-like people, i.e. people of love, joy, peace, patience, kindness, generosity, fidelity, gentleness, and selfcontrol (Gal 5:22), the more does the Church shine out as an event of grace."[141] The church as a redeemed and redeeming community, is a sacrament, an event of grace only if through her actions the lives of her "members are transformed in hope, in joy, in self-forgetful love, in peace, in patience, and in all other Christ-like virtues."[142]

Christian witnessing both in word and in action in the church that is seen as sacrament "appears as the expression of a heartfelt conviction inspired by the grace of the Holy Spirit."[143] Bernard P. Prusak avers that the church must be open to possibility and to newness in the realization that "faith may empower a struggle to bring forth what may now be just a dream."[144] According to him, the church as the sacrament of Christ will lose its sacramental efficacy and becomes a negative sign if it is not open to newness and possibility. Prusak views the church as the unfinished church. Being the unfinished church with the possibility of newness, "we are called prayerfully to ponder what new insights God's Spirit, ever present in our midst, might be drawing the Church toward."[145] Considering the fact that Christianity proclaims the centrality of the cross—the event of God's self-emptying or kenosis—Prusak argues that "the Church must be reshaped by its proclamation of the God who ever seeks to empower the powerless and to overcome the suffering of the victims of our history."[146]

Theologically and intellectually, this is apparently the ecclesiology that Pentecostals uphold, as noted above. It is, of course, the ecclesiology of some mainline churches that some charismatics belong to. These charismatics, therefore, uphold the same ecclesiology as other members of their churches. The difference is that charismatics and Pentecostals believe that theology in general and ecclesiology in particular is a theology of an encounter that is praxis-oriented and experiential. Because of this, they,

---

141. Gleeson, "Church as Sacrament Revisited," 2.
142. Dulles, *Models*, 65.
143. Dulles, *Models*, 67.
144. Prusak, *Church Unfinished*, 6.
145. Prusak, *Church Unfinished*, 6.
146. Prusak, *Church Unfinished*, 6.

in praxis, embark on actions that truly make the charismatic and Pentecostal churches the redeeming, the sanctifying, and the healing presence of the Triune God among his people through the indwelling of the Holy Spirit. And this is the basis on which this work is using the charismatic and Pentecostal theology and praxis to argue for the renewal of the Nigerian Catholic Church. The next section focuses on how this ecclesiology of experiential encounter plays out in praxis in the case of the Nigerian charismatic renewal and Pentecostalism.

Ecclesiology of Experiential Encounter Vis-à-vis the Nigerian Charismatic Renewal and Pentecostalism

Ecclesiology for charismatics and Pentecostals, as mentioned earlier, is characterized by an encounter with the Triune God made possible by God's empowering presence, the Holy Spirit, which makes it praxis-oriented and experiential. This ecclesiological belief not only empowers them with a radical openness to God's presence and power, but also turns them, as a church, into a living sign of God's presence with his people. Through this ecclesiology, Pentecostals and charismatics as God's family, God's temple, the body of Christ, and as redeemed and unredeemed churches, have been empowered by the indwelling Spirit to be the redeeming presence of God amidst his people. As a redeeming community, they are to become the instruments through which God will continue to redeem his people from sin, sickness, death, poverty, discrimination, oppression, and from all that dehumanizes his people.

For charismatics and Pentecostals to fulfill their soteriological mandate as redeeming, sanctifying, and healing communities through the empowerment of the Holy Spirit, they practically embraced in earnest their missiological function of witnessing to the Triune God in all the earth. This empowerment for mission rightly characterizes them in praxis as missionary communities or churches. The Nigerian charismatic and Pentecostal churches know this very well and in praxis embark on actions that will make it a reality. They take the missionary work very seriously. As Ayuk Ayuk attests, "The Pentecostals have not only made the gospel alive in Nigeria, but they are also sending missionaries all over the world to preach the gospel, despite financial upheaval in the country. The Pentecostal churches in Nigeria have sent out more missionaries in the late twentieth century than any other denomination in Nigeria."[147] Ayuk compares the charismatic and Pentecostal churches in Nigeria with the churches described in the Acts of

---

147. Ayuk, "Portrait of a Nigerian Pentecostal," 119.

the Apostles. Quoting DAWN (Discipling A Whole Nation) Fridayfax, he maintains that "What has been described as a 'book of Acts-like' move of God is sweeping through Nigeria and spreading overseas. Large meetings and confirmed healings are order of the day."[148]

The Nigerian charismatics and Pentecostals know that for the missiological and soteriological functions of the church to continue, they will not only preach the gospel, but will also establish churches that will carry on the continuity. Hence, the Nigerian charismatics and Pentecostals as missionary churches are vigorously preaching the gospel and establishing churches in Africa and beyond. As Ayuk attests, "Nigerian missionaries are presently going beyond Africa to plant and grow big churches that no one ever imagined was possible. . . . They are not only evangelizing African nations, but they are also evangelizing people in Europe, Asia and America."[149] Financial constrains have been slowing down the missionary zeal and work of these Nigerian charismatics and Pentecostals. In fact, "Many Pentecostal churches in Nigeria have grown in numbers, but only a few are actually taking the initiative to send missionaries to other nations due to financial constraints."[150] Among Pentecostal churches in Nigeria that have made a serious breakthrough in mission is the Redeemed Christian Church of God. It "is one of the strongest churches in the area of missions in Nigeria and abroad. This church is said to be the largest Pentecostal church in Africa. It counts eighty-two parishes in the United States. . . . The church has about 5,000 parishes in eighty countries."[151]

As empowered or missionary communities or churches, Nigerian charismatics and Pentecostals believe that empowerment for mission is for all believers, male and female old and young. Hence, every believer is encouraged to preach the gospel. They do not allow obstacles to deter them from doing so. The case of Sunday Adelaja, a young Nigerian cleric who "went to study with the hope of doing missions as directed by God through dreams and visions, and arrived in the Ukraine with only a $20 bill,"[152] attests to this. Within "eight years, he was able to establish a church of 20,000 members."[153] To achieve this, Adelaja in praxis allowed some flexibilities in his strategy, which is what the charismatic and Pentecostal churches do to make sure that people encounter and experience the

148. Ayuk, "Portrait of a Nigerian Pentecostal," 119.
149. Ayuk, "Portrait of a Nigerian Pentecostal," 121.
150. Ayuk, "Portrait of a Nigerian Pentecostal," 121.
151. Ayuk, "Portrait of a Nigerian Pentecostal," 122.
152. Ayuk, "Portrait of a Nigerian Pentecostal," 125.
153. Ayuk, "Portrait of a Nigerian Pentecostal," 125.

redeeming, sanctifying, and healing God. Ayuk quotes Godwin Ifijeh's reports of Adelaja's strategy. He says:

> There was the fear that religion could enthrone them in another form of detention. So, to get around that, we went to the prostitutes, the outcasts, drug addicts, the alcoholics and social outcasts. It worked out. We preached the ministry to them and tried to restore them. With those people delivered and cleansed up to once again become normal people, their parents started coming to the church to find out what happened. It dawned on them that there must be something about what we were trying to do.[154]

The charismatic and Pentecostal ecclesiology of experiential encounter spurred charismatics and Pentecostals in Nigeria into getting involved in people's real-life situations. "Getting involved in the real life situations of people," according to Ayuk, "can actually pay off in missions. People want to see the reality of God in their lives, not just by word of mouth. The words uttered by God must be authenticated with action."[155]

In fact, if charismatics and Pentecostals should effectively carry out their missiological function as empowered or missionary churches or communities, they must take very seriously the soteriological function of the church which makes her the redeeming, sanctifying, and healing Community or church. From the perspective of the baptism in the Holy Spirit as noted in chapter 1, these two functions are inseparable. The Nigerian charismatic and Pentecostal churches seem to be fully aware of this and do everything possible to demonstrate it in praxis. Through the indwelling of the Holy Spirit they move into actions that make people to encounter and experience God—make them have a foretaste, the firstfruit, and a down payment of the redeeming, sanctifying, and healing presence of God's kingdom here on earth while waiting for its fullness in the eschaton.

The Nigerian Pentecostal cleric Sunday Adelaja did not stop at preaching the gospel to the poor and hungry in Ukraine. "The next thing he did," according to Ayuk, "was to make sure the restored dejects in the society would be well taken care of, and so he decided to start a feeding program."[156] Charismatics and Pentecostals believe that the "ministry of God is never complete without signs and wonders."[157] Ayuk notes that God performed some miracles which helped the people through Adelaja's church by the power of the indwelling Spirit. Ayuk's story about Sunday Adelaja's mission

154. Ayuk, "Portrait of a Nigerian Pentecostal," 126.
155. Ayuk, "Portrait of a Nigerian Pentecostal," 126.
156. Ayuk, "Portrait of a Nigerian Pentecostal," 126.
157. Ayuk, "Portrait of a Nigerian Pentecostal," 127.

in Ukraine is corroborated by J. Kwabena Asamoah-Gyadu, who visited this mission and wrote an article about it. In his article, "An African Pentecostal on Mission in Eastern Europe: The Church of the 'Embassy of God' in the Ukraine," Asamoah-Gyadu narrates his encounter and what he feels about Sunday Adelaja and the church of the "Embassy of God" in Ukraine. He notes his conversation with the taxi driver who took him to the Dynamo Kiev Stadium, where the Jesus March which Pastor Sunday Adelaja organized was to begin. According to him, the "driver did not speak much English, he was not churched himself, but he knew about and highly respected Pastor Sunday of whom he had heard so much. 'He is doing great work in our country,' he told me. 'So, what do you think about this church?' I asked. 'Well, I don't go (to) church myself, but looking at the many Ukrainians in it, it certainly must be something good; that (an) African pastor has become more popular than the politicians.'"[158] Asamoah-Gyadu recalls Adelaja stating "in one of his more than thirty popular Christian publications, 'though I am a foreigner, God has given me the ability to go and minister beyond race, culture, and denominational barriers.'"[159] Explaining how he eventually succeeded in his mission, Adelaja, according to Asamoah-Gyadu, said that "the Lord told him: 'pay attention to the neglected, downtrodden, and outcasts of Ukrainian society, and I will give you those in the higher echelons of power.'"[160] Asamoah-Gyadu goes on to elaborate:

> Starting the new ministry with seven people as a home fellowship, Pastor Sunday Adelaja began to reach out to the "outcasts," which, as he explained to me, meant those whose human dignity had been eroded through addiction to narcotics, armed robbery, prostitution, and alcoholism. These were people whose families were ashamed of them, and whom the Ukrainian establishment was finding it difficult to deal with and rehabilitate.[161]

Adelaja, like other Pentecostals and charismatics, believes that it is God who in Christ Jesus saves his people and establishes his kingdom on earth, but he does it through his empowering presence, the Holy Spirit. This is evident in Adelaja's tone of prayer as Asamoah-Gyadu observes: "'Let your grace come, let your Spirit come, let your power come, Lord. Let this nation seek your face; let doors be open; we need your power and Spirit so that people may come into your kingdom.'"[162] Asamoah-Gyadu notes some

---

158. Asamoah-Gyadu, "African Pentacostal," 298.
159. Asamoah-Gyadu, "African Pentacostal," 302.
160. Asamoah-Gyadu, "African Pentacostal," 303.
161. Asamoah-Gyadu, "African Pentacostal," 303.
162. Asamoah-Gyadu, "African Pentacostal," 308.

testimonies given by people as signs and wonders that God worked for his people through Sunday Adelaja and the church of the "Embassy of God" in the Ukraine.[163] These signs and wonders contribute in making Asamoah-Gyadu aver that "One of the major contributions of African Christianity, particularly in its Pentecostal and charismatic forms, to Western Christianity is the attention it draws to the fact that Christianity is about experience and that the power of God is able to transform circumstances that Western rationalist theologies will consider the preserve of psychology and scientific development."[164] In fact, the thrust of this essay by Asamoah-Gyadu is that "God's Embassy provides incontrovertible evidence that in African hands, Christian mission is truly in reverse gear, showing that the Kingdom of God comes with power."[165] In other words, Christian mission is going back to what it used to be during the time of the apostles and the early Christians when it was characterized with charismatic manifestations.

The Nigerian charismatics and Pentecostals believe that an ecclesiology of experiential encounter in which believers encounter the Triune God through the power of the indwelling Spirit "gives power and knowledge to contest the world and the life-threatening forces in it. Thus, sanctification would lead to health and prosperity for those who believe and act upon their belief."[166] Charismatics and Pentecostals believe that Jesus went about proclaiming the good news of the kingdom and healing every disease and sickness. They also believe that Jesus empowered his disciples and believers to drive out evil spirits and to heal every disease and sickness. But they do not only believe, they act on their belief. This explains why the Nigerian charismatics and Pentecostals take the work of preaching the gospel, healing, and deliverance very seriously as shown in the previous chapter. They, however, believe that God does not only work in extraordinary or supernatural ways but also in ordinary and natural ways. It is no surprise that some Pentecostal churches in Nigeria "own banks, business companies and operate NGOs, health-care facilities and universities."[167] In fact, according to Ogbu Kalu, Nigerian "Pentecostals aid the people 'to see, to know and to experience Jesus Christ as the victor over the powers and forces from which Africa knows no means of deliverance' such as poverty, witchcraft, sorcery, anxiety, sickness and death."[168] For Kalu, Nigerian charismatics

---

163. Asamoah-Gyadu, "African Pentacostal," 311–12.
164. Asamoah-Gyadu, "African Pentacostal," 314.
165. Asamoah-Gyadu, "African Pentacostal," 314.
166. Kalu, "Pentecostal and Charismatic Reshaping," 94.
167. Kalu, "Pentecostal and Charismatic Reshaping," 94.
168. Kalu, "Pentecostal and Charismatic Reshaping," 96.

and Pentecostals "offer an exit or resolution to the problems of bondage to witchcraft, ancestral spirits and curses inherited through the generations. God's power, mediated through the name and blood of Jesus, liberates the afflicted and brings salvation."[169]

As churches that believe in experiential encounter with God, the Nigerian charismatic and Pentecostal churches believe there is no real power other than the power of Jesus through the indwelling Spirit. They believe and exemplify in praxis that "this power encounters the hollow powers of demons, spirits, witches or sorcerers, and likewise the powers of sickness, poverty, and death, that is: the powers of evil in all its individual and structural manifestations."[170] This resonates well with the Nigerian people and the Nigerian worldview where "evil refers to anything limiting, besetting or destroying life—including infertility, sickness and death as well as droughts and famines, but likewise jealousy, envy or everyday life misfortunes."[171]

Klaus Hock maintains that the breathtaking success story of movements like William Kumuyi's Deeper Life or Benson Idahosa's Church of God Mission "is at least partly linked to the fact that African ideas of power and power encounter are to a much higher degree a constitutive element of their message than is the case in other denominations."[172] It is no surprise that the "Thursday Evangelism Training" of William Folorunso Kumuyi's Deeper Life Bible Church turned into the "Miracle Revival Hour."[173] For Klaus Hock, "the work of the Spirit, proven by the visible presence of God's power, is seen as a benchmark for 'Church'" in Benson Idahosa's Church of God Mission.[174] He reports that "Whenever Bishop Idahosa starts praying, people fall on the floor—due to the spiritual powers he has set free, 'slain by the spirit,' as it is called."[175]

The Nigerian charismatics and Pentecostals do not only believe that the church is an empowered or missionary church or community, a redeeming, sanctifying, and healing community, they act in praxis on their belief. This is evident particularly in the activities of the new-wave Pentecostalism in Igboland (the Eastern Nigerian territory where the Igbo people live) during the early 1970s, which was a response to the crisis engendered by the Nigerian Biafran Civil War. According to Richard Burgess, "It began as an evangelical revival associated with the Scripture Union but quickly acquired

---

169. Kalu, "Pentecostal and Charismatic Reshaping," 96.
170. Hock, "'Jesus Power-Super-Power!,'" 62.
171. Hock, "'Jesus Power-Super-Power!,'" 64.
172. Hock, "'Jesus Power-Super-Power!,'" 65.
173. Hock, "'Jesus Power-Super-Power!,'" 60.
174. Hock, "'Jesus Power-Super-Power!,'" 58.
175. Hock, "'Jesus Power-Super-Power!,'" 62.

a Pentecostal spirituality as participants sought for practical answers to their current dilemmas."[176] Burgess notes that:

> Immediately prior to the Civil War, a nominal form of Christianity dominated the Igbo religious landscape, and most people claimed affiliation to one of the mainline Protestant denominations or to the Roman Catholic Church. There was a growing interest in the prayer houses and Aladura churches because of their close affinity to Igbo traditional piety and their pragmatic approach to religion. . . . Okorocha believes that during the Biafran crisis, many Igbos were "reconverted" to a more radical form of Christianity. Sometimes this involved a change of denomination and adoption of a more Pentecostal spirituality.[177]

It is no surprise that the theology and praxis of the charismatic and Pentecostal churches in Igboland, as churches that hold on to an ecclesiology of an encounter with the Triune God, which is praxis-oriented and experiential, appealed more to the Biafran people during the Civil War crisis. According to Burgess, "Insecurities caused by social dislocation, lack of food and medical facilities, air raids, growing fatalities, and the threat of genocide all helped to heighten popular stress among the Igbos during the war."[178] In situations like this, bearing witness to and preaching about the God who saves, sanctifies, and heals, and demonstrating to churches that in praxis are the continuous presence of the redeeming, sanctifying, and healing God among his people through the power of the Holy Spirit, certainly resonated with people whose worldview is ontologically pragmatic and experiential. Burgess insists that "Despite the resistance of Scripture Union leaders in Biafra to Pentecostal doctrine and practices, the movement was phenomenologically Pentecostal during its Civil War phase. It exhibited many of the features of Pentecostal spirituality associated with the experience of the Holy Spirit. Intense religious experiences were relatively common."[179] When it comes to relief operation during the Nigerian/Biafran Civil War, both "Catholic and Protestant churches played a significant role in this."[180]

A new Irish documentary, "Biafra: Misean Dearmadta (Forgotten Mission),"[181] corroborates this. It reveals how Irish missionaries risked their lives to save millions from starvation during the Nigerian Civil War.

176. Burgess, "Crisis and Renewal," 206.
177. Burgess, "Crisis and Renewal," 207.
178. Burgess, "Crisis and Renewal," 207.
179. Burgess, "Crisis and Renewal," 222.
180. Burgess, "Crisis and Renewal," 219.
181. Kelly, "How Irish Missionaries Fought."

It could be argued that this is one of the reasons why Christianity in general was and is still very strong in the Eastern part of Nigeria. While the mainline churches relaxed back to their usual type of Christianity after the war, charismatics and Pentecostals became vibrant with their type of spirituality, which is experiential and praxis-oriented. They continued to uphold, preach, and in praxis demonstrate a holistic view of salvation that resonates well with the cosmological worldview of the people of Eastern Nigeria and Nigeria in general. The result is that many Christians of the mainline churches embraced the spirituality and style of worship of the charismatic groups in their churches while many others continue to resort to indigenous religion to solve their problems. Bishop Anthony Obiefuna attests to this when he reaffirmed:

> Times without number the rumour reaches us that our Christians are worshipping "idols," false gods. They swear on idols. They erect shrines in their homes, in their compounds. They hide fetishes in their shades in the market places and in their workshops. . . . At every retreat, (they) bring out from their homes fetishes and charms of all kinds. Idol worship, superstitious practices, fear of witchcrafts, charms, and all sorts of vain observances are realities among our (Christians). We cannot simply deny they obtain.[182]

In charismatic and Pentecostal churches, God ceases to be a distant figure but a reality that is encountered. Believers and participants in these churches speak of Jesus and God not only as someone who is very real but as someone who can be counted on to help in the day-to-day struggle for life. All these show that the charismatic and Pentecostal churches in Nigeria demonstrate in praxis to be the redeeming, sanctifying, and healing presence of God among his people through the power of the Holy Spirit. They are in praxis the sign of God's kingdom among God's people. Through them, God's people enjoy the firstfruit, the down payment, and the foretaste of the kingdom here on earth while waiting for its fullness in the eschaton. It is this praxis-oriented and experiential character of the charismatic and Pentecostal churches that is the reason this work is using the charismatic and Pentecostal theology and praxis to argue for the renewal of the Nigerian Catholic Church. The next chapter shows how this theology of experiential encounter plays out in the charismatic and Pentecostal worship.

---

182. Obiefuna, *Idolatry*, 11.

CHAPTER 3

Charismatic and Pentecostal Theology of Worship

THE ONTOLOGY OF THE charismatic and Pentecostal theology which makes it a theology of encounter that is praxis-oriented and experiential, influenced their pneumatology. In accord with the nature of their theology in general, it turned their pneumatology into a pneumatology of an encounter with the Triune God through the indwelling Spirit as evident in their concept of the baptism of the Holy Spirit. This experiential encounter with the Triune God through the power of the Holy Spirit, shaped the charismatic and Pentecostal ecclesiology making it an ecclesiology of experiential encounter with God. In this ecclesiology, the charismatic and Pentecostal churches become empowered or missionary communities or churches, redeemed and redeeming churches, sanctified and sanctifying churches, and healed and healing churches. As churches viewed theologically in this manner, they become in praxis the redeeming, sanctifying, and healing presence of the Triune God amidst his people through the power of the Holy Spirit. In other words, as these churches carry out their missiological function, which is ontologically interconnected with their soteriological function, they become the sign, the foretaste, and the down payment of the kingdom of God among God's people as they wait for the full realization of the kingdom in the eschaton. As redeeming, sanctifying, and healing communities, the charismatic and Pentecostal churches allow some flexibility in their worship in such a way that in praxis, worship becomes for them a medium for an experiential encounter with the Triune God through the power of the Holy Spirit.

This chapter focuses on the charismatic and Pentecostal theology of worship. As noted in the previous chapter, this work recognizes that charismatics intellectually follow the theology of worship of their mainline churches, which to some extent vary from the theology of worship of Pentecostals. However, both charismatics and Pentecostals believe in the central role of the Holy Spirit in worship and go on in praxis to live out their belief as it is evident in their style of worship. It is at this backdrop that this work is discussing charismatic and Pentecostal theology of worship in this chapter. It will project the Pentecostal theology of worship as a theology of experiential encounter. It will show that the trinitarian character of the charismatic and Pentecostal theology of worship is different from that of the mainline churches. More importantly, it will demonstrate that the emphasis of charismatics and Pentecostals on the essential role of the Holy Spirit in liturgy makes their worship ontologically pneumatocentric. It will also explore the charismatic and Pentecostal style of preaching, music, and praying. Finally, the chapter will show how this plays out in the case of the Nigerian charismatics and Pentecostals.

The Charismatic and Pentecostal Worship of Experiential Encounter

In his study of the Holy Spirit in the letters of Paul, Gordon Fee observes that "for Paul the gathered church was first of all a worshiping community; and the key to their worship was the presence of the Holy Spirit."[1] For Fee, "What is most noteworthy in all the *available* evidence is the free, spontaneous nature of worship in the Pauline churches, apparently orchestrated by the Spirit himself."[2] The uniqueness of the charismatic and Pentecostal worship is centered on the fact that charismatics and Pentecostals understand worship as "a *felt* experience of being in the presence of God—an experience made possible by the Spirit."[3] This understanding of worship is evident in their style of prayer, preaching, healing, and lively and joyous expressive ways of worship.

Jacqueline Grey avers that early Pentecostal perceptions of worship stress an affective engagement with the Spirit.[4] The early Pentecostals according to her critiqued and abandoned formal liturgies which they perceived as empty worship in preference to what they see as spontaneous "and therefore (supposedly) sincere expressions of worship."[5] Contemporary Pentecostals she avers hold the same view of worship with their predecessors as what

1. Fee, *God's Empowering Presence*, 884.
2. Fee, *God's Empowering Presence*, 884.
3. Archer, "Worship," 115.
4. Grey, "Book of Isaiah," 37.
5. Grey, "Book of Isaiah," 37.

matters to them in worship is "the need for personal and dynamic encounter with God—to enter the throne room and meet with the Holy Spirit."[6] In worship therefore, charismatics and Pentecostals allow themselves to be led by the Holy Spirit into the "throne room" where they encounter God. The entering of the "throne room" where the encounter with God takes place in worship can be emotional no doubt. And there is nothing wrong with that as emotions are a genuine part of worship. When the people of God gather at worship, the totality of the human person is involved. In other words, genuine worship involves the person's mind (*nous*), the soul (*psyche*), the spirit (*pneuma*), the body (*soma*), and the heart (*kardia*). In fact, psychologists primarily identify three manners of conscious activity during worship: emotion, knowledge, and will. There should, however, be a balance between intellectual and emotional activities during worship.[7] Worshipers should endeavor not to always associate their own emotions with the power of the Holy Spirit. In addition to this, there is always a need to test emotional expressions arising during worship by biblical teachings, by reason, and by prayer.[8] Charismatics and Pentecostals choose to be influenced and guided by Luke/Acts' narrative which itself is part of biblical teachings. The charismatic and Pentecostal worship in Nigeria is not only influenced by Luke/Acts' narrative but also by the Nigerian worldview, as will be demonstrated in the next chapter, which of course corroborates Luke/Acts' story as indicated in chapter 1. In line with this, Grey admonishes that "new forms and appropriate indigenous practices in worship need to be embraced and encouraged to celebrate the unpredictable moving of the Spirit globally and to speak immanently to these new contexts in their own language."[9] Elochukwu E. Uzukwu corroborates this when he avers that worship entails movement in which "humans move toward God in response to God's movement to humans."[10] This motion toward God and other humans is done by the entire human person, that is, a person with body and spirit together.[11] He argues that "our motions or gestures, and the way we generally interpret human rhythmic movement, are bound to an ethnic experience."[12] He, therefore, maintains that "our praise or thanksgiving, adoration or contemplation, prayer of quiet or measured ritual dance, which display the assembled body of worshippers

6. Grey, "Book of Isaiah," 38.
7. Segler and Bradley, *Christian Worship*, 62.
8. Segler and Bradley, *Christian Worship*, 63.
9. Grey, "Book of Isaiah," 45.
10. Uzukwu, *Worship as Body Language as Body Language*, ix.
11. Uzukwu, *Worship as Body Language as Body Language*, ix.
12. Uzukwu, *Worship as Body Language as Body Language*, ix.

before God or spirits, have meaning within an ethnic group."[13] Hence, the gestures with which humans express their relationship with the God of Jesus Christ must always be homegrown.[14]

In worship the assembled community recounts its foundation story which sometimes is the ritual re-enactment of past events "that are lived in the present."[15] In this way the worshiping community is created and re-created during worship time.[16] The charismatic and Pentecostal style of worship in itself involves pressing prayer, regular testimonies, excessive praise, manifestations of hope of answered prayers, and the reenactment of the Christian foundation story. Lee Roy Martin attests to this when alluding to the Psalms suggesting that "worship should include urgent prayer, frequent testimonies, extravagant praise, hopeful content, and recitals of the Church's story."[17]

The charismatic and Pentecostal worship is trinitarian in character but not in the sense of the dominant trinitarian faith of Prosper of Aquitaine's *ut legem credendi lex statuat supplicandi*: "that the law of praying establishes the law of believing." Or in the sense of the oldest rule of trinitarian Prayer, Canon 23 of Council of Hippo, rule 393, reproduced in Council of Carthage: "In prayers let no one name [address] the Father instead of the Son, or the Son instead of the Father. And when one stands at the altar let prayer always be directed to the Father."[18] Their worship is trinitarian in character in the sense that what they do in worship is what Frans Jozef Van Beeck describes as "the doxological encounter, in *ecstatic immediacy*, with God the Father; mediated by Christ risen and embodied in him, and carried by the Spirit."[19] This makes the charismatic and Pentecostal worship an encounter with the Triune God through God's indwelling presence, the Holy Spirit. The emphasis they lay on the Holy Spirit, however, makes their worship Pneumatocentric as they believe that it is through the Holy Spirit that God is present in worship.[20] Kimberly E. Alexander puts it succinctly when she avers that charismatic and Pentecostal worship is experiential and dynamic and not motivated by doctrine or reliant on having right theology first. According to her, it is an encounter and a communion with the Spirit and with God's

13. Uzukwu, *Worship as Body Language*, ix.
14. Uzukwu, *Worship as Body Language*, ix.
15. Uzukwu, *Worship as Body Language*, x.
16. Uzukwu, *Worship as Body Language*, 41–77.
17. Martin, "Book of Psalms," 87.
18. Spinks, *Place of Christ*, 58.
19. Van Beeck, *God Encountered*, 218.
20. Segler and Bradley, *Christian Worship*, 53–54.

people through which the worshipers are led into God's glory, the fullness of which is to be realized eschatologically.[21]

Charismatics and Pentecostals believe in experiential encounter with the divine through the power of the Holy Spirit. As redeeming, sanctifying, and healing churches, they make their liturgical services or worships in praxis to provide the scenario, the ambient through which worshipers encounter and experience the redeeming, sanctifying, and healing presence of the Triune God by the indwelling Spirit. Their worship is marked with intensity and liveliness, as evident in their loud prayer and loud and joyous singing and clapping, or in their preaching, which is often full of interjections of "Amen," "hallelujah." Ma attributes this intensity and liveliness in charismatic and Pentecostal worship to a high expectancy of experiencing God. According to him, "Both 'expectancy' and 'experience' can immediately prompt enthusiastic responses. God is never abstract, but concrete; He is never static, but dynamic."[22]

The charismatic and Pentecostal style of worship which is characterized by an experiential encounter between God and worshipers is seen through the lens of Acts, as a way of "reaching all the way back to apostolic times, characterized by heroic faith and daily experience of God's miraculous power."[23] Charismatics and Pentecostals believe that worship is an encounter with the Triune God through the power of the Holy Spirit who animates worship. Consequently, the charismatic and Pentecostal worship is characterized by spontaneity in which worshipers, despite plans and previous rehearsals, allow themselves to be led by the Holy Spirit. Ma notes that "During the 'worship and praise,' although songs were pre-selected and the music team rehashed previously, the leaders are prepared to be 'led by the Spirit,' a common expression among Pentecostals to refer to an unexpected urge to do something not planned at all."[24]

The sensitivity to the move of the Holy Spirit is very crucial in charismatic and Pentecostal worship. Hence, "a singing segment can turn into a season of congregational prayer or corporate worship, often with individuals voicing their praises and thanksgiving to the Lord, or 'singing in the Spirit.' . . . Anyone among the congregation may arise and share his or her experience with the rest of the church."[25] Humanly speaking, Ma insists that pastors

---

21. Alexander, "'Singing Heavenly Music,'" 220.
22. Ma, "Pentecostal Worship," 141.
23. Ma, "Pentecostal Worship," 142.
24. Ma, "Pentecostal Worship," 145.
25. Ma, "Pentecostal Worship," 145.

"should be open to the changing scenes of human responses and be able to lead the congregation into a suitable mode of worship."[26]

Daniel E. Albrecht corroborates the view that the charismatic and Pentecostal worship is a worship of encounter with God, which is experiential and praxis-oriented. He notes that for charismatics and Pentecostals, "worship is not strictly a human activity. . . . Believers expect God to come and meet with them. Pentecostals believe that God alone inaugurates such a meeting by God's gracious acts and presence" through his Spirit.[27] Worshipers in charismatic and Pentecostal worship are prepared to encounter God. They do pray for the indwelling of the Holy Spirit and are usually prepared for what the Spirit can do as "God 'comes' to meet with God's people," listening and responding to them as they worship him.[28]

Within the context of the charismatic and Pentecostal worship, there is the expectation of an encounter with God's presence throughout the period of the worship. It is no surprise that the personal encounter with the holy God through God's empowering presence, the Holy Spirit, remains at the epicenter of charismatic and Pentecostal spirituality and worship. No doubt, the expectation of an encounter with God's presence "heightens the sensitivity of worshipers to what God speaks to individuals and to the collective gathering. Impressions in the heart, audible voice, dreams, visions, any scriptural passage or words of a song 'that stand out' are all perceived as means of God speaking to his people."[29]

Due to the experiential nature of charismatic and Pentecostal worship, which creates room for spontaneity, most charismatic and Pentecostal churches do not have any prescribed liturgy. As Ma attests, alluding to Hollenweger, "Pentecostals do have rich liturgical components in their worship, but they are primarily non-verbal and unprescribed."[30] There is, no doubt, an experiential aspect in the religious life of other Christian traditions. However, "what stands out in the Pentecostal tradition is more than cognitive awareness of God's being. It is rather a tangible encounter with the great God, and such an experience affects the whole human being including one's feelings and will power."[31] This is evident in the report of tangible experiences of

---

26. Ma, "Pentecostal Worship," 145.
27. Albrecht, "Anatomy of Worship," 72.
28. Albrecht, "Anatomy of Worship," 74.
29. Ma, "Pentecostal Worship," 146.
30. Ma, "Pentecostal Worship," 147.
31. Ma, "Pentecostal Worship," 147.

healing, repentance, and baptism in the Holy Spirit which worshipers report during charismatic and Pentecostal worships.³²

"Prayers are often offered for the healing of family members who are not present in the worship service, family problems (such as financial matters), relationship issues, and even for tuition payments for their children.... God is believed to be not only good, but also capable, indeed answering their prayers in the 'here and now.'"³³

When Pentecostals celebrate the Lord's supper or communion in remembrance of the Lord's body and blood, they expect to encounter God through the celebration. In fact, "it is often expected that through this experience physical healing takes place. Passages such as 'By his wounds, you have been healed' (Isa 53:5; 1 Pet 2:24, NIV) are often recited by the minister to remind the congregation that communion is a special occasion with its powerful ritual elements when healing indeed takes place."³⁴

It is in worship that charismatics and Pentecostals live out their theology particularly, their pneumatology and their ecclesiology in a tangible manner. In worship, they encounter and experience God through the power of the Holy Spirit. In worship, empowered by the Holy Spirit, the charismatic and Pentecostal churches truly become the redeeming, sanctifying, and healing presence of God.

For charismatics and Pentecostals, "worship is also a place where theological revision, reinterpretation and even alteration take place. This can take place in various ways: 1) inclusion or choice (of certain songs, sermon topics, etc.), 2) emphases, 3) reinterpretation (particularly in a changing social context), and more seriously, 4) by omission. The decreasing message of the Lord's return, for example, is a case of the latter."³⁵ Ma sees what happens in charismatic and Pentecostal worship as a formation of theology. His assessment of the role of testimonies during charismatic and Pentecostal worship is worth quoting in detail. He says:

> Even in tribal churches in the Cordillera mountain region of the Philippines, old and young members stand or come forward to the pulpit to share their experiences with God. Sometimes this lasts more than an hour.... This tradition provides a place not only for participation in theology-making, but also for the rest of the congregation to reflect, evaluate, and commonly share, once accepted as genuine and valid, the theological experiences

---

32. Ma, "Pentecostal Worship," 147.
33. Ma, "Pentecostal Worship," 147–48.
34. Ma, "Pentecostal Worship," 148.
35. Ma, "Pentecostal Worship," 151.

of one member as a community possession. This has made Pentecostal theology inevitably a "people's theology." The uniqueness of this feature should be understood in the context where theologizing has been left exclusively in the hands of theological and ecclesial elites in most Christian traditions.[36]

The above quotation corroborates an earlier statement, which observes that the charismatic and Pentecostal worship is not trinitarian in the sense the Catholic Church, for example, would understand trinitarian worship. For worship to be most effective, charismatics and Pentecostals insist, it must connect with the worshiper holistically, that is, heart, mind, and body. Charismatics and Pentecostals believe that for a transforming encounter to take place during worship, worshipers must allow worship and consequently themselves to be transformed by the power of the Holy Spirit.

Jerome Boone notes that "Encountering the eternal and transcendent God demands images, signs, and symbols. Yet, transformation requires more than well-planned liturgy; the real issue is, 'Do we allow the transforming power of the Spirit into our worship and into our lives?' Liturgy and rituals are essential to worship but the Spirit is the true agent of transformation."[37]

The book of Revelation confirms the charismatic and Pentecostal claim "that true worship is experiential, involving the whole person—body, mind, and spirit—in encounter with God *in the Spirit*."[38] Archer argues that "Pentecostals can find an invitation to a *Spirited* sensory experience of worship—an experience of worship as 'ritual play' whereby the Spirit takes them into the throne room to worship before God and the Lamb" just as John is able through the power of the Holy Spirit to see the Lamb, hear the trumpets, smell the incense, taste the scroll, and touch the measuring rod.[39] In worship, charismatics and Pentecostals experience as a redeemed, sanctified, and healed community or church the foretaste of the future kingdom of God; and as a redeeming, sanctifying, and healing community or church they invite others to share in this experience. Archer notes that "It is through their rituals that Pentecostals experience communally a foretaste of the future and invite others to participate in that for which they were designed—worship."[40]

Frank Macchia perceives charismatic and Pentecostal worship as signs of grace in a graceless world. According to him, "the worship-driven church

36. Ma, "Pentecostal Worship," 151.
37. Boone, "Worship and the Torah," 23.
38. Archer, "Worship," 121.
39. Archer, "Worship," 122.
40. Archer, "Worship," 126.

celebrates grace in celebrating the presence of the gracious God among us" who graciously redeems, sanctifies, and heals his people.[41] He avers that

> worship is the context in which the church lives the biblical story in resistance to the world and in witness to an alternative reality. . . . In a world convinced that it has its own lords and power, the church celebrates Jesus as Lord of all. In the midst of a world dominated by a grab for power and influence, guided by the illusion of autonomy and self-sufficiency, the church yields in thanksgiving and praise to God as creator, redeemer, and giver of life.[42]

In other words, the charismatic and Pentecostal churches in praxis show themselves in worship to be truly signs of the presence of the redeeming, sanctifying, and healing God among his people. In this theology of worship, Macchia maintains that "Worship is not simply the expression of a leader backed by a monolithic 'amen'. Worship is an orchestra of colorfully diverse expressions," in which the charismatic structure of the church manifests itself.[43] Macchia notes that the charismatic and Pentecostal churches "have traditionally stressed the Charismatic structure of the church as essential to the strength of the church's worship and witness."[44]

The flexibility which charismatics and Pentecostals permit in their worship—for instance, the paying of attention more to oral rather than a written communication, which gives room for spontaneity—allows a wider range of participation in charismatic and Pentecostal worship. This wider range of participation is further strengthened by the fact that charismatics and Pentecostals in praxis live out their belief that all believers are gifted in one way or another by the Holy Spirit "to contribute to all facets of the church's worship."[45]

Using Walter Hollenweger as a dialogue partner, Macchia argues that "Orality, narrativity, visions, dreams, healing, and bodily movements imply a charismatically-diverse worship service that is holistic (involving the subconscious mind as well as rationality, story as well as confession of beliefs, body as well as spirit)."[46] If there is one thing that is vital to the charismatic and Pentecostal perception of worship, it is the presence of the Holy Spirit of God. Charismatics and Pentecostals do not only "believe that God's Spirit should

---

41. Macchia, "Signs of Grace," 154.
42. Macchia, "Signs of Grace," 154.
43. Macchia, "Signs of Grace," 156.
44. Macchia, "Signs of Grace," 157.
45. Macchia, "Signs of Grace," 157.
46. Macchia, "Signs of Grace," 158.

always be integrally involved in Christian worship,"⁴⁷ they also go in praxis to make this a reality. It is no surprise that during a worship service, especially "in giving a testimony or getting ready to pray for someone's healing, a Pentecostal worshiper will remind himself or herself as well as fellow worshipers that 'the Spirit is here, right here, now; Jesus is here.'"⁴⁸

The role of the Holy Spirit in worship makes expectancy of the presence of the Holy Spirit often palpable during charismatic and Pentecostal worship. Although the charismatic and Pentecostal worshipers know that the Holy Spirit, the Spirit of Jesus, comes every time and anywhere two or three gather in the name of Jesus as Jesus promised, yet, "they are also keenly aware that their attitudes and sensibilities make a difference in how God's presence is manifested and how it affects the worshipers." Hence, they "seek radical receptivity to the Holy Spirit, i.e., openness, vulnerability, and docility before God. Their liturgical rites and sensibilities encourage becoming consciously present to God—even as God's presence is expected to become very real in worship."⁴⁹ Albrecht notes that this kind of radical openness and sensitivity marks the charismatic and Pentecostal "vision and the experience of worship in the Spirit and the Spirit's role in worship."⁵⁰

Charismatics and Pentecostals know that the Spirit blows where the Spirit wills. Yet, they believe and exemplify in praxis that to "worship authentically and to experience the close presence of the Holy Spirit, worshipers must seek God with an open spirit toward God."⁵¹ Encounter with God through God's empowering presence, the Holy Spirit, is for charismatics and Pentecostals an integral part of worship experience. Hence, they believe that in "the midst of radical receptivity an encounter with the Holy may occur."⁵²

Despite worshipers' liturgical services and works during worship, charismatics and Pentecostals believe that genuine worship is the work of the Holy Spirit through whom the Triune God manifests his presence among worshipers. They believe that God speaks to his worshipers during worship through the power of his Holy Spirit. Hence, they prepare themselves to listen to God's Holy Spirit. "They hear the Spirit in the words of the Bible, through preaching, within testimonies, prophecies, and other Charismatic words in and for the congregation."⁵³

47. Albrecht, "Worshiping and the Spirit," 239.
48. Albrecht, "Worshiping and the Spirit," 239.
49. Albrecht, "Worshiping and the Spirit," 239.
50. Albrecht, "Worshiping and the Spirit," 239.
51. Albrecht, "Worshiping and the Spirit," 239.
52. Albrecht, "Worshiping and the Spirit," 240.
53. Albrecht, "Worshiping and the Spirit," 240.

The Holy Spirit cannot be manipulated in any way. Charismatics and Pentecostals know this as much as they know too that the Holy Spirit calls them for participation in God's works through empowerment. Such knowledge inspires them to "exhort one another to be sensitive to the Lord's leadings, to 'step out in faith' and follow the Holy Spirit's lead. To 'move in the Spirit' is to be sensitive to the Spirit's direction and desires within the more spontaneous moments in the service." According to Albrecht, "That may mean speaking out 'in the Spirit' with a message from the Holy Spirit, a gift for that moment in the service. It may mean laying hands on a fellow congregant and praying the 'prayer of faith' for healing or deliverance."[54] Such flexibility born out of openness to the direction of the Holy Spirit makes an encounter with God in worship palpable. It is this that makes the charismatic and Pentecostal worship unique and, consequently, the reason for which this work is using the charismatic and Pentecostal theology and praxis to argue for the renewal of the Nigerian Catholic Church. In fact, to "move in and with the Spirit," during charismatic and Pentecostal worship, "may be embodied in contemplative modes of adoration and love, or in exuberant worship filled with vocal praise and kinesthetic movement."[55]

There is always a felt need of freedom by worshipers to most effectively and authentically worship God. Charismatics and Pentecostals believe that "having the room" to freely express their worship without "being 'boxed in' by restrictive human structures" will greatly aid worshipers to really encounter God in worship. They, no doubt, believe in maintaining decency and order during worship, "but the order should be in line with the Spirit's work and direction; it should accommodate spiritual worship, not inhibit it."[56] As Albrecht notes, "freedom in worship means that God by the Holy Spirit is free to move in the ways that the Holy Spirit wishes. God is sovereign, yet worshipers can inhibit God's desire for and movements in the service."[57] It is no surprise that one of the charismatic and Pentecostal famous choruses says, "Let the Lord have His way."[58]

The charismatic and Pentecostal encounter in worship with the Triune God through the indwelling of the Holy Spirit is concretized by the experience of healings, deliverances, etc. These liturgical experiences help to give the charismatic and Pentecostal churches a new self-understanding. They help the charismatic and Pentecostal churches to see themselves as

---

54. Albrecht, "Worshiping and the Spirit," 241.
55. Albrecht, "Worshiping and the Spirit," 241.
56. Albrecht, "Worshiping and the Spirit," 242.
57. Albrecht, "Worshiping and the Spirit," 242.
58. Albrecht, "Worshiping and the Spirit," 242.

redeemed, sanctified, and healed churches or communities empowered by the Holy Spirit to become in turn the redeeming, sanctifying, and healing presence of God among his people. Charismatics and Pentecostals "reason that Jesus is the same yesterday, today, forever, and everywhere; that Jesus still saves, heals, speaks by his Spirit; that by the Spirit he meets men and women wherever they seek him."[59] Motivated by this, and coupled by the fact that "their liturgies are an expression of who they are, how they see and relate to God—that is, how they worship in the Spirit," they take their liturgies everywhere.[60]

In describing the contemporary charismatic worship he observed in the Vineyard Church, James Steven notes that the "first period was marked by a renewal called 'baptism in the Spirit' accompanied in corporate worship by Pentecostal practices such as praying or singing in tongues, new musical styles that matched the more extemporary forms of prayer, and a new physical expressiveness in worship such as raising of hands."[61] All these are in response to the felt experience of the presence of the Holy Spirit as worshipers experience healing and deliverance. In fact, Steven notes about the worshipers in Vineyard movement that emphasis was prominent "upon the power of Spirit for healing, expressed ritually in what is called the 'Ministry Time' where the Spirit is called upon the assembly and participants receive prayer, often associated with visible and ecstatic demonstrations of the Spirit's presence in power."[62] The style of worship of charismatics and Pentecostals is shaped by their theology of experiential encounter as played out in their pneumatology and ecclesiology, as much as their ritual realities shape their theological understanding. In fact, as Steven observes, "the Charismatic understanding of Spirit has been formed by the experience of Pentecostal styles of ritual encounter in and with the Spirit."[63]

Pinnock maintains that the charismatic and Pentecostal "Church services provide the context for mystical encounter, for experiencing the divine and the inbreaking of the supernatural which overwhelms humans."[64]

In charismatic and Pentecostal worships, preaching, prayers, and singing are rendered in a manner that they become vehicles to open the worshipers up for the indwelling Spirit, thereby actualizing the encounter between them and God. Pinnock puts it succinctly, he says, "In the preaching and singing,

---

59. Albrecht, "Worshiping and the Spirit," 244.
60. Albrecht, "Worshiping and the Spirit," 244.
61. Steven, "Spirit in Contemporary Charismatic Worship," 245.
62. Steven, "Spirit in Contemporary Charismatic Worship," 246.
63. Steven, "Spirit in Contemporary Charismatic Worship," 246.
64. Pinnock, "Church in the Power," 158.

with tongues and with dancing, with prayers and healing, and with the casting out of demons, they experience the touch of God and are grasped by a power that can put their lives together and support them in life's struggle."[65] Just as a dynamic faith was provided for people centuries ago through the hearing of the message of God's forgiveness, a redeeming, sanctifying, and healing experience of the presence of the Spirit of God in power are provided for the people today. The issue, as Pinnock avers, "is not primarily a doctrinal one, as if it were just a matter of learning something that one did not know intellectually. The thrust is thoroughly experiential—God is not a vague and distant figure but a reality that can be encountered."[66]

Theologically and doctrinally speaking, the charismatic and Pentecostal theology of worship is not totally different from those of other Christians. For instance, the Second Vatican Council Fathers in describing the nature of the sacred liturgy and its importance in the church's life note in Constitution on the Sacred Liturgy, *Sacrosantum Concilium*, no. 5:

> God who "wills that all men be saved and come to the knowledge of the truth" (1 Tim. 2:4), "who in many and various ways spoke in times past to the fathers by the prophets" (Heb. 1:1), when the fullness of time had come sent His Son, the Word made flesh, anointed by the Holy Spirit, to preach the gospel to the poor, to heal the contrite of heart, to be a "bodily and spiritual medicine," the Mediator between God and man. . . . The wonderful works of God among the people of the Old Testament were but a prelude to the work of Christ the Lord in redeeming mankind and giving perfect glory to God.

The Council Fathers go on in no. 6 to state:

> Just as Christ was sent by the Father, so also He sent the apostles, filled with the Holy Spirit. This He did that, by preaching the gospel to every creature, they might proclaim that the Son of God, by His death and resurrection, had freed us from the power of Satan and from death, and brought us into the kingdom of His Father. His purpose also was that they might accomplish the work of salvation which they had proclaimed, by means of sacrifice and sacraments, around which the entire liturgical life revolves.

The first sentence of no. 7 is very revealing. In this, the Council Fathers maintain that to "accomplish so great a work, Christ is always present in His Church, especially in her liturgical celebrations." In no. 33 the

---

65. Pinnock, "Church in the Power," 158.
66. Pinnock, "Church in the Power," 158.

Council Fathers insist that "in the liturgy God speaks to His people and Christ is still proclaiming His gospel. And the people reply to God both by song and prayer." The charismatic and Pentecostal theology of worship harmonizes with Romano Guardini's concept of worship where he sees liturgy as the play of the children of God before God their father.[67] Wolfgang Vondey decries the inability of the Roman Catholic Church to develop a comprehensive theology of the liturgy based on Guardini's insights in spite of the fact that his work formed the foundation for much of Roman Catholic liturgical renewal before Vatican II.[68] He "proposes that Pentecostalism offers resources to revitalize Guardini's heritage, since the development of classical Pentecostal liturgy has exposed many of the discrepancies between the traditional liturgical world of performance and the Pentecostal sensitivity to liturgical action that is best characterized as the susceptibility to engage in play."[69] Vondey's view on this will be reviewed in much detail in the final chapter when it will be used to argue for the renewal of the Nigerian Catholic Church.

David Peterson, an Australian Anglican minister and a scholar of the New Testament, views Christian worship as an "'engagement' with God, in which he acts towards us and we act towards him—in the context of a fellowship or mutual bond between the various people taking part."[70] For him, Christian worship "is essentially the engagement with God that he has made possible through the revelation of himself in Jesus Christ and the life he has made available through the Holy Spirit."[71] He maintains that the doctrine of the Trinity is the center of true Christian worship because it is through the ministry of the Son and the Spirit that the Father obtains true worshipers.[72]

Geoffrey Wainwright, a British Methodist minister and a scholar of Christian theology, uses the letter to the Romans and other scriptural passages to show how Christian worship, which comes in various forms like prayers, hymns, breaking of the word and the bread, and mutual service, etc., is directed to the Triune God.[73] He avers that in "characteristically modern terms, it might be said that the liturgy affords the opportunity for human beings to 'discover meaning' and 'make sense' of their lives and the world—provided always that the anthropological and cosmological

---

67. Guardini, *Spirit of the Liturgy*, 71.
68. Vondey, *Beyond Pentecostalism*, 131–32.
69. Vondey, *Beyond Pentecostalism*, 132.
70. Peterson, *Engaging with God*, 9.
71. Peterson, *Engaging with God*, 100.
72. Peterson, *Engaging with God*, 285.
73. Wainwright, "Christian Worship," 2–28.

categories be embraced within a divine transcendence that, according to the Christian faith, is the gracious being and action of the Triune God."[74] Wainwright had in earlier work shown how Christian doctrine and life are "firmly shaped and strongly coloured by the Christian liturgy."[75] According to him the biblical and traditional notion of humanity made in the image of God expresses a creature Creator relationship. While creatures depend on this relationship to be, God "transcends his creation and therefore transcends this relationship."[76] Wainwright therefore argues that "the proper relationship between creature and Creator is, in Christian eyes, the relationship of worship."[77] As the true image of God, Wainwright avers that Christ occupies "a central place and function in the Christian cult, he is seen as a recipient of worship, a mediator in worship, and a pattern of worship."[78] He insists that the Holy Spirit enables worship in accordance with the pattern of Christ, while "Christian worship is seen to give ritual expression to the eschatological tension"[79] that marks the church on the way to realize God's purpose. Christian worship is therefore understood "as the Church's worship of God through Christ in the Spirit."[80]

The theology of Christian worship which Franklin M. Segler and Randall Bradley present is theologically and doctrinally in line with the charismatic and Pentecostal theology of worship. They perceive Christian worship as an act of faith springing from Christians' willing response to God's revelation of himself.[81] As the earliest Christians were Jews they argue that Christian worship is rooted in Jewish religious practices, teachings, and symbolism along with Jesus' practices and teachings.[82] In spite of its root in Jewish practices, Segler and Bradley aver that Christian worship has its own distinctions. Some of these distinctions include: a) the use of the writings and teachings of Christian leaders, b) the addition of new hymns to the Psalms used in praise and worship, c) the addition of Baptism and Communion, d) the expression of zeal produced by the awareness of the presence of

---

74. Wainwright, "Christian Worship," 27.
75. Wainwright, *Doxology*, 1.
76. Wainwright, *Doxology*, 16.
77. Wainwright, *Doxology*, 16.
78. Wainwright, *Doxology*, 6.
79. Wainwright, *Doxology*, 6.
80. Wainwright, *Doxology*, 6.
81. Segler and Bradley, *Christian Worship*, 8.
82. Segler and Bradley, *Christian Worship*, 19.

the Holy Spirit, and e) the fact that "Christian worship was held at different times and places than Jewish worship."[83]

Although no particular order is found in New Testament worship, Segler and Bradley identify some elements of New Testament worship. These include hymns, scriptural readings, prayers, the people's "amens," sermons, exhortations, offerings, doxologies, confessions, and the rules of baptism and the Lord's Supper.[84]

From the historical perspective they explore Christian worship in the early churches down through the contemporary time. If there is anything, these eons revealed a considerable latitude and series of reforms in Christian worship.[85] Since theological worship according to Segler and Bradley is "a revelation and a response which springs from God's initiative in redemption," they argue that "Christian worship depends on the revelation of God in Christ Jesus."[86] While Christian worship is theocentric, the worship of God is made possible in God's Son Jesus Christ who is the object of Christian faith and worship. Hence, they maintain that all true worship must be Christocentric.[87] Here emerges another major difference between the theology of worship of the mainline churches, especially the Catholic Church, besides their view of trinitarian worship that was pointed out earlier, and the charismatic and Pentecostal theology of worship.

Although charismatics and Pentecostals acknowledge the christological aspect of worship, they do not accept that true worship must be christocentric. For them, the crucial role the Holy Spirit plays in worship makes worship pneumatocentric. Even Segler and Bradley acknowledge this essential role of the Holy Spirit in the church and in the church's liturgy when they observe that the Holy Spirit animates the church and the church's worship; and that it is through the Holy Spirit that God is present in worship.[88]

As noted already, Frans Jozef Van Beeck's presentation of Christian worship as encounter with God corroborates the charismatic and Pentecostal theology of Christian worship. Christian worship according to him "centers on Jesus Christ, present as the One whom God has raised to life, revealed as the Holy and Just One, and exalted in Glory."[89] He avers that Christian worship comprises and engages the whole dynamic of Christian

---

83. Segler and Bradley, *Christian Worship*, 21–22.
84. Segler and Bradley, *Christian Worship*, 23–24.
85. Segler and Bradley, *Christian Worship*, 25–47.
86. Segler and Bradley, *Christian Worship*, 50.
87. Segler and Bradley, *Christian Worship*, 49–53.
88. Segler and Bradley, *Christian Worship*, 53–54.
89. Beeck, *God Encountered*, 154.

life.⁹⁰ In this case Christian worship is trinitarian in nature. However, at the heart of Christian worship "is the doxological encounter, in ecstatic immediacy, with God the Father; mediated by Christ risen and embodied in him, and carried by the Spirit."⁹¹ He also maintains that Christian worship has an eschatological dimension. This, according to him, is evidenced "by the fact that the Church worships with hands lifted up, with eyes closed or raised to heaven, and with hearts groaning in expectancy."⁹²

Unlike the mainline churches, particularly the Catholic Church that insists that all true worship must be Christocentric, the charismatic and Pentecostal churches believe that all true worship must be pneumatocentric. They do not only believe this, they go a step further in praxis to act on their belief. In other words, charismatics and Pentecostals would show in praxis that the church is not only a redeemed, sanctified, and healed community, but also by the power of the Holy Spirit, a sign of the redeeming, sanctifying, and healing presence of Christ among his people. Charismatics and Pentecostals, unlike the mainline churches, believe that if Christ is always present in his church especially in her liturgical celebrations, worshipers should encounter and experience him. This experiential encounter, they maintain, is made possible only by God's empowering presence, the Holy Spirit. This is where the difference lies. It is the thrust for which this work is using the charismatic and Pentecostal theology and praxis to argue for the renewal of the Nigerian Catholic Church. The rest of this section will focus on a brief exposé of: a) the charismatic and Pentecostal style of preaching, b) the charismatic and Pentecostal style of singing, and c) the charismatic and Pentecostal style of praying respectively.

The Charismatic and Pentecostal Style of Preaching

No doubt, the charismatic and Pentecostal theology of experiential encounter influences the style of preaching of charismatics and Pentecostals. However, to really understand the style of preaching of charismatics and Pentecostals, one needs to comprehend the charismatic and Pentecostal understanding of the Bible which is also influenced by their theology of experiential encounter.

Keith Warrington notes that "Pentecostals believe that the main purpose of the Bible is to help them develop their experience of and relationship with God, to be more available to the ministry of the Spirit and to be

---

90. Beeck, *God Encountered*, 158.
91. Beeck, *God Encountered*, 218.
92. Beeck, *God Encountered*, 218.

drawn closer to Jesus."⁹³ For charismatics and Pentecostals, the Bible is primarily more of a place of encounter with the divine author than a resource for the identification and embellishment of various doctrines. When they read the Bible, they read it with the expectation to encounter God's words speaking directly to their life's situations. Warrington corroborates this when quoting Ellington, noting that "Pentecostals expect 'to encounter in the Scripture the very words of God speaking directly to their needs and guiding them.'"⁹⁴ Quoting Anderson, Warrington insists that charismatics' and Pentecostals' "'purpose in reading the Bible is to find there something that can be experienced as relevant to their felt needs,'" which according to him Wagner views as accounting "for the growth of Pentecostalism, in part, due to the 'extensive Bible-teaching ministry which is focused on the *felt needs* of church members.'"⁹⁵

In fact, the cosmology of charismatics and Pentecostals includes a dynamic God who impacts his people now as he impacted his people then. Hence, for charismatics and Pentecostals, the "Bible is anticipated as being for the purpose of teaching the readers emotionally, not simply to teach them intellectually; to result in an experience, not merely better exegesis; to facilitate an exposure of God not only an exposure of truth."⁹⁶ Charismatics and Pentecostals, in reading the Bible appropriate and adopt biblical promises and messages given to the followers of God and make them their own as long as they relate to their life's situations. They have no regrets doing this. After all, that is how the early Christians adopted some of the promises and messages given to the Jewish people in the Old Testament. Warrington notes, quoting Ebojo, that the "'reality was that early Christians reflected on the 'Word' and made it relevant in *their* own 'world' even if it meant 'rewriting' Scripture.'"⁹⁷

Charismatics and Pentecostals place high value on biblical narratives. While these narratives attest to what God has done in the past, charismatics and Pentecostals believe that they have "normative theological value" as they indicate what God can and will still do for his people in every generation. Hence, for charismatics and Pentecostals, "stories in which people have encountered God are generally preferred to didactic sections that explore the theology of that encounter. Thus, traditionally, they have related more easily to the Gospels and Acts than the epistles;

---

93. Warrington, *Pentecostal Theology*, 188.
94. Warrington, *Pentecostal Theology*, 189.
95. Warrington, *Pentecostal Theology*, 189.
96. Warrington, *Pentecostal Theology*, 189.
97. Warrington, *Pentecostal Theology*, 191.

they have enjoyed pausing with the historical books before Psalms more than the prophetic books that follow."[98]

The prominence on narratives by charismatics and Pentecostals resounds with their own storytelling journeys as evident in the majority of anecdotes and narrative in their preaching. As members of churches that believe in experiential encounter with God and in the God who is willing to do now what he did then, charismatics and Pentecostals are comfortable with expressions of various emotions provoked by biblical narratives that speak to their context during worship. For instance, "the stories of the wanderings of the Israelites, the travails and joys of the Psalmists, the sufferings of the prophets who stood for God and righteousness and the emphasis on a holy God who responded to his people with hot rage and tender compassion," resonates with the experiences of charismatics and Pentecostals "in their relationship with God and the world in which they live."[99]

Their experience with God determines how charismatics and Pentecostals interpret biblical texts. In other words, the theology of experiential encounter of charismatics and Pentecostals "inevitably affects their hermeneutics as they interpret the text with an expectation that God may similarly move in their lives now just as he did then."[100] It is common to see how experience bridges the text and its application and informs how a charismatic or Pentecostal preacher interprets the text. Warrington notes, "At all times, the sermon must be judged, not only on its presentation and style but also on its effectiveness and aftermath. The model of Jesus, the Galilean teacher is valued above that of the Jerusalem scribe for contemporary Pentecostal preaching."[101]

When it comes to the interpretation of the Scripture, a charismatic or Pentecostal preacher would not want the human mind to "militate against the work of the Spirit who has been given to lead believers into truth."[102] The ontology of the charismatic and Pentecostal theology, which is experiential and praxis-oriented, spurs charismatic and Pentecostal preachers to take the various contexts of the charismatic and Pentecostal worshipers into consideration when interpreting scriptural passages. Warrington observes that "the Pentecostal community brings its own unique comment on the text, based on its social and religious contexts and belief in the dynamic nature of the Spirit and experiential aspect of their faith, such a context being

---

98. Warrington, *Pentecostal Theology*, 191.
99. Warrington, *Pentecostal Theology*, 192.
100. Warrington, *Pentecostal Theology*, 193
101. Warrington, *Pentecostal Theology*, 194.
102. Warrington, *Pentecostal Theology*, 195.

as important to the hermeneutical process as any exegetical or theological method."[103] The charismatic and Pentecostal preachers believe that with the inspiration of the Holy Spirit who is the principal teacher of believers and whose job is to lead them into truth, a biblical text is illuminated, leading to the possibility of multidimensional interpretations. In this sense, "the Spirit is centrally valued in the creation, transmission, reception, and application of the text. This pneumatic hermeneutic is a valuable means of restoring to the text the integral characteristic of the Spirit who is the most important element of the transmission process from God to the believer."[104] Charismatics and Pentecostals are worried that the encounter with the Triune God might not be possible if the charismatic and prophetic dimension of interpreting a scriptural text is lost, consequently, blocking the Holy Spirit from doing that which he desires to do most—encounter the worshipers through the word of God.

In charismatic and Pentecostal preaching, both the preacher and the audience believe that the Holy Spirit has already spoken in the Bible. However, they believe too that "the timeless Spirit also continuously provides guidance for behavior and praxis and this pneumatic hermeneutic needs to be borne in mind in one's hermeneutical deliberations."[105] For them, the "dynamic Spirit speaks today through the ancient word but often in fresh, new and innovative ways—sometimes with the revelations that are additional to those received by the original readers."[106] The charismatic and Pentecostal preachers, therefore, work hard in their hermeneutics and preaching to guide and help "believers to be aware that the Spirit is not as silent as many may assume but that he desires to enlighten and encounter them as they listen to him speaking to them through the text."[107]

The charismatic and Pentecostal hermeneutic is, therefore, fundamentally inspired by the Holy Spirit. They see their preaching and sermons "not simply as opportunities to impart truth but to communicate life."[108] It is no surprise that "they use stories and personal testimony to illustrate and apply the truths they seek to express."[109] In fact, charismatic and Pentecostal "preachers are often emotional and extemporaneous communicators, engaging in storytelling to make a point, retelling the biblical narratives in their

---

103. Warrington, *Pentecostal Theology*, 198–99.
104. Warrington, *Pentecostal Theology*, 199.
105. Warrington, *Pentecostal Theology*, 200.
106. Warrington, *Pentecostal Theology*, 200.
107. Warrington, *Pentecostal Theology*, 200–201.
108. Warrington, *Pentecostal Theology*, 202.
109. Warrington, *Pentecostal Theology*, 202.

own words, often packaged in lengthy sermons."[110] Warrington rightly defines Charismatic and Pentecostal preaching by quoting Hocken, who views it "as comprising 'a use of Scripture and the style of preaching and ministry that was more anecdotal and narrative than schematic and doctrinal.'"[111] Charismatic and Pentecostal preaching anticipates leading the hearers, the believers to an experiential encounter with the Triune God through the power of the Holy Spirit who illuminates the text.

Alluding to Clark's description of charismatic and Pentecostal preaching, Warrington portrays it "as 'kerygmatic, par excellence' in that, although it may contain exposition, it is a dynamic event that anticipates a change in the hearers, be it conviction, challenge, encouragement or guidance."[112] In essence, in charismatic and Pentecostal preaching, "the preacher attempts to identify that which the text means for now and for the particular group of people to whom the sermon is being preached. There is an expectation that the preacher and hearer will 're-experience the text,' learning old lessons as presented in the text for the benefit of the original readers but also be open to the possibility of hearing from God in a new way."[113] In this way, an individual hearer listening to a Pentecostal or charismatic preacher may receive the preaching as a specific communication from God without the knowledge of the preacher.

In charismatic and Pentecostal preaching, neither human eloquence, wisdom, nor persuasion is of primary importance. Of fundamental importance for charismatics and Pentecostals is the empowerment of the Holy Spirit. Hence, as Vincent Leoh notes, they "hold that the only kind of preaching that matters is the Pauline model of preaching—in the power and demonstration of the Spirit (1 Cor 2:1, 4) and 'by the power of signs and miracles, through the power of the Spirit' (Rom 15:19)."[114] For this to happen and consequently initiate an encounter with the Triune God, charismatics and Pentecostals "prize a sense of dynamic freedom and sensitive flexibility in their worship and preaching."[115] It does not mean, however, that the charismatic and Pentecostal preachers eschew human preparations. For they believe that there "is the anointing that comes as a result of human preparation, and there is also that blessed prophetic anointing that comes spontaneously as God gives the preacher an urgent,

---

110. Warrington, *Pentecostal Theology*, 202.
111. Warrington, *Pentecostal Theology*, 202.
112. Warrington, *Pentecostal Theology*, 203.
113. Warrington, *Pentecostal Theology*, 203.
114. Leoh, "Pentecostal Preacher," 37.
115. Leoh, "Pentecostal Preacher," 40.

unpremeditated message."[116] In other words, true charismatic and Pentecostal preaching combines both human preparation and reliance on the empowerment of the Holy Spirit. For the "Holy Spirit operates both in the study and in the pulpit. The baptism of the Holy Spirit is not a substitute for careful planning and thoughtful preparation; neither is it a labor-saving device."[117] Charismatic and Pentecostal preachers believe that "the human personality is sanctified, enhanced, anointed and taken to a level of effectiveness beyond human finiteness."[118] They, therefore, take into cognizance "their dual responsibilities of using their God-given faculties and at the same time yielding to the dynamic unction and power of the Spirit, without which all human efforts would be fruitless."[119] In fact, it is very unlikely that any charismatic or Pentecostal preacher would object that LeRoy Bartel's statement about the Spirit-filled teacher applies to the Spirit-anointed preacher. He says, "The Holy Spirit can enhance the teacher's presentation. Plans should be made, methodology mastered, and public speaking skills improved, keeping in mind, however, that the Holy Spirit is able to lift the teacher's efforts to new levels of effectiveness. He can provide the clarity of thought, the stability of emotions, and the personal poise so necessary to persuasive presentation."[120]

As far as charismatic and Pentecostal preaching is concerned, Leoh corroborates Bartel's view of the interconnectedness between human preparation and the empowerment of the Holy Spirit. According to him, "the Holy Spirit in sermon preparation opens to the preacher the whole range of possibilities of imaginative approaches to preaching. The Holy Spirit may move upon the heart and mind of the preacher to deal in certain topics of needs. Divine wisdom may be brought to bear on crucial individual and societal problems."[121] He, therefore, insists that charismatic and Pentecostal preaching "must be viewed as a divine-human process and cooperative venture" devoid of any "dichotomy between intensive preparation and direct illumination."[122]

Although charismatic and Pentecostal preachers believe and do embark on human preparations for sermons or preaching, they believe that it is the Holy Spirit who makes preaching or sermon produce the

---

116. Leoh, "Pentecostal Preacher," 41–42.
117. Leoh, "Pentecostal Preacher," 42.
118. Leoh, "Pentecostal Preacher," 42.
119. Leoh, "Pentecostal Preacher," 42.
120. Bartel, "Holy Spirit," 122.
121. Leoh, "Pentecostal Preacher," 43.
122. Leoh, "Pentecostal Preacher," 43.

desired effect—encounter between God and the hearer. Leoh is right when he notes that the "process of sermon preparation should be initiated by prayer, enlightened by study, strengthened by homiletical techniques, and guided by the Holy Spirit. For the Pentecostal, even after all human preparation has been thoroughly done, the dependence for real success is on the Spirit of God."[123]

Charismatic and Pentecostal preaching is characterized by its forcefulness. Indeed, charismatics and Pentecostals "have always eschewed stiff, formal, 'emotionless religion,' 'emotionless audience,' and 'emotionless sermons.'"[124] While charismatics and Pentecostals value emotion in preaching, they eschew emotionalism. For them, there "is a distinct difference between the use of emotion in preaching, which is almost always encouraged, and merely being emotional, which is always to be avoided." "The former," they argue, "is genuine, passionate, expression of intense feeling in response to significant truth, whereas emotionalism is simulated feeling momentarily indulged as an end in itself, or artificial, untrue sentimentalism calling attention to itself and serving its own ends."[125] In sum, authentic charismatic and Pentecostal preaching is "both cognitive and emotive. It is a matter of moral feelings and intuitions as well as rational standards; it is a matter of personal experience as well as reasonable reflection. All these activities are carried out under the influence of the Spirit," charismatics and Pentecostals would emphasize.[126]

Charismatics and Pentecostals expect to encounter God through the power of the Holy Spirit when the word of God is preached. Hence, charismatic and Pentecostal "preaching is successful when the people feel good, blessed, spiritually nourished and motivated to serve God. Pentecostal preachers might not go as deeply into the biblical texts as their counterparts in mainline churches do, but the response of the listeners will indicate that they have been 'touched' in general or specific ways."[127] They believe that "signs and wonders" and other supernatural evidences promised in the Gospel of Mark and made manifest in the book of Acts "will follow an anointed ministry." It is a common belief among charismatics and Pentecostals that when the word of God is preached with power and under the anointing of the Holy Spirit, "there will be a manifestation of spiritual gifts. Healings may take place, deliverances may occur, the needs of the congregation will be

---

123. Leoh, "Pentecostal Preacher," 44.
124. Leoh, "Pentecostal Preacher," 45.
125. Leoh, "Pentecostal Preacher," 45.
126. Leoh, "Pentecostal Preacher," 52.
127. Leoh, "Pentecostal Preacher," 57.

met in supernatural ways or they will at least be ministered to, and people will develop an awesome respect for spiritual things."[128]

Preaching, singing, and praying are all interconnected in charismatic and Pentecostal worship. Each adds strength to the other and helps it to achieve the desired goal, which is, leading the worshipers into an encounter with the Triune God through the power of the Holy Spirit. The enthusiasm and expectancy that characterize charismatic and Pentecostal preaching are very conspicuous in their style of singing and praying. It is to these that attention is now turned respectively.

The Charismatic and Pentecostal Style of Music

In noting the place of singing in Pauline churches, Gordon Fee, a Pentecostal scholar that has been referred to above, observes that as "with prayer, song had become the special province of the Spirit (1 Cor 14:14-15, 26; Col 3:16; Eph 5:19)."[129] The principle of experiential encounter, which influences the charismatic and Pentecostal theology in general and their pneumatology, ecclesiology, and worship in particular, is the same principle that influences their music during worship. Charismatics and Pentecostals expect to encounter the Triune God during worship by the power of the indwelling Spirit.

For charismatics and Pentecostals music prepares the worshipers during worship and takes them to encounter God through the power of the Holy Spirit. Robert Webber corroborates the charismatic and Pentecostal concept of and approach to music when he observes that "music is the wheel upon which the Word and Eucharist ride."[130] It is no surprise that Daniel Albrecht observes, "Many Pentecostal ritualists report that during the worship they sense the proximity of the Holy Spirit and the reality of close communion with the divine heightened during the singing, listening and participating in the music and the other sounds of worship."[131] As people who await an experiential encounter with their God during worship, music not only disposes charismatic and Pentecostal worshipers for such encounter, but also awakens them to the reality of the presence of God in their midst. Richard Griggs rightly notes that in charismatic and Pentecostal worship, "music itself becomes a cry of maranatha, and it is the expectation of the worshiping

---

128. Leoh, "Pentecostal Preacher," 57–58.
129. Fee, *God's Empowering Presence*, 885.
130. Webber, *Worship Old & New*, 195.
131. Albrecht, *Rites in the Spirit*, 143.

community that begins to make that presence a reality."¹³² David Mosely is perhaps right when he states that "music is a participatory experience that links worldly existence with its transcendent ground in God's loving, reconciling self-revelation in Christ."¹³³ For charismatics and Pentecostals, music is part and parcel of worship. Hence, they believe that worship spiced with music establishes in the words of Steven J. Land a "connectional reality of the presence of the Holy Spirit in the life of the Church and the power of the Spirit's influence upon people's hearts and minds."¹³⁴

Charismatics and Pentecostals believe that charismatic and Pentecostal music is a medium through which God invites worshipers during worship to an experiential encounter of him. Mark J. Cartledge attests to this when he explains that "Songs associated with Charismatic spirituality display a conviction that God Himself is the primary agent in worship and that through them He is establishing and sustaining a personal relationship with the worshippers."¹³⁵ As in the case of preaching, charismatic and Pentecostal music directors make all necessary human preparations while at the same time create room for spontaneity as the Holy Spirit gives the lead. They re-enact the biblical stories in songs, making them their own stories as they relate to their life situations.

In fact, musical worship engages charismatic and Pentecostal "spirituality by facilitating the discovery of personal and communal narratives, allowing worshippers to identify their own stories as part of the grand metanarrative of scripture without losing sight of the breadth and diversity of the human experience."¹³⁶ Lee Roy Martin puts it succinctly when he says, "The Pentecostals' appreciation for the narrative quality of scripture meant that they became a part of the story. Therefore, they no longer looked at the Bible from the outside; instead, they entered the world of the Bible, and the world of the Bible shaped their world."¹³⁷ This charismatic and Pentecostal mode of re-enacting biblical realities through music establishes for them a mutual dependence between knowledge and lived experience. Land puts it distinctly when he notes that "These ways of remembering the biblical world mediated the biblical realities in a kind of Pentecostal sacramentality in which there was a constant, mutually conditioning interplay between knowledge and lived experience, where learning about God and directly

132. Griggs, "Musical Worship," 53.
133. Mosely, "'Parables' and 'Polyphony,'" 269.
134. Land, *Pentecostal Spirituality*, 147.
135. Cartledge, *Encountering the Spirit*, 67.
136. Griggs, "Musical Worship," 62.
137. Martin, *Pentecostal Hermeneutics*, 5.

experiencing God perpetually inform and depend upon one another."¹³⁸ In fact, charismatics and Pentecostals "engage both their own stories and the divine story while singing hymns that recount the narrative of redemption and highlight the ups and downs in the lives of participants."¹³⁹

Charismatics and Pentecostals give meaning to their lives' situations by re-enacting the scriptural narratives and relating them to their experiences in life. In fact, according to Griggs, charismatics and Pentecostals "sing their theology, reenacting the biblical narrative within their liturgy of planned spontaneity. Music simultaneously creates an atmosphere of receptivity to and participation with God's presence while articulating that experience in one single action."¹⁴⁰ Land thinks in the same vein. He says:

> By interpreting their daily life and worship in terms of the significant events of biblical history, their own lives and actions were given significance. Everybody became a witness to Calvary and his or her own crucifixion with Christ, the biblical Pentecost and a personal Pentecost, the healings of the disciples and his or her own healing and so on. The singing reflected this idea of the present normativity of biblical events and therefore, for that very reason, the necessity of existential appropriation and participation.... Thus, for them Calvary was not only a specific historical event but also a testimony and focus for daily life.¹⁴¹

Charismatics and Pentecostals no doubt would agree with Erik Contzius, a Jewish musician and composer whom Griggs quotes as saying, "Singing expresses that which words and thoughts alone cannot. We sing in joy and in sorrow. Singing moves us in ways inexplicable. When we hear others sing, we can glean their innermost emotions. When we sing ourselves, we experience release and sometimes, relief."¹⁴² Charismatics and Pentecostals attest to music being "a vehicle of this release and relief, present when chains are loosened in freedom, fear removed in celebration, and walls torn down in obedient trust," as in the case of Paul and Silas and the falling of the walls of Jericho.¹⁴³

From the early times of charismatic renewal and Pentecostalism, charismatic and Pentecostal musicians boldly "take their new-found faith and express it with the cultural context of their native musical forms," according

---

138. Land, *Pentecostal Spirituality*, 75.
139. Griggs, "Musical Worship," 65–66.
140. Griggs, "Musical Worship," 63–64.
141. Land, *Pentecostal Spirituality*, 73.
142. Griggs, "Musical Worship," 64.
143. Griggs, "Musical Worship," 64.

to Kelly J. Godoy de Danielson and Robert Danielson.[144] Danielson and Danielson, using the Christian songs and music of Juan Luis Guerra, show that charismatics and Pentecostals, in songs and music, acclaim Christ as the savior, the sanctifier, the healer, and the coming Lord.[145]

In his study of the development of early Spanish Pentecostal music, Daniel Ramírez observes:

> In contrast to historic Protestantism's disdainful distancing, Pentecostal hymnody redeemed the fiesta of Mexican and Latino culture. It brightened the previously dark view—held by Protestant missionaries—of popular culture that saw this as hopelessly enmeshed in intractable pathologies of alcoholism and unbridled machismo. Pentecostals returned popular musical culture to the sacred place of ritual, performance, and spectacle. They forged a new sonic universe that replaced the earlier popular Catholic visual world of saints, candles, gilded altars, and paintings—stimuli that had been erased by iconoclastic Protestantism—with intense sonic and sensory stimulation. Against mainline missionary censure, Pentecostals reintroduced a measure of the carnivalesque (laughter, weeping, body movement, profane instruments, feasts, etc.) into liturgical space and time.[146]

Charismatic and Pentecostal music establishes in worship a communication and an encounter between not only the worshiping community with God, but also the individual worshiper with God. Warrington observes that "Music in Pentecostal worship is often very personal in terms of endearment and communication between the singer and God and songs are increasingly viewed as 'vehicles for people to communicate directly with God.'"[147]

The charismatic and Pentecostal style of music mimics the biblical Psalms in the sense that through music the charismatic and Pentecostal worshipers express various forms of emotions to God. The emotions range from praise, worship, adoration, and thanksgiving to God, to lamentation, confession of sins, asking for pardon, for protection, deliverance, healing, blessings of all kinds, and so on. As Warrington notes, the "songs have increasingly taken the form of more directional expressions to God than doctrinal reflections on his character. They function as modern day psalms expressing a

---

144. Danielson and Danielson, "Pentecostal Music," 62.
145. Danielson and Danielson, "Pentecostal Music," 64–69.
146. Ramírez, *Migrating Faith*, 178.
147. Warrington, *Pentecostal Theology*, 224.

wide range of emotions, requests and statements of praise to God."[148] The charismatic and Pentecostal music is more experientially and emotionally oriented than doctrinally based. Warrington, still referring to the charismatic and Pentecostal style of music, observes that the "doctrinally based hymns of past decades have been largely replaced by simpler songs that are easier to memorize and contain more emotionally charged lyrics of affection for God, readiness to serve him and praying for his increasing involvement in the lives of the singers."[149] For charismatics and Pentecostals, music is less an entertainment and exhibition of talent than singing in the Spirit in line with Paul's admonition to sing in Ephesians 5:19. Ray H. Hughes, commenting on the role of music in charismatic and Pentecostal worship through the lens of Paul's admonition to sing in the Spirit, observes:

> Therefore, singing in the Spirit is not an exhibition of talent, nor is it entertainment for the hearers. It is making melody in the heart to the Lord. This accounts for the apparent lack of inhibition of Pentecostal worshipers. They lift their souls to God, completely caught up in the ecstasy of the moment, wafted the way on the wings of songs. Often they are oblivious to fellow worshipers or to bystanders. This also accounts in part for their beaming, shining countenances as they are enraptured in song.[150]

While this kind of music which inspires the congregation or the worshipers and glorifies God is often sung spontaneously, it "does not preclude training. Intellectual refinement when touched by the Spirit often makes the singing even more edifying."[151] Alexander, quoting Delton L. Alford, observes that music in the early Pentecostal tradition was "'exuberant and spirited singing of gospel hymns. . . . Their singing was joyful in spirit and consisted primarily of congregational expressions of praise and testimony.'"[152]

Charismatic and Pentecostal music prepares worshipers and helps them to open themselves up for an encounter with the Triune God through the power of the Holy Spirit. In this encounter, the worshipers experience the loving mercy of God the Father made manifest in his only begotten Son Jesus Christ through the power of the Holy Spirit by experiencing Jesus as the Savior, Sanctifier, Healer, and the Coming King. This is an experiential encounter that not only makes them a saved, sanctified, and healed

---

148. Warrington, *Pentecostal Theology*, 224.
149. Warrington, *Pentecostal Theology*, 224.
150. Hughes, *Classical Pentecostal Sermon Library*, 51.
151. Hughes, *Classical Pentecostal Sermon Library*, 51.
152. Alexander, "'Singing Heavenly Music,'" 215.

community but also a saving, sanctifying, and healing community in this life while not losing sight of the fact that they are at the same time unsaved, unsanctified, and unhealed community waiting for the fullness of their salvation, sanctification, and healing when they finally meet with their coming Lord and King in the eschaton.

The Charismatic and Pentecostal Style of Prayer

Most of the things discussed about the charismatic and Pentecostal style of preaching and music apply to their style of prayer. Hence, much will not be discussed in this section. Like the style of preaching and music of charismatics and Pentecostals, the expectation to encounter God in prayer influences their style of praying. Gordon Fee, in his study of the Holy Spirit in the Letters of Paul notes that the coming of the Holy Spirit radically transformed prayer as far as Paul is concerned. He observes that while it cannot be determined whether set prayers were said in the Pauline churches, "spontaneous prayer by the Spirit is the norm."[153] It is the Holy Spirit who assists in our prayer because, "in our present weakness we don't know for what to pray, the Spirit himself makes intercession for us with 'inarticulate groanings' (Rom 8:26–27)."[154] Fee maintains that "Praying 'in the Spirit,'" which Paul admonished his churches to be doing and which he himself was doing, "(however that is to be understood) is also God's provision for his people in another area of weakness—in the ongoing struggle 'against the principalities and powers.'"[155]

Fee observes that besides "the defensive armor provided by the gospel, Paul urges believers to use their two 'Spirit weapons' as they engage the enemy: the message of the gospel (penetrating the enemy's territory and rescuing people who are captive to him) and 'praying in the Spirit' (Eph 6:18–20)."[156] In this, Paul showed that the role of the Holy Spirit in prayer is indispensable. And "because we do not know how to pray as we ought we need to lean more heavily on 'praying in/by the Spirit' so as to carry on such 'spiritual warfare' more effectively."[157] For Fee, "Prayer, therefore, is not simply our cry of desperation or our 'grocery list' of requests that we bring before our heavenly *Abba*; prayer is an activity inspired by God himself, through his Holy Spirit. It is God siding with his people and, by his own

---

153. Fee, *God's Empowering Presence*, 866.
154. Fee, *God's Empowering Presence*, 867.
155. Fee, *God's Empowering Presence*, 867.
156. Fee, *God's Empowering Presence*, 867.
157. Fee, *God's Empowering Presence*, 867.

empowering presence, the Spirit of God himself, bringing forth prayer that is in keeping with his will and his ways."[158]

Charismatics and Pentecostals "base their beliefs relating to prayer on the Bible, though temperament and church tradition also play a part in forming the motivation for and practice of prayer."[159] Charismatics and Pentecostals believe that the Holy Spirit has an essential role in prayer as prayer is seen as an encounter with the Triune God through the power of the Holy Spirit. For them, prayer "is intended to be a God-conscious moment when the transcendent God opens a window into the world of the believer and announces his presence—maybe in a cataclysmic setting but more often in a whisper, so quiet that it may be missed. But in that encounter, a prayer is born."[160]

Charismatics and Pentecostals prefer to articulate their individual prayer requests loudly during communal worship as a way of sharing them with others. "Praying aloud is a means of sharing one's request with others, their spoken affirmation of it as it is being uttered providing communal and personal significance. Not only is extemporary prayer common in Pentecostal gatherings, but so also is the corporate nature of such prayer in unison, either in tongues or in the first language of the individuals concerned."[161]

The charismatic and Pentecostal prayer is more informal and less liturgical due to the fact that charismatics and Pentecostals tend to see God as their personal Father, Jesus as their personal Lord and Savior, and the Holy Spirit as their personal guide.[162] Encouraged by scriptural passages where God listened and answered the prayers of his people, charismatics and Pentecostals pray with confidence that God listens and will answer their prayer. Hence, they pray with expectation of God's "intervention into their lives and in response to their prayers."[163] However, they believe that "prayer is not an opportunity to encourage God to change his mind or the future but of engaging with God and bringing the future into a reality in the present."[164]

In their prayer and praise, charismatics and Pentecostals often make use of biblical verses as part of their prayer and praise. They often refer to biblical stories and promises as part of the embroidery of their prayer. "Such narratives provide examples of how to pray and what to pray for as

---

158. Fee, *God's Empowering Presence*, 867.
159. Warrington, *Pentecostal Theology*, 214.
160. Warrington, *Pentecostal Theology*, 214–15.
161. Warrington, *Pentecostal Theology*, 216.
162. Warrington, *Pentecostal Theology*, 216.
163. Warrington, *Pentecostal Theology*, 216.
164. Warrington, *Pentecostal Theology*, 217.

well as encouragement and reasons to pray. The experiences of OT believers and the promises spoken by the earthly Jesus are drafted into modern prayers by many who would seek to ascribe those experiences and promises to themselves."[165] Charismatics and Pentecostals, however, understand that "this belief does not assume that all prayer requests will always be granted by God. There are other issues to be considered including the appropriate nature of the prayer (1 John 5.16), its relationship to the will of God (1 John 5.14) and the possibility that the delay in response may result in the prayer not being answered in the way hoped for."[166] Charismatics and Pentecostals believe that God not only answers prayers made with faith through the power of the Holy Spirit, but also provides wisdom on how to pray. For them, prayer is "an opportunity not only for requesting healing but also for listening to divine advice and guidance as to how one should pray in contexts of sickness as well as other settings."[167] Charismatics and Pentecostals believe that 'the prayer of faith' in James 5:15 and its closest parallel of trust in God's promises in James 1:6 shows that the "prayer of faith can only thus be offered if the will of God is in keeping with the prayer," in which case, there is an expectation that the request will be granted.[168] Warrington observes that

> It is possible that Jas 5.15 finds its closest parallel in 1.6 in as much as the shared context is a prayer of request. The faith that is anticipated in 1.6 is trust in God's promise that he will provide wisdom, on the basis of which one is encouraged to pray and expect a positive response. It is in this respect that faith, as recorded in 5.15, is most appropriately interpreted as trust that God will do as he has promised.[169]

In the light of this, charismatics and Pentecostals identify prayer of faith "as knowledge of God's will for a particular situation. The faith referred to is thus equivalent to a divine assurance or revelation to pray in a particular way. Resulting from such divinely imparted knowledge, an individual may confidently expect that the outcome, as revealed, will occur."[170] Hence, when charismatics and Pentecostals offer prayer, they make an attempt "to ascertain the will of God in order to pray most appropriately (1.6)."[171]

165. Warrington, *Pentecostal Theology*, 217.
166. Warrington, *Pentecostal Theology*, 217.
167. Warrington, *Pentecostal Theology*, 288.
168. Warrington, *Pentecostal Theology*, 288.
169. Warrington, *Pentecostal Theology*, 288.
170. Warrington, *Pentecostal Theology*, 288.
171. Warrington, *Pentecostal Theology*, 288.

Charismatics and Pentecostals believe that prayer should still be offered even when there is no certainty that healing will take place. As Warrington says quoting Opoku Onyinah, "the healing ministry of Jesus is to encourage people to pray for healing but also 'to trust him to bring good out of every situation whether he cures or not.'"[172] The style of prayer of charismatics and Pentecostals "is powerful, not because it is related to the meritorious nature of the one praying but because the one praying is willing and able to discern how best to pray."[173] According to James Steven, "The language of desire permeates Charismatic prayer and is often found in song lyrics."[174] In their style of prayer, charismatics bring "together the spontaneous mode of prayer with the 'objective' public prayer of the church."[175] In this sense, Mass for the Catholic charismatics is transformed from 'saying Mass' to 'praying Mass.' In other words, the gift of the Holy Spirit in prayer enables Catholic charismatics "to enter more deeply, emotionally, and intentionally into the spirit and content of the prayer of the Mass."[176] Compared to the seventeenth-century dissenting prayer, Steven maintains that "Charismatic prayer is more concerned to establish free prayer as the sign of God's spontaneity, and less interested with free prayer being a sign of the spiritual status of those who pray."[177] This shows that for charismatics and Pentecostals, "prayer is more of divine event than it is human. This is not to deny that the human is important—worshipers are to be passionate, and the raising of hands, for example, signifies the intensity of engagement in prayer—but the prime significance of these so-called postural artifacts lies in their character as icons of God's presence in and through the Spirit."[178]

Whatever prayer is to others, it is to charismatics and Pentecostals an experiential encounter with God by the indwelling Spirit. Alluding to the importance of prayer in charismatic and Pentecostal worship, Albrecht observes, "To pray is to experience God. Experience is primary for Pentecostals in their view of worship. The focus and desire of all worship experience is God. Prayer is the vehicle, the conduit; it is the interaction itself between the worshipers and God. It is the joining of the human and divine experiences."[179]

---

172. Warrington, *Pentecostal Theology*, 289.
173. Warrington, *Pentecostal Theology*, 289.
174. Steven, "Spirit in Contemporary Charismatic Worship," 249.
175. Steven, "Spirit in Contemporary Charismatic Worship," 251.
176. Steven, "Spirit in Contemporary Charismatic Worship," 251.
177. Steven, "Spirit in Contemporary Charismatic Worship," 251.
178. Steven, "Spirit in Contemporary Charismatic Worship," 251–52.
179. Albrecht, "Worshiping and the Spirit," 237.

The role of prayer in charismatic and Pentecostal worship cannot be overemphasized as prayer opens the door for the saving, sanctifying, and healing power of God through the power of the Holy Spirit. For charismatics and Pentecostals, "prayer services can involve music, sharing from the Word, testimony, and other rites, but they focus on prayer—mostly unwritten, spontaneous, fully participatory, and often loud. They are filled with sounds as believers' voices together crescendo and diminish in waves of corporate prayer."[180] The charismatic and Pentecostal worship embellished with its style of preaching, music, and prayer, aims at an experiential encounter with the redeeming, sanctifying, and healing love of God the Father made manifest in his Son Jesus Christ through the power of the Holy Spirit. The next section portrays how this plays out in the context of the Nigerian charismatic renewal and Pentecostalism.

Charismatic and Pentecostal Worship in the Context of the Nigerian Charismatic Renewal and Pentecostalism

In a cosmological worldview like that of Nigeria, where the deities, the spirits, and the ancestors deeply get involved in human affairs by constant interaction with humans, either bringing them blessings or curses, Christian worshipers would want their Christian God to interact with them, listen to their prayers, respond to their worship, and provide for their needs. This is what the charismatic and Pentecostal worships have done for the people, "which," according to Ma, "is quite different from the version of Christianity which Western missionaries once propagated."[181] Nigerian charismatic and Pentecostal worshipers worship with the expectation of encountering the Triune God through the power of the Holy Spirit. In this encounter, they expect to experience the redeeming, sanctifying, and healing power of God. The preaching, music, and prayer that form part of their worship are done in such a way that they facilitate this encounter with the divine. In fact, Nigerian charismatic and Pentecostal hermeneutics, like the hermeneutics of charismatics and Pentecostals in general, is praxis-oriented with experience and Scripture being maintained in a dialectical relationship. The Holy Spirit maintains the ongoing relationship. The truth must be fulfilled in life experiences. The emphases are on experiential, relational, emotional, oral faith, immediacy of text, and a freedom to interpret and appropriate the multiple meanings of the biblical texts. By a pneumatic illumination, it recognizes a spiritual kinship between the authors and readers and an

180. Albrecht, "Worshiping and the Spirit," 237.
181. Ma, "Pentecostal Worship," 142.

ongoing continuity with the New Testament church. Personal and corporate experience was not to be divorced from the hermeneutical task. This is the dialogical role of experience.[182]

In this kind of hermeneutics, Kalu observes alluding to the work of Cheryl Bridges Johns on *Pentecostal Formation* that "the Christian story serves as a source of critique for the present. Then, there is a movement from present praxis to the story, bringing its own consciousness and needs to the appropriation of the story. Next, there is a dialectic between the vision that arises out of the meaning of the story and our present praxis. Finally, the vision shifts from the present praxis to the future being shaped by our appropriation."[183] To understand the style of preaching of the Nigerian charismatic and Pentecostal preachers, take a look at the illustration Ogbu Kalu gave using the pericope in Luke 13:10–17, where Jesus healed the crippled woman. According to Kalu:

> If a Nigerian or African Charismatic and Pentecostal preacher was to preach on this pericope, he or she would first describe the sad fate of the woman until everyone would recognize a similar case in the home village. There may be an interlude with a plaintive song from a traditional dirge or folk-tale. Then, the entry of Jesus into the context would be portrayed in such vivid colors that each person would feel the same presence. The past is given life in the present. The healing occurs as the whole congregation stands to sing that "in the word of God, there is power; in the name of Jesus, every knee shall bow." Other victory choruses would follow before the coup de main in verse 16. Jesus calls the woman, "the daughter of Abraham," that is, one in whose body the promise of God was powerfully at work. Her social context had constructed her otherwise-crippled, ugly, dysfunctional and worthless. She accepted the verdict for life. Jesus renames her and imbues her with an imagination of being much different. She accepts the counter-verdict, "stood up straight and began to praise God" (verse 13). Jesus roots himself in the enduring covenant of God and, rejecting manifest givens, voices a different reality that is borne on the counter-text in Genesis.[184]

Indeed, Nigerian charismatic and Pentecostal preachers in their hermeneutics "surf the counter-verdicts of God and use these to conscientize the people of God in the midst of life's debilitating contexts."[185] Alluding

182. Kalu, "Pentecostal and Charismatic Reshaping," 99.
183. Kalu, "Pentecostal and Charismatic Reshaping," 99.
184. Kalu, "Pentecostal and Charismatic Reshaping," 100–101.
185. Kalu, "Pentecostal and Charismatic Reshaping," 101.

to the work of Lewis R. Rambo on *Understanding Religious Conversion*, Kalu maintains that "the songs and dances, yells and elicitation of audience participation" that accompany charismatic and Pentecostal preaching "aid the believers to 'perform religiously' before rationalizing the process. Such rituals offer knowledge in a distinct form that enables the believers to understand, experience and embody the new way of life."[186]

Nigerian charismatic and Pentecostal preachers "craft language in a transformative manner so that the believer would begin to speak differently and soon, through biographical testimonies, share and validate the religious belief system being advocated."[187] Kalu maintains that this "process of turning text into oral and experiential models is a recovery of what the Bible originally had been."[188]

The Nigerian charismatic and Pentecostal worship as demonstrated in the style of preaching, music, and prayer of the Nigerian charismatics and Pentecostals arouses "the senses, permeating the unconscious and quickening the body, giving it new life as Paul would say in I Cor 6:19ff."[189] For Nigerian charismatics and Pentecostals, worship as exemplified in their style of preaching, music, and prayer is designed to bring the foretaste of the kingdom of God on earth and to restore God's peace.

It has been noted that the Nigerian worldview knows no dichotomy between the spiritual and the physical. Hence, in worship, the spirituality of the Nigerian charismatics and Pentecostals uses "musical rhythm to communicate a holistic experience of human existence."[190] To understand the importance of music for the Nigerian charismatics and Pentecostals and their style of music, one needs to understand the role and style of music in Nigerian traditional religious worship. In the Nigerian worldview as in the worldview of most African Nations, music is deeply interconnected with the "verbal expression of religious transcendence, which is often expressed as spirit-possession."[191] In fact, music opens the door for worshipers in traditional Nigerian religion, to experientially encounter the Supreme Being through the intermediary spirits. At "the heart of traditional African religions is the emotional experience of being filled with the power of the spiritual universe."[192] This is often made possible in worship through the power

---

186. Kalu, "Pentecostal and Charismatic Reshaping," 101.
187. Kalu, "Pentecostal and Charismatic Reshaping," 101.
188. Kalu, "Pentecostal and Charismatic Reshaping," 101.
189. Kalu, "Pentecostal and Charismatic Reshaping," 102.
190. Mills, "Musical Prayers," 113.
191. Mills, "Musical Prayers," 114.
192. Mills, "Musical Prayers," 114.

of music. It is no surprise that Albert J. Raboteau referring to worship in traditional West African religion observes that worship that ends up in Spirit possession "consists in prayer, praise, songs, offerings of food and drink."[193] According to him, "drumming plays a paramount role in calling the powers and facilitating possession. The drums are of African type, played in trio. The music of the ceremonies employ(s) polyrhythms, antiphonal responses . . . bodily swaying and hand-clapping."[194]

For the Nigerian charismatics and Pentecostals, the importance of music in worship cannot be overemphasized. As Clement E. Udok and Fumilayo A. Odunuga observed, music plays a vital role in the relationship between man and God. For Christians, music forms one of the fundamental elements in church liturgy and it plays an integral part in worship service. However, music has a propelling effect of inspiring one's soul to God, but it all depends on the kind and style of music performed. In the early years of missionary work in Nigeria, music in liturgical service was developed and centered with such features as hymn singing, chant, and anthem with no application of indigenous musical accompaniment.[195]

The mainline churches in Nigeria embraced the European style of music and worship that could not effectively elevate worshipers to an experiential encounter with God. The Nigerian charismatic renewal and Pentecostalism on the contrary opted for "the adaptation of new musical genre of emotional expression by lifting up of hands prostrating and other exciting and emotional gestures in form of worship to God. . . . The solemn expression marked and conveyed by strict seriousness during church services are replaced by new contemporary styles of worship."[196] The Nigerian charismatic and Pentecostal music resembles more in style, the mode of music obtainable in contemporary Nigerian society than the usual hymns and chants the mainline churches are known for. "Its typical usage is based on pop, rock or praise and worship styles, arranged with the lyrics of the themes to include—message of salvation, faith and encouragement, spirit renewal, praise and worship."[197] Nigerian charismatic and Pentecostal churches

> are known for a distinctive style of singing choruses which is referred to as praise and worship. This is often done spontaneously with handclapping, singing, shouting, dancing, speaking in tongues and prophesying. Praise worship being one of the

193. Raboteau, *Invisible Institution*, 46.
194. Raboteau, *Invisible Institution*, 55.
195. Udok and Odunuga, "Music and Pentecostalism," 54.
196. Udok and Odunuga, "Music and Pentecostalism," 55.
197. Udok and Odunuga, "Music and Pentecostalism," 55.

exuberant characteristic activities of the Pentecostal churches, has from its inception realized its performance as spiritual electric current with emotional switch that can ignite power.[198]

Nigerian charismatics and Pentecostals, indeed, charismatics and Pentecostals all over, lay great emphasis on the importance of music and dance as part of worship. They believe that there are examples of the inclusion of music and dance as part of liturgical worship contained both in the Old and New Testaments scriptural passages.[199] The lyric and the musical features of most charismatic and Pentecostal "songs are characterized by emphasis on the Holy Spirit and personal relationship with God. Lyrically, words showing the intimate relationship with God are often used (the words You and I). Sometimes, slangs are used (I wanna thank you Lord). Most times, physical response follows the lyrics, expressing and demonstrating accordingly to the lyrics of the music, all these are accompanied with the use of drums and popular rhythms."[200] The Nigerian charismatic and Pentecostal "principles and ideology on the work of the Holy Spirit has prompted the development of different musical styles, such as gospel music, Christian pop, gospel rock, and Christian punk especially among youths."[201] For Nigerian charismatics and Pentecostals, music is more an act of praying and ministering than a mere entertainment tool. As Floribert Patrick Calvain Endong observes, most Nigerian charismatic and Pentecostal "gospel singers have often sought to mobilize both their lyrical text and the melody of their songs, not just as mere entertainment tools, but as veritable weapons of impactful ministering."[202] This statement should not be seen as negating the fact that the Nigerian charismatic and Pentecostal music is an entertainment tool. Rather, it should be understood in the sense that the Nigerian charismatic and Pentecostal music, particularly when used in worship, while a tool of healthy entertainment, aims primarily at opening the worshipers up for an encounter with the Triune God through God's empowering presence, the Holy Spirit. In fact, in Nigerian charismatic and Pentecostal worship, "the dispositions that attract God's Spirit are prayer, songs and sustained percussion with the talking drum," as Uzukwu rightly observed.[203] This will be revisited in the next chapter in more detail.

---

198. Udok and Odunuga, "Music and Pentecostalism," 56.
199. Udok and Odunuga, "Music and Pentecostalism," 56.
200. Udok and Odunuga, "Music and Pentecostalism," 59.
201. Udok and Odunuga, "Music and Pentecostalism," 60.
202. Endong, "Glossolalia," 18.
203. Uzukwu, *God, Spirit and Human Wholeness*, 202.

According to Matthews Ojo, the "first and most successful Gospel musical group on the Nigerian scene was the Good Women Choir of the Christ Apostolic Church (an indigenous Pentecostal church which seceded from the British Apostolic Church about 1937), Ibadan and District, led by Mrs. D.A. Fashoyin."[204] All their songs, although rendered in Yoruba language, convey "the conventional African themes of victory over one's enemies and in the spiritual world, prayers for success and for children, prayers for long life and health, which are basic to African cosmology."[205]

The Nigerian charismatic and Pentecostal style of music is a repetition of phrases of simple words accompanied by joyful drumming and dancing. As Matthews Ojo observes, the "themes of their songs included the success and peace which Christians have in Jesus Christ, the dominion of Jesus' power over that of Satan, overcoming the adversities of life, and health and peace in the country."[206] When in use in worship, this style of music connects the worshipers to the spiritual realm, consequently making an experiential encounter between them and God a reality through the power of the Holy Spirit. Nigerian charismatic and Pentecostal "Gospel musicians constantly reflected their concern with the crises confronting individuals and as well as society at large, not only by commenting on them but also by proffering solutions. Consequently, Gospel music became popular because it created the much needed space necessary for social reconstruction within a purely Christian milieu."[207] The Nigerian charismatics and Pentecostals believe and in praxis try to demonstrate that when they pray and sing during worship, the walls of sickness, barrenness, poverty, and the walls of all that dehumanizes them will fall as the walls of Jericho fell when Joshua and his men marched around them with the sound of trumpets. They believe that the foundations of satanic kingdoms will be shaken, the doors thrown open, and the chains of those held captive in these kingdoms fall off as the foundations of the prison house shook, the doors were thrown open, and the chains of the prisoners fell off their hands when Paul and Silas prayed and sang hymns of praise to God.

For the Nigerian charismatics and Pentecostals, it is the dynamism that is seen in charismatic and Pentecostal worship services rather than the preaching of doctrine that makes the church and life itself meaningful for the people. They believe that the styles of music, preaching, and prayer that characterize the charismatic and Pentecostal worship facilitate

204. Ojo, "Indigenous Gospel Music," 214.
205. Ojo, "Indigenous Gospel Music," 214.
206. Ojo, "Indigenous Gospel Music," 215.
207. Ojo, "Indigenous Gospel Music," 216.

an experiential encounter with the Triune God through the power of the Holy Spirit in which worshipers experience the redeeming, sanctifying, and healing power of God. Ayuk attests to this when in quoting Leiblich and McCann he observes, "The African Pentecostals are characterized by their use of music and dance in the liturgy, their belief that prayer will solve problems, and their attempts to adapt Christian values to African beliefs and ways of life."[208] The dynamism that characterizes the Nigerian charismatic and Pentecostal worship has been very helpful not only in facilitating the experiential encounter between God and the worshipers which is indeed the primary goal, but it has also helped in making the young people to be active in charismatic and Pentecostal churches. According to Ayuk, "This dynamism is helping young people to be involved in church activities today in Nigeria. The use of drums and other musical instruments is very attractive to young people who like to move and dance instead of sitting down in one place."[209] The Nigerian charismatic and Pentecostal worship is characteristically vibrant and full of emotions as the worshipers experience and encounter the redeeming, sanctifying, and healing power of the Triune God through the indwelling Holy Spirit. This is not a surprise, as Ayuk observes, "Nigerians are very active people. They like to sing and swing and move. Such is the nature of a Nigerian, which invariably is the nature of Pentecostalism."[210]

Nigerian charismatics and Pentecostals pray enthusiastically with the expectation that their prayers will be answered. Their prayers of supplication are usually accompanied by prayers of thanksgiving and praise as a demonstration of faith that their supplications are already answered and in praise of God's goodness. Some of their pastors and leaders of prayer meetings make "use of anointing oil for prayers for healing and deliverance."[211] Another characteristic feature of the Nigerian charismatic and Pentecostal prayer is what Moses O. Oladeji calls "the practice of mass prayer. This may be loud, spontaneous or simultaneous congregational prayers which are often accompanied by 'speaking in tongues.'"[212] In fact, for Nigerian charismatics and Pentecostals, "'worship is a celebration of the Lordship of Jesus Christ and a celebration of God's power.'"[213] Hence, in their worship, "Christ is exalted and testimonies of God's greatness and goodness are

208. Ayuk, "Portrait of a Nigerian Pentecostal," 123.
209. Ayuk, "Portrait of a Nigerian Pentecostal," 123.
210. Ayuk, "Portrait of a Nigerian Pentecostal," 131.
211. Oladeji, "Charismatic Movement," 160.
212. Oladeji, "Charismatic Movement," 161.
213. Oladeji, "Charismatic Movement," 162.

given."[214] Their "mode of worship is always very lively and interesting,"[215] full of spontaneity, as the Holy Spirit is believed to lead and guide worship. The Nigerian charismatics and Pentecostals, indeed, charismatics and Pentecostals everywhere, "make much of the statement of Paul that where the (S)pirit of God is, there is freedom. The freedom runs through every aspect of worship—songs, choruses, hymns, prayers, even dancing."[216]

The Nigerian charismatic and Pentecostal worship is conducive to the Nigerian culture. Their "approach to musical expression is appealing and inviting to both young and old. Worshippers sing choruses, clap hands and dance vigorously. They become excited and happy."[217] More importantly, they are led into an experiential encounter with God through the power of the indwelling Spirit in which they experience the redeeming, sanctifying, and healing power of God. The Nigerian charismatic and Pentecostal "emphasis on the living power of Jesus as (S)aviour, Healer, Deliverer and Provider has greatly helped in making Christianity more relevant to human conditions"[218] in Nigeria. Their style of worship, preaching, music, and prayer no doubt helps to facilitate the experiential encounter between worshipers and the Triune God through the power of the Holy Spirit. In fact, as Oladeji observes, "No matter what the critics of the Charismatic movement have said about their doctrines and mode of worship, the truth is that they have affected the spiritual life of Nigerians. No matter what critics may say about their prayers and unrepentant deliverance ministries, they have contributed greatly to church growth in Nigeria."[219]

Not only is the Nigerian charismatic and Pentecostal style of worship conducive to the Nigerian traditional religious culture, the worldview of the charismatic renewal and Pentecostalism resonates with African/Nigerian worldview. It is no surprise that charismatic renewal and Pentecostalism are interpreted by some scholars within the context of African worldview as an African religion that flows from African roots and addresses African issues and realities. Its experiential and praxis-oriented theology of encounter is interpreted to harmonize with the African religious experience of God, deities, spirits, and ancestors. The next chapter, therefore, focuses on how charismatic renewal and Pentecostalism are interpreted within the Context of African Worldview.

214. Oladeji, "Charismatic Movement," 162.
215. Oladeji, "Charismatic Movement," 162.
216. Oladeji, "Charismatic Movement," 162.
217. Oladeji, "Charismatic Movement," 162.
218. Oladeji, "Charismatic Movement," 163.
219. Oladeji, "Charismatic Movement," 163.

CHAPTER 4

Charismatic Renewal and Pentecostalism within the Context of Nigerian Worldview

CHARISMATIC RENEWAL AND PENTECOSTALISM are interpreted within the context of African worldview as an African religion that flows from African roots and addresses African issues and realities. Its experiential and praxis-oriented theology of encounter is interpreted to harmonize with the African religious experience of God, deities, spirits, and ancestors. No wonder Ogbu Kalu would not link the origin of African Pentecostalism to the spur from the North American Pentecostalism. While he agrees with the tracing of the genealogy of the early Pentecostals to the recovery of the character of the early church, particularly, the event on the day of Pentecost, he disagrees with tracing the genealogy of African Pentecostalism to the spark from the North American Pentecostalism.[1] He avers that African Pentecostalism is rooted in the image of encounters Africans had with the Holy Spirit in an African universe that is filled with many spirits, and in Africans' "expressions of conversions that enabled the Holy Spirit to perform in better ways the roles that the indigenous spirits played in the individual and communal lives."[2] In fact, Kalu's argument is that "mental and material cultures are shared" as the gospel spreads and encounters different peoples; and that these peoples' worldviews and cultures become the prism through which the message and new ideas and material cultures are appropriated.[3] In this way, the people are able to indigenize the gospel, using it to answer questions that are raised within the interiors of their cultures while weaving "emergent cultures that create new challenges in daily living."[4] For Kalu, "indigenous

1. Kalu, *African Pentecostalism*, 7.
2. Kalu, *African Pentecostalism*, 17.
3. Kalu, *African Pentecostalism*, 16.
4. Kalu, *African Pentecostalism*, 16

worldview still dominates contemporary African experience and shapes the character of African Pentecostalism."[5]

Nimi Wariboko corroborates the arguments of Kalu on the origins and character of charismatic renewal and Pentecostalism of Nigeria. He traces the origin of Nigerian Pentecostalism to indigenous worldview of Nigerians and maintains that its character is derived from the mode of response Nigerians have given to Christianity at least since the nineteenth century.[6] He argues that Nigerian political and social characters played a vital role in shaping the message and structures of meaning of Nigerian Pentecostalism.[7] This chapter focuses on charismatic renewal and Pentecostalism within the context of Nigerian worldview. Its goal is to portray the fundamental reason behind some scholars' interpretation of charismatic renewal and Pentecostalism within the context of Nigerian worldview as an African religion that flows from African roots and addresses African issues and realities. It is the same reason attributed to the rapid growth of the Movements in the region by some scholars. Ironically, it seems to be the same reason some Nigerian theologians see the Movements as a phenomenal disorder; Christianity without memory dressed in borrowed robes. However, Nigerian charismatics and Pentecostals would not accept such interpretations about their Movements. The chapter will be discussed under the following subheadings:

- Nigerian Religious Experience of God, Divinities, and Spirits
- Nigerian Traditional Concept of Soteriology
- Nigerian Mode of Traditional Religious Worship
- Nigerian Charismatic Renewal and Pentecostalism and Nigerian Traditional Religious Experiences of God, Divinities, and Spirits

Nigerian Traditional Religious Experiences of God, Divinities, and Spirits

The Nigerian worldview is full of the experiences of God, divinities, and spirits, who are in constant interaction with humans. This section focuses briefly on Nigerian concepts of God, divinities, and spirits and their relationships with humans. It does not pretend to get into details on these concepts. It focuses only on what is relevant to the section and the work in general. The section is treated under the following subheadings:

5. Kalu, *African Pentecostalism*, 170.
6. Wariboko, *Nigerian Pentecostalism*, 18.
7. Wariboko, *Nigerian Pentecostalism*, 18.

- God in Nigerian Traditional Religious Worldview
- Divinities in Nigerian Traditional Religious Worldview
- Spirits, Ancestors, and Human Mediators in Nigerian Traditional Religious Worldview

God in Nigerian Traditional Religious Worldview

The universe and the forces of nature in it made Nigerians/Africans to believe in the existence of a Supreme Being or God who created the universe and all that is in it. Emeka Ekeke and Chike Ekeopara maintain that "God is real to Africans: Africans do not perceive of God as an abstract entity whose existence is in the mind. He is seen and perceived as a real personal entity whose help is sought in times of trouble and who is believed to be the protector of the people."[8]

The names by which God is known and called in various parts of Africa attest to the reality of God to Africans. Ekeke and Ekeopara enumerated some of them.[9] For instance, they note that the Igbo people of Nigeria call him *Chukwu*, "Source Being," which means "the Great One from whom being originates." They also call him *Chineke*, meaning, "The Source Being Who creates all things." The Yoruba of Nigeria address God as *Olodumare* or *Edumere*, "The King or Chief unique who holds the sceptre, wields authority and has the quality which is superlative in worth, and he is at the same time permanent, unchanging and reliable." They also call him *Olorun*, "the owner of heaven" or "the Lord of heaven." Still in Nigeria, the Edo people call him *Osanobua* or *Osanobwa*, which means "the source of all beings who carries and sustains the world or universe" while the Nupe refer to him as *Soko*, which means "the creator or supreme deity that resides in heaven." In Dahomey the Ewe and the Fon people call God *Nana Buluku*, which means "the great ancient Deity," while the Akan and Ga people of Ghana address him as *Odamankoma*, meaning "He who is uninterruptedly, infinitely and exclusively fully of grace" or "He who alone is full of abundance or completeness" or "He who in His grace has completed everything in heaven and on earth." They as well know him as *Nyame* or *Onyame*, meaning "if you possess or get him, you are satisfied."[10] God is

---

8. Ekeke and Ekeopara, "God, Divinities, and Spirits," 211.
9. Ekeke and Ekeopara, "God, Divinities, and Spirits," 211–12.
10. Ekeke and Ekeopara, "God, Divinities, and Spirits," 211.

known and called *Ngewo* among the Mende people of Sierra-Leone, which means "the eternal one who rules from above."

God is not only seen as unique in Africa "but He is also seen as permanent, unchanging and reliable. This is why in Africa there are no images attributed to the Supreme Being. In most cases there are no temples except in a few places, dedicated to the Supreme Being."[11] Bolaji Idowu attests to this when he observes that "The uniqueness of Deity is one reason why there are no images—graven or in drawing or in painting of him in Africa. Symbols there are copiously, but no images. The African concept of God, in this regard is an emphatic 'No one' and 'None' to the question, 'To whom then will you liken God or what likeness compare with Him?"[12] Africans see God as a transcendent and immanent Being. For them God is transcendent but at the same time immanent. Ekeke and Ekeopara, alluding to David Brown's *A Guide to Religions*, note what it means when Africans say that God is transcendent. According to them, "it means that (a) God is not limited to a particular place and time as human beings are. (b) It means that God lives outside the natural world in which human beings live. (c) It also means that human beings can never fully comprehend the will or thoughts of the Supreme Being. He is beyond their understanding."[13] They go further to indicate that as a transcendent Being, "(d) God is always there first: He is the creator of all things and the initiator of all events. (e) Finally, it means that human beings feel awe when they remember the presence of God. He is good and trustworthy in a way that they are not."[14] Africans believe that God's transcendent nature does not prevent God from being encountered and experienced as God is in constant relationship with humans. Hence, God, while being transcendent, is also immanent. "As an immanent God, Africans see Him as God whose presence is felt by people within the natural world. This means that they feel his presence around their surroundings, and through what happens to them and their families. Africans see God as very present within the natural world to help protect and deliver his creation, although at the same time, He transcends the natural realm."[15] Evans-Pritchard is right when expressing his view of God, known as *Kwoth* among the Nuer people of Sudan he observes:

> The Nuer word we translate "God" is *Kwoth*, Spirit. . . . We may certainly say that the Nuer do not regard the sky or any celestial

---

11. Ekeke and Ekeopara, "God, Divinities, and Spirits," 212.
12. Idowu, *African Traditional Religion*, 152.
13. Ekeke and Ekeopara, "God, Divinities, and Spirits," 212.
14. Ekeke and Ekeopara, "God, Divinities, and Spirits," 212.
15. Ekeke and Ekeopara, "God, Divinities, and Spirits," 212–13.

phenomena as God, and this is clearly known in the distinction made between God and the sky in the expression "spirit of the sky" and "spirit who is in the sky." Moreover, it would even be a mistake to interpret "of the sky" and "in the sky" too literally.... They may address the moon, but it is God to whom they speak through it, for the moon is not regarded, as such, as Spirit or as a person. Though God is not (sky, moon, rain, and others) . . . He reveals Himself through them.[16]

Who and what are these spiritual beings through whom God the Supreme Being reveals himself? It is to this that attention is turned now.

Divinities in Nigerian Traditional Religious Worldview

The beings named divinities in African especially West African traditional religious cosmology "have been given various names by various writers such as 'gods,' 'demigods,' 'nature spirits,' divinities, and the like."[17] John Mbiti maintains that the term divinities "'covers personification of God's activities and manifestations, the so-called 'nature spirits,' deified heroes, and mythological figures."[18] As spiritual beings with immaterial bodies, all divinities or deities are spirits, but not all spirits are divinities or deities, as will be seen in the next section.

Divinities or deities are functionaries or intermediaries of God. As such, they are perceived by Africans, particularly the West Africans, as the vehicles through whom the transcendent God makes his presence felt by his people.[19] Some of these divinities include the earth, the rivers, the mountains, storms, thunder and lightning, and other phenomena such as day and night, the firmament, the sun, moon, and stars. These divinities are not God, but they embody God's presence. As complex and ambiguous as it is, they are the manifestations of the Supreme Being; and act as intermediaries between humans and the Supreme Being. They are, therefore, channels through which sacrifices, prayers, and offerings are offered to the Supreme Being.

In Nigerian mysticism, deities and spirits are believed to descend or mount devotees and use them to involve themselves in acts of communication with humans. The relationship between devotees and vodhun during acts of possession has been described in African cosmology with

16. Evan-Pritchard, *Nuer Religion*, 12.
17. Ekeke and Ekeopara, "God, Divinities, and Spirits," 213.
18. Mbiti, *Concepts of God*, 117.
19. Ekeke and Ekeopara, "God, Divinities, and Spirits," 212.

the sexual idioms used in describing the intercourse between men and women. Lovell Nadia observes that

> Women who are possessed consider the gods to be their partners in a cosmological marriage, and they are readily penetrated, having their flesh "entered into" and mounted by the deities. Devotees are described as the spouses (vodhunsi) of the gods, although such unions do not preclude human alliances. Yet if women are invaded in this way, possession remains one of the most potent avenues for grounding the deities among humans, and involving them in acts of communication.[20]

Getting vodhun to possess or mount devotees is one of the means to bring it to earth in order to make it more accessible to the needs and demands of humans, and to satisfy its own expectations.[21] Nadia observes, "The act of possession enables the deities to become detached from the metaphysical realm which they normally inhabit, bringing them down to earth, for them to be contained in human form for the duration of the trance. This allows them to express their wishes through the women whom they inhabit, and to receive, in exchange, a direct act of devotion."[22]

As Uzukwu observes, there are many West African myths that "declare without ambiguity that 'God' does not diminish the agency of deities or spirits and ancestors."[23] According to him, divinities or "*Deities* are divine beings living with God as consultors or collaborators; they are also described as related to or as being identical with natural forces—'nature deities': 'they are personal, spiritual and powerful beings, and exercise immense power over human life and destiny.'"[24]

Although the Old Testament and African traditional religious approaches to divinities take different trajectories, divinities as God's functionaries and intermediaries between humans and the Supreme Being, and as manifestations of God can be likened to what Benjamin D. Sommer refers to as the "Bodies of God" in the world of Ancient Israel. Based on numerous instances within the Old Testament that portray God as having a discrete form, Sommer concludes that God has more than one body "located in sundry places in the world that God created."[25] He defines body as "'something located in a particular place at a particular time, whatever its shape or substance,'" and

20. Nadia, *Cord of Blood*, 72.
21. Nadia, *Cord of Blood*, 74.
22. Nadia, *Cord of Blood*, 80.
23. Uzukwu, *God, Spirit and Human Wholeness*, 61.
24. Uzukwu, *God, Spirit and Human Wholeness*, 61–62.
25. Sommer, *Bodies of God*, 1.

qualifies God's body as "immaterial" which differentiates it from human bodies.[26] Sommer identifies two sorts of fluidity of divine selfhood. The first is a fluidity in which "it was possible for various local and even heavenly manifestations of a single god to be effectively identical with each other and also distinct from each other."[27] The second sort of fluidity of divine selfhood "involves the overlap of identity between gods who are usually discrete selves"[28] as seen in several Akkadian texts or in *Enuma Elish*.

While evidences of this fluidity of divine selfhood abound in Yahwistic and Elohistic traditions, priestly and deuteronomic traditions "reject both the notion of fluid divine selfhood and the concept of multiple divine embodiment."[29] Sommer, however, insists that "the theological intuition found in JE [Yahwistic and Elohistic traditions] and elsewhere did not simply disappear, in spite of the dominant role that deuteronomic and priestly literature play in the biblical canon."[30] Unlike in the vast majority of ancient Near Eastern texts, for example, "in biblical texts," according to Sommer, "divinity is not subject to the cosmos and its powers, except when divinity voluntarily limits its might to allow freedom of action for some of the creatures it has fashioned."[31] This is what Uzukwu means in the case of African Traditional Religion and worldview when he avers that multiplicity of spirits or divine beings "does not undermine hierarchy; rather it redefines hierarchy, making it flexible or malleable."[32] He maintains that in African Traditional Religion and worldview, "Multiple deities, complementary roles, relationality, and flexibility maximize the agency of deities, spirits, ancestors, and human mediators, in dynamic relationship to the benevolent purpose of the one Creator God, for integral human wellbeing."[33] Unfortunately, the weaknesses of some human mediators or agents make the reverse painfully true as some of them exploit and instrumentalize the powers or deities for selfish ends which jeopardize the good of humans and question moral integrity of such mediators.[34] The fact is that all human "mediators, diviner-doctors and/or priests, draw their power from the same source as the sorcerer and the witch. They are not destined to be evil,

26. Sommer, *Bodies of God*, 71.
27. Sommer, *Bodies of God*, 14.
28. Sommer, *Bodies of God*, 16.
29. Sommer, *Bodies of God*, 62.
30. Sommer, *Bodies of God*, 79.
31. Sommer, *Bodies of God*, 173.
32. Uzukwu, *God, Spirit and Human Wholeness*, 60.
33. Uzukwu, *God, Spirit and Human Wholeness*, 59.
34. Uzukwu, *God, Spirit and Human Wholeness*, 59.

rather they decide to be evil."³⁵ Uzukwu affirms Mary Douglas to be right when she described the witch in her article "Problem of Evil among the Lele" as "a spoiled priest." Douglas's argument according to Uzukwu is that "As power is one, and knowledge is one, the sorcerer taps into the same channels as the priest and diviner. . . . the more he is trained in religious techniques for more ensuring fertility, curing sickness, and sterility, the more he has at his fingertips the techniques for striking with barrenness and killing. The difference is entirely moral."³⁶

Both Benjamin D. Sommer and Elochukwu E. Uzukwu aver that the fluidity of divine selfhood in the religions and worldviews of the ancient Israel and Africa respectively, adds value and credibility to the trinitarian notion of Christian theology. Viewing Christianity through the lens of Judaism's embodied God, Sommer avers that "a religion whose scripture contains the fluidity traditions, whose teachings emphasize the multiplicity of the *shekhinah*, and whose thinkers speak of the *sephirot* does not differ in its theological essentials from a religion that adores the triune God."³⁷ Uzukwu admits that multiplicity of spirits or divine beings in African Traditional Religion "does not undermine hierarchy; rather it redefines hierarchy, making it flexible or malleable."³⁸ He, therefore, maintains that the relationality among the multiple divine beings in African worldview which rules out any fight for supremacy among these divine beings exemplifies the relational God-Christ-Spirit in Christian trinitarian theology.³⁹

Spirits, Ancestors, Human Mediators in Nigerian Traditional Religious Worldview

The existence of spirits is a common belief in Nigerian religious cosmology. The spirits discussed in this section are those spiritual beings that are not ranked among the divinities or deities. Rather, they are what Idowu observes as "those apparitional entities which form separate category of beings from those described as divinities."⁴⁰ For John Mbiti they are the "'common' spiritual beings beneath the status of divinities, and above the status of men. They are the 'common populace' of spiritual beings."⁴¹ Ekeke and Ekeopara

35. Uzukwu, *God, Spirit and Human Wholeness*, 59.
36. Uzukwu, *God, Spirit and Human Wholeness*, 59.
37. Sommer, *Bodies of God*, 135.
38. Uzukwu, *God, Spirit and Human Wholeness*, 60.
39. Uzukwu, *God, Spirit and Human Wholeness*, 151–224.
40. Idowu, *African Traditional Religion*, 173.
41. *African Religions*, 78.

observe that spirits like divinities or deities "are nondescript, immortal and invisible entities. This is because they do not possess material body through which they could be seen but they may incarnate into any material thing in order to make themselves seen for any reason or purpose."[42]

Nigerians believe there are good and bad, or evil, spirits. And both are in the same environment with humans. Hence, Nigerians believe that spirits can positively or negatively influence human lives and activities. "This," according to Ekeke and Ekeopara, "means that man has to try in one way or the other to protect himself from the activities of the spirits knowing that the spirits are stronger than him. He uses the various means available to him such as magical powers, sacrifices, and offerings to appease, control and change the course of their action."[43] Nigerians believe that in some cases good spirits may possess people just as divinities or deities do, using them to bring healings and all kinds of blessings for the good of individuals and the community in general. In like manner, they believe that evil spirits do possess people using them to cause havoc in the society and in people's lives.

Mbiti observes that "During the height of spirit possession," as in the case of deities, "the individual in effect loses his own personality and acts in the content of the 'personality' of the spirit possessing him."[44] When a good spirit possesses a person, the spirit "may give the person information for the larger society in the case of a prophet or soothsayer." Once it is noticed that an evil spirit has possessed a person, "the traditional doctors and diviners may be called to exorcise that spirit from the person thereby setting him free from his captor."[45] Nigerians believe that the spirit of witches "is real, active and powerful yet very dangerous and disastrous in its actions and activities."[46] The concept of witchcraft in Africa, according to Idowu, consists "in the belief that the spirits of living human beings can be sent out of the body on errands of doing havoc to other persons in body, mind, or estate; that the witches have guilds or operate singly, and that the spirits sent out of the human body in this way can act either invisibly or through a lower creature—an animal or a bird."[47]

The "born-to-die" spirit known as *Ogbanje/Ndi-Otu/Ogbonuke*, or *Abiku* among the Igbo and the Yoruba of Nigeria, respectively, and aquatic spirits, otherwise known as *Mammy-water*, are among the dangerous and

42. Ekeke and Ekeopara, "God, Divinities, and Spirits," 216.
43. Ekeke and Ekeopara, "God, Divinities, and Spirits," 217.
44. Mbiti, *African Religions*, 82.
45. Ekeke and Ekeopara, "God, Divinities, and Spirits," 217.
46. Ekeke and Ekeopara, "God, Divinities, and Spirits," 127.
47. Idowu, *African Traditional Religion*, 175.

disastrous spirits in Nigerian worldview believed to have negative influences on humans. However, in some parts of Africa, aquatic spirits or *Mammy-water* are believed to be benevolent. See Lovell Nadia's work[48] referred above, for instance. See also Sabine Jell-Bahlsen's article, "The Lake Goddess, Uhammiri/Ogbuide: The Female Side of the Universe in Igbo Cosmology,"[49] and book.[50] As Christopher Ejizu observes, there are "numerous reported cases of ladies who have been prevented from getting husbands or children by *Ogbanje*, as well as young boys with stories of protracted illnesses attributed to the same malevolent spiritual being."[51] He goes on to note that "the most devastating form of *Ogbanje* is found in people who are believed to be in mythical league with *Ogbanje* to make repeated trips to families ('born-to-die') by dying prematurely and re-incarnating as many times as possible thereby bringing terrible agony to people."[52] Ejizu observes that as "in the case of *Ogbanje*, women, particularly pretty ones, are very vulnerable to the attack of aquatic spirits. Such attacks could come in many ways. But issues relating to family life are most common."[53]

Nigerians believe that ambivalent or malevolent spirits and deities are "behind misfortunes which people suffer, like loss of jobs and property, motor accidents, family disputes and various types of illnesses."[54] Nigerians also believe that every person "has a guardian spirit which if it is good, works to bring prosperity and good luck to its double but if the guardian spirit is not in good state, it will rather bring obstacle to the ways of its double."[55] Different people in Africa call this guardian spirit by various names. While the Igbo of Nigeria call it *chi*, the Edo and the Yoruba call it *ehi* and *ori* respectively. "In most cases, it is this spirit that helps to ward off evil spirits that may want to derail the individual from achieving his ultimate in life. This is why most Africans will make sure they sacrifice and appease their guardian-spirit whenever they want to take any important decision or they want to go on a journey."[56]

In African cosmology, ancestors are human spirits or the living-dead who fulfilled all the qualifications for an ancestor. Hence, they are regarded

---

48. Nadia, *Cord of Blood*, 80.
49. Jell-Bahlsen, "Lake Goddess," 38–53.
50. Jell-Bahlsen, *Water Goddess*, 2008.
51. Ejizu, "Cosmological Perspectives," 168.
52. Ejizu, "Cosmological Perspectives," 168.
53. Ejizu, "Cosmological Perspectives," 169.
54. Ejizu, "Cosmological Perspectives," 169.
55. Ekeke and Ekeopara, "God, Divinities, and Spirits," 217.
56. Ekeke and Ekeopara, "God, Divinities, and Spirits," 217.

as good spirits and are venerated. Yet, they do punish for correction as noted earlier. Those who do not qualify "are generally regarded as malignant spirits and are driven away by rites of exorcism."[57] In other words, death by itself does not qualify one as an ancestor. As Ikenga-Metuh observes, there are some requirements that qualify one for ancestorhood. In some African societies these include, old-age (relatively speaking), offspring, good moral life, and appropriate funeral rites that serve as "rites of passage."[58] To become an ancestor, one must live an upright life according to the moral standard of the society. He or she must have at least an offspring who will continue his or her lineage and must live up to a relatively old-age before dying. Dying at such relatively old age is regarded as a good and natural death, while not living up to that is considered as a bad and unnatural death. In many African societies, it is necessary for one who has fulfilled the above requirements to receive appropriate funeral rites as the rites "are regarded as 'rites of passage' by which the dead are installed as ancestors."[59]

Ancestors are intermediaries between humans and the Supreme Being and the deities as they are believed to be closer to the Supreme Being and the deities. "With their better knowledge of the affairs of the spirit world, they constantly warn their descendants and kinsmen of an impending disaster and counsel them on what to do to attract the most favourable fortunes."[60] In fact, ancestors are "believed to be custodians of traditional laws and customs on which the survival of the clan depends, and would punish with sickness or misfortune anybody who flouted them."[61] In general, the Nigerian indigenous worldview "has been referred to as heavily anthropocentric (that is primarily and largely centered on human beings and their general well-being). Human life, its success and full enhancement, is the foremost good as well as the most vital and sacred value around which most other things and movements in the universe gravitate."[62] It is no surprise that the traditional Nigerian cosmology is this-worldly. In this worldview, one's personhood is determined by one's ability to have offspring, raise a family, make success and achievement in one's profession, etc. Even the hope of one attaining the position of an ancestor in the afterlife is largely predicated and dependent on one's uprightness and achievements in this life.[63] In this

---

57. Ikenga-Metuh, *Comparative Studies*, 136.
58. Ikenga-Metuh, *Comparative Studies*, 137.
59. Ikenga-Metuh, *Comparative Studies*, 137.
60. Ikenga-Metuh, *Comparative Studies*, 139.
61. Ikenga-Metuh, *Comparative Studies*, 139.
62. Ejizu, "Cosmological Perspectives," 171.
63. Ejizu, "Cosmological Perspectives," 171.

worldview, God, divinities, spirits, ancestors, humans, and every other thing in the cosmos exist in dialectical relationship. In fact, Ejizu notes that the Nigerian "indigenous worldview is essentially an integrated, holistic and dynamic one in which the two orders of reality—visible and invisible, the human world and the spiritual world—are believed to be intricately interrelated and intensely influence one another."[64]

Despite being at the center of focus and being considered the greatest good, humans and their world are considered more inferior to the spiritual beings and their world. In fact, "the invisible world of spiritual beings and other entities is believed to be superior, while spirit beings and mythical forces in their various hierarchies (benevolent and malevolent ones), are said to wield tremendous powers and influence over human life and vital interests."[65] Hence, the spiritual beings have enormous positive and negative influences over humans and their world. Humans, therefore, depend on benevolent spiritual beings and their agents for protection. To succeed here in life and attain the position of an ancestor, humans must work hard to be at peace with the spiritual beings, especially the benevolent ones and with fellow humans, while keeping to the ethics of the society. Ejizu maintains that "Conformity with all the norms of acceptable behavior in one's society; peace with gods and peace with men, helps the maintenance of the delicate equilibrium of the cosmos and assures divine favors, very necessary for a successful life. Whereas infringement, either by way of commission or omission, is most likely to provoke the anger of gods or the ruin of evil spirits."[66]

An essential premise of the traditional vision of reality in Nigerian cosmology is the principle of double causality which holds that every effect has a physical and spiritual cause. Like many other parts of Nigeria and Africa, the Igbo of Nigeria would say *ihe adighi eme na nkiti* (nothing happens by chance). So, while they work hard to be successful in life, "they know too well that they have constantly to seek the aid of good gods, patron ancestors, magic and divination and elaborate propitiatory rituals as counters to the evil forces. In the final analysis, whatever success one makes is regarded as a favorable nod from the gods."[67] Just as all kinds of fortunes, blessings, successes, and achievements are attributed to the favors of benevolent spiritual beings, "all forms of misfortunes, including sickness, barrenness, mental illness, failure of crops, drought, premature death, unhappy family life, etc. are explained by the

---

64. Ejizu, "Cosmological Perspectives," 171.
65. Ejizu, "Cosmological Perspectives," 172.
66. Ejizu, "Cosmological Perspectives," 172.
67. Ejizu, "Cosmological Perspectives," 172.

activities of ubiquitous evil spirits, angry gods, revengeful ancestors and evil forces operating through man and nature."[68]

Laurenti Magesa corroborates the interconnected relationship between spiritual beings and humans in African worldview. He agrees that "'Nothing moves in the universe of forces without influencing other forces by its movement. The world of forces is held like a spider's web of which no single thread can be caused to vibrate without shaking the whole network.'"[69] Magesa maintains that the ancestors or the living-dead have been granted by God a qualitatively more powerful life force over their descendants due to their proximity to God orchestrated by their death. They, therefore, form the principal strand in this web of network without which the fabric collapses.[70] They are powerful figures in the society who see that the moral standard of the community is observed. They bring protection and blessings to those who live according to the ethics of the society and punish those who contravene them. "The operating principle is that of presence. The ancestors, though dead, are present and continue to influence life in their erstwhile communities on earth . . . the presence of the dead is assumed and invoked when the life of the tribe is threatened with disaster."[71]

Magesa agrees in the existence of benevolent and malevolent spirits in African cosmology who can bring blessings and protection and disaster and punishment to humans respectively. "Spirits thus become an important factor in the practice of harmful or good medicine and healing. They are also a factor when one acquires through possession supra-human powers for the benefit of life or, as in the case of witches, for its destruction."[72] Benevolent spirits such as the Supreme Being, the deities or divinities, and the ancestors ontologically do not cause evil to humans and their societies. However, they can punish or cause evil for correction. As Ikenga-Metuh observes, "They are believed to be committed to the over-all good of the individual and the community, so that when they send a misfortune, it is for the welfare of the sufferer or his community. Like a father, they punish in order to save."[73] On the other hand, malevolent spirits are believed to be working assiduously against the wellbeing of humans and their communities to thwart the paths of humans entering the ancestral bliss. Confronted with these negative forces and influences, humans do not simply sit down, fold hands and watch

68. Ejizu, "Cosmological Perspectives," 172.
69. Magesa, *African Traditional Religion*, 46.
70. Magesa, *African Traditional Religion*, 47.
71. Magesa, *African Traditional Religion*, 48.
72. Magesa, *African Traditional Religion*, 57.
73. Ikenga-Metuh, *Comparative Studies*, 151.

them ruin their lives. They do everything possible to "resist them with all the resources available to him, including placating gods and spirits. They are not only antithetical to a successful and fully enhanced life here on earth, they pose the greatest threat to the attainment of ancestorhood, which is the burning desire of most traditional people."[74]

Christopher Ejizu is right when he avers that

> The practice of medicine and healing are, therefore, perceived as essentially religious. The physical cause of illness or other misfortunes may be known or at least suspected. But, there is often the felt-need to decipher the socio-moral and/or mystico-spiritual causation or connection. The role of diviners is indispensable while medicine practitioners and ritual experts are the greatest gift to any community.[75]

Diviners and specialists in medicine, known as herbalists or medicine-doctors, are among the human agents who, through the aids of benevolent spirits who possess them, reveal the cause of illnesses and other afflictions and provide remedy for them respectively. Both diviners and medicine doctors rely often on divination for their practices which makes it difficult sometimes to differentiate between diviners and "pure" medicine doctors. The diviner "is a diagnostician who is concerned with the spiritual causes of the affliction, and the medicine-doctor or herbalist is a therapeutist who is more concerned with treating the physical effects of the affliction."[76] Like the diviner, the medicine doctor or herbalist "depends on his spirit to find the appropriate cure, and the spirit may convey, usually in dreams, which herbs to look for, and where and how to apply them."[77] Because "divination is prognosis in order to right wrongs and enhance the vital life force," and herbalism "uses medicine to protect or restore life," any diviner or herbalist who uses his or her practice to harm others thereby diminishing the force of life is regarded as sorcerer.[78]

Through temporary spirit possession often induced by drumming and singing, diviners decipher the cause of the problem and identify means to restore health and harmony. Magesa rightly observes that "in mediumistic divination the diviner always goes into a state of possession and becomes an instrument of speech for the possessing spirit. Yet, at the same time the diviner becomes, in a sense, possessor of the spirit because he or she can

---

74. Ejizu, "Cosmological Perspectives," 173.
75. Ejizu, "Cosmological Perspectives," 173.
76. Magesa, *African Traditional Religion*, 212.
77. Magesa, *African Traditional Religion*, 212.
78. Magesa, *African Traditional Religion*, 209–10.

induce it to speak when need be."⁷⁹ Describing divination possession among the Shona, he notes that

> At the sound of music played for the purpose, and while people sing and dance, the medium becomes possessed. "As the music continues the medium's head begins to shake, his limbs move up and down, almost vibrating with the music, and the muscles become taut. Many emit sighs and grunts as if inspiring deeply. . . . the medium may sing, move around. . . ." At this time, questions are put to the spirit, who may respond. The spirit may also enumerate specific moral irregularities in the community which must be rectified.⁸⁰

Elochukwu E. Uzukwu is right when he notes that "In the West African universe, specialists or experts inspired (or possessed) by tutelary deities (like *agwu* of the Igbo or *orunmila-ifa* of the Yoruba) render services for the overall health and progress of the human community."⁸¹ The importance of the role of these human agents or specialists makes them indispensable in African cosmology. They become men and women of power in a universe of multiple and ambivalent deities, offering communities and individuals "relative freedom to choose from alternative centers of power."⁸²

These human agents or experts are called by various names in different parts of Africa. For instance, the Igbo and Yoruba of Nigeria call them *dibia* and *babalawo* respectively. The Bantu of Central and Southern Africa call them *nganga*. As malevolent spirits unleash their anger and violence on humans and their societies, "the Nganga wages a continuous and relentless war on them and the evils they cause in various ways. The powers of the Nganga are believed to be given him by God and his ancestors for the benefit of the people."⁸³ In the same vein, John A. Umeh observes that the *dibia* works under the influence or possession of *Agwu* for the good of the individuals and the community.⁸⁴ Umeh understands *Agwu* to be the same as the Christian Holy Spirit.⁸⁵ For Umeh, when the *dibia* is possessed by *Agwu* he or she acts under the influence of *Agwu* whether in speaking, hearing, seeing, thinking, or in healing. He observes:

---

79. Magesa, *African Traditional Religion*, 230.
80. Magesa, *African Traditional Religion*, 231.
81. Uzukwu, *God, Spirit and Human Wholeness*, 88.
82. Uzukwu, *God, Spirit and Human Wholeness*, 88.
83. Ikenga-Metuh, *Comparative Studies*, 216.
84. Umeh, *After God*, 103–28.
85. Umeh, *After God*, 78.

> Being blessed with *Agwu*, the Holy Spirit's possession, the *Dibia*, sometimes is so taken with complete possession that he or she virtually becomes *Agwu*. He or she speaks the voice of the Holy Spirit, thinks the thought of the Holy Spirit, performs the skills, miracles and the feats of *Agwu* the Holy Spirit, sees with the vision of the Holy Spirit and hears with the divine Ears of the Holy Spirit.[86]

Umeh insists that *Agwu*, whom he identifies as the Holy Spirit, "does not do evil. And that is the reason why all great *Dibias* in Igboland desist from doing evil in the face of extreme provocation."[87] These human agents or experts are men and women who receive their gifts from God the Supreme Being through God's intermediaries for the fulfilment of their destinies or vocations for the wellbeing of the people and the society. Hence, it is not God the Supreme Being who possesses these experts but his emissaries or intermediaries. Some of the human agents pass through great suffering and conflict at the beginning of their call as a shakeup and awakening call to embrace their vocations or destinies. The suffering and conflict usually cease once he or she embraces the call and is initiated.[88]

In a cosmological worldview devoid of the Greco-Christian polarity between the physical and the spiritual, the body and the soul, and in a universe filled with multiple spiritual beings who have powerful influences on humans for good or for bad, one can imagine how salvation is conceptualized. The next section focuses on what salvation means in African worldview.

Nigerian Traditional Concept of Soteriology

It was observed in chapter 1 that sin or evil in the African worldview is seen "as the violation of God's 'laws' for social order and human interaction." In fact, the goal of life for any African is the attainment of ancestorhood. The worst thing that could happen to one is not to enter the ancestral bliss. For the African, to become an ancestor is to be saved. That is, saved from all that can debar someone from becoming an ancestor, from attaining salvation. That, as has already been noted, include but are not limited to dying without reaching a relatively old-age, which is considered to be an unnatural death; dying without an offspring that will continue one's lineage; failure to live a good moral life according to the moral standard of

---

86. Umeh, *After God*, 78.
87. Umeh, *After God*, 107.
88. Uzukwu, *God, Spirit and Human Wholeness*, 91–94.

one's society; and in some societies, not receiving appropriate funeral rites that serve as "rites of passage."

This reveals two dimensions of soteriology in African worldview which, is at the same time 'this-worldly' and 'other-worldly'. In other words, salvation for the African begins here on earth and reaches its fulfilment with the entering of the ancestral bliss. This resonates with the reality of the African worldview where the sacred and the secular are interconnected and taken as a unified whole. Entering the ancestral bliss is so important to the African that he or she does everything within his or her power to be saved from whatever that will debar him or her from achieving it.

As Chirevo V. Kwenda observes, this is so important "that both the living and the living-dead will do everything in their power to ensure its achievement."[89] He maintains that "Mbiti is correct in intoning that the greatest tragedy that could befall an African is to be cast away from the community both of the living and the living-dead."[90] He, however, could not understand how Mbiti could turn around to declare that there is no notion of salvation in African traditional religion after outlining the meaning of salvation in the same religion. For, according to him, Mbiti lamented:

> Yet behind these fleeting glimpses of the original state and bliss of man, whether they are rich or shadowy, there lies the tantalising and unattained gift of the resurrection, the loss of human immortality and the monster of death. Here African religions and philosophy must admit defeat they have supplied no solution. This remains the most serious cul-de-sac in the otherwise rich thought and sensitive religious feeling of our peoples. It is perhaps here then, that we find the greatest weakness and poverty of our traditional religions compared to world religions like Christianity, Judaism, Buddhism or Hinduism.[91]

Kwenda thinks that Mbiti is partially right when he observed that African traditional religions "do not offer for mankind at large, a way of 'escape,' a message of redemption (however that may be conceived)"; and correct when he added that the redemption he had in mind "involves rescue from the monster of death (and) regaining immortality."[92] However, Kwenda maintains that Mbiti "is wrong in thinking that salvation can or must only take the form of an 'escape.'"[93] To him, salvation in African

89. Kwenda, "Affliction and Healing," 1.
90. Kwenda, "Affliction and Healing," 2.
91. Kwenda, "Affliction and Healing," 2.
92. Kwenda, "Affliction and Healing," 2.
93. Kwenda, "Affliction and Healing," 2.

traditional religions "can, and does, take the form of courage to face the harshness of the reality of mortality"; and the fact that it is "different from the prescriptions of the world religions," according to him, does not mean that African traditional religions have no notion of salvation neither does it make their notion of salvation absurd.[94] Kwenda insists that "Mbiti is also wrong in thinking that 'rescue from the monster of death' can only be achieved through a mythology of future bodily resurrection" as this is embodied in the notion of reincarnation in African traditional religious cosmology.[95] For Kwenda, whether it is partial or complete reincarnation, it "is no less serious a proposition than future bodily resurrection."[96] He warns that the notion of reincarnation should not by any calculation "be dismissed as a mythology of the deep past (*Zamant*)."[97]

For this particular section of this work, the debate of whether African traditional religious worldview has a notion of salvation or not is completely out of the question. It maintains that soteriology in African traditional religious cosmology is the attainment of ancestorhood. In other words, to be saved for the African is to be saved or redeemed from whatever can debar one from entering the ancestral bliss. It is no surprise that traditional Africans do everything within their power to achieve this goal, as evident in their relationships with benevolent spirits and the works of human agents or experts. In fact, this kind of soteriology is embodied in what Uzukwu calls "human wholeness," "the full realization of human destiny" which traditional Africans work hard to achieve through the benevolence of benevolent spirits that operate within the African cosmos and gifted human agents or experts.[98] The "human wholeness" begins here in this life.

Observing the indispensable roles of benevolent spiritual beings who use human experts to help humans achieve wholeness of life in African traditional religious worldview, Uzukwu maintains that "Deities, spirits, and ancestors, ambivalent in behavior, are closer to the community and mediated for the community the experience of what one expects of a concerned (providential) God."[99] Based on this, he avers that in Africa, particularly "West African Christianity, the liberating, healing or therapeutic hand of God is best

---

94. Kwenda, "Affliction and Healing," 2.
95. Kwenda, "Affliction and Healing," 2.
96. Kwenda, "Affliction and Healing," 2.
97. Kwenda, "Affliction and Healing," 2.
98. Uzukwu, *God, Spirit and Human Wholeness*, 52–104.
99. Uzukwu, *God, Spirit and Human Wholeness*, 135.

experienced through the Holy Spirit."[100] In this sense, soteriology or salvation is portrayed to be human wholeness or abundant life.

While decrying Pentecostalism's heightening of the foundation for dualism laid by missionary Christianity, which is alien to African traditional religious worldview, and African Independent Churches (AICs) and charismatic movements' trinitarian intuitions, which he says do not "align with trinitarian intuitions of the great Christian tradition," Uzukwu notes that "the dramatic focus on demons diametrically at war with God (especially in Pentecostalism) and the radical focus on the Holy Spirit (AICs, charismatic movements, and Pentecostalism), indicate the continuing relevance of West African cosmological ideas and opens a window for a fertile encounter between Christianity and West African ATR."[101]

This will be revisited in the later part of this chapter and in the final chapter. This notion of salvation in African religious cosmology is what Omaka Ngele et al. identify in the traditional religion of the Igbo people of Nigeria as *ubandu* (wholeness of life).[102] They maintain that "it is a core belief in ITR (Igbo Traditional Religion) that acceptance or rejection in the ancestral world is, in part, the effect of humans' interaction with the spiritual world while alive. Being accepted into the ancestral homeland is the ultimate eschatological experience of *ubandu* (salvation) in ITR, just as achieving the best life one can offer here on the earth is an important part of the experience of *ubandu* as salvation for the practitioners of the religion."[103] They are in effect saying in a different way what has already been noted above that salvation in African traditional religious worldview is attaining human wholeness or abundant life and being saved and redeemed in this life from all that can debar one from achieving this goal. Ngele et al. go on to aver from the foregoing "that salvation in ITR is experienced in concrete visible forms. These include general well-being and provisions of life in forms of good health, prospering households, bountiful harvests, large number of children who continue family lineages, peace and harmony and longevity."[104] Due to the interconnectedness in the web of relationship in African traditional worldview, which makes humans inseparable from their community, the African traditional experience of salvation is world-affirming, personal and physical, relationship-based, and communal, holistic, and eschatological. "Hence, communal peace and harmony, prosperity and general thriving of

---

100. Uzukwu, *God, Spirit and Human Wholeness*, 135.
101. Uzukwu, *God, Spirit and Human Wholeness*, 134.
102. Ngele et al., "Sōteria," 1–7.
103. Ngele et al., "Sōteria," 2.
104. Ngele et al., "Sōteria," 5.

the community are all manifestations of salvation."[105] Ngele et al. observe that "in recent times, ancestorhood as eschatological salvation in ITR (as in African Traditional Religion, ATR) is being likened to the Christian idea of being eschatologically saved into the kingdom of God through belief in Jesus during the end of time."[106] Alluding to their personal communication with Iheonu, they maintain that "both eschatological salvation in Christianity and ITR (ATR) point towards the direction of eternal, blissful 'rest'; as such, both religions' ideas of spiritual eschatological salvation relate with each other."[107] They acknowledge that *sōteria* as salvation in Christianity has many aspects, however, they maintain that their "discussion revealed that it encompasses physical deliverance in forms of healing of sicknesses and illness, deliverance from enemies and dangers and general providence in life."[108] This notion of salvation in Christianity portrays charismatics and Pentecostals especially in Nigeria as being on right track as will be seen later; and it resonates "well in Igbo traditional religious experience of *ụbandu* as salvation"[109] in particular and the notion of salvation in African traditional religious worldview in general.

According to Godson Ahortor salvation or redemption among the Tongu Mafi people of Ghana is *dagbe*. *Dagbe* (*de-agbe*) which etymologically means "to redeem life" connotes abundant life. Ahortor gathers from his discussants that "the good things one can pray for or request from the ancestors such as good health, prosperity, fertility, peace, success, bumper harvest etc. or prayer against inimical effects, barrenness, ill-health, untimely death, poverty, frustration etc. are all summed up in the expression *dagbe neva* meaning '*dagbe* or abundant life should come.'"[110] According to him, "*Dagbe* as abundant life connotes total well-being; of mind, body and in spirit."[111] In other words, to experience *dagbe* is to be redeemed in this life from all that can debar one from entering the ancestral bliss, which ranges from not being able to live up to a relatively old age. This means to die an unnatural death, not having offspring that will continue one's lineage, not being able to live a morally good life, and failure of one to receive appropriate funeral rites. Ahortor notes that "The salvation experienced in the mundane is regarded as an extension of the soteriological goal of joining the

---

105. Ngele et al., "Sōteria," 5.
106. Ngele et al., "Sōteria," 6.
107. Ngele et al., "Sōteria," 6.
108. Ngele et al., "Sōteria," 6.
109. Ngele et al., "Sōteria," 6.
110. Ahortor, "Salvation and Morality," 223.
111. Ahortor, "Salvation and Morality," 223–24.

ancestors after death. . . . The blessing of living to an old age, exemplary life devoid of misfortunes and evil, is a symbol of *dagbe* and an experience of what holds in the ancestral home."[112]

Salvation among the Shona people of Zimbabwe, like in most other countries of Africa, is viewed holistically. Henry Mugabe observes that "Salvation in Shona religion, for example, does not relate specifically to the afterlife."[113] He notes that all the "words used to translate salvation or redemption have to do with preserving and sustaining the life of the individual or community in this present life."[114] For instance, the Shona word *ruponeso*, which is commonly used by the Shona people to translate salvation, according to Mugabe "comes from the verb *kupona* which means to give birth, to survive, to sustain life, to rescue, or to deliver a baby."[115] In other words, for the Shona people, as for most Africans, to have an offspring; to survive and live up to a relatively old age; to be rescued in this life from sickness, untimely or unnatural death, and from all that can hinder one from entering the ancestral bliss are all considered as salvation. For Mugabe, Abraham Akrong is right when he averred that salvation among the Akan of Ghana "has to do with protection, preservation of life both physical and spiritual from the threats of evil doers like witches, sorcerers, vengeful spirits and all those who seek to destroy life."[116] From the religious worldview of the Akan,

> Salvation, therefore, means the condition, context or space in which human well-being and the ultimate fulfillment of the individual destiny are made possible. It means the absence of everything that threatens and destroys human life or disturbs the conditions that guarantee prosperity and well-being. Finally, salvation means the conditions that preserve or restore the harmonies of creation so that the "rhythm of life" may go on undisturbed in order that human beings may have the space to be human.[117]

Emmanuel Asante is correct when he insists that salvation in African traditional religious cosmology includes "getting answers for the problems of life and overcoming the agents of evil and the hard realities of life."[118] Salvation in the African religious worldview resonates with what Laurenti

112. Ahortor, "Salvation and Morality," 224.
113. Mugabe, "Salvation," 32.
114. Mugabe, "Salvation," 32.
115. Mugabe, "Salvation," 32.
116. Mugabe, "Salvation," 32–33.
117. Mugabe, "Salvation," 33.
118. Asante, "Gospel in Context," 361.

Magesa sees as abundant life in African traditional religion.[119] For Chirevo V. Kwenda salvation in the African traditional worldview "refers to preventive as well as remedial strategies in relation to one's prospects of attaining ancestorhood."[120]

It has been demonstrated so far in this section that salvation in African traditional religious cosmology is holistic and involves being saved or redeemed in this life from all that can debar one from attaining ancestorhood. However, the question that might be asked is this: what happens to those who did everything they could in this life to be saved, that is, to have ubandu, dagbe, wholeness of life, or abundant life, and for no fault of theirs could not, and hence were denied entrance into the ancestral bliss? These are those who fall within the categories Kwenda refers to as accidents, miscarriage, and sabotage. According to him,

> the accidents are those occurrences and factors for which the individual concerned may not be held morally responsible, such as dying as an unmarried adult, or married but childless. To this category also belong those who die "a bad death," that is an unnatural death. . . . Miscarriage may refer to damnation by default, due to a technical error, such as failure by the living to carry out the bringing back ritual (or the funeral rite of passage). By sabotage is meant deliberate acts of interference with one's well-being and progress to ancestral bliss, for instance what has been called witchcraft and sorcery.[121]

There are some provisions in some parts of Africa, as Kwenda noted, for such people to help them enter the ancestral bliss a place of rest and peace. In fact, Kwenda avers that "If salvation means achieving a complete and fulfilled life (in terms of lifecycle experiences) and, despite all the preventive and remedial efforts to secure success, many still fall by the wayside, then there ought to be a net to catch those who fall through the cracks."[122]

One of the nets to catch those who fall through the cracks is the affliction healing in the Chihamba cult among the Ndembu of northwestern Zambia. Among the Ndembu of northwestern Zambia it is believed that the spirit of a person who for no fault of his is denied ancestorhood afflicts a member of the family or community with sickness or disaster in protest. Through the Chihamba cult, rituals are performed to pacify the protesting spirit consequently granting the spirit of the dead person entrance into the

119. Magesa, *African Traditional Religion*, 231.
120. Kwenda, "Affliction and Healing," 2.
121. Kwenda, "Affliction and Healing," 3.
122. Kwenda, "Affliction and Healing," 3.

ancestral bliss and setting the afflicted person or community free.[123] Kwenda maintains that "whatever else they may be doing, cults of affliction are there primarily to create ancestors out of otherwise disqualified candidates. However, these are not normative ancestors (normances) but ancestors by protest, protesting ancestors (protances). Ancestorhood is such a key to salvation that if one cannot attain it by the normal channels, one struggles for it through protest."[124] Their protest through affliction on the living is a way of calling attention to the situations that unjustly keep them restless in the land of the dead. Kwenda insists that "To call afflicting spirits 'protesters' is to suggest that far from taking their condition lying down, unfairly damned spirits demand at the hands of society and the whole cosmic order a chance to self-fulfill. This they do by afflicting one of the community's or society's own members.[125] He, therefore, argues that "in the cults of affliction Africans are articulating this ontological inadequacy, as well as registering their pragmatic response to the crisis."[126]

Kwenda averred that protesting ancestors are not normative ancestors. He is right on one hand in the sense that they did not attain it by the normal channels. But on the other hand, they are normative ancestors, for they help to reinvent the tradition, which is the reason Kwenda sees cults of affliction as the African way of articulating this ontological inadequacy, as well as registering their pragmatic response to the crisis.

In a similar vein, there is a belief among the Igbo of Nigeria that a man who for no fault of his is denied *okwukwu* the funeral rites of passage would afflict a member of his family, particularly his first son, with sickness or disaster to protest the situation that unjustly keeps him restless in the land of the dead. The affliction or its fear makes family members perform the *okwukwu* for the dead member of their family, consequently offering him an entrance into the ancestral bliss. This is implied in the statement of Elochukwu A. Nwankwo and Okechukwu Anozie when alluding to J. Ossai and C. Anoruo's "The Cost of Burial Ceremonies in Igboland," they observe, "In the Igbo Nation, full burial rites are accorded to the dead, in order to prevent the disturbances from the dead, not minding the cost implications on the living."[127] Referencing Chinwe Nwoye's article, "Igbo Cultural and Religious Worldview: An Insider's Perspective," they maintain that "in a place where this particular ceremony is omitted the dead will not have a smooth journey to the great

---

123. Kwenda, "Affliction and Healing," 4–10.
124. Kwenda, "Affliction and Healing," 4.
125. Kwenda, "Affliction and Healing," 4.
126. Kwenda, "Affliction and Healing," 4.
127. Nwankwo and Okechkwu, "Igbu-Efi," 63.

beyond—rather he/she could come back in visions as ghosts to disturb the living until such a time when they would complete the send-off ceremony, which is the burial rite."[128] Maduawuchi S. Ogbonna avers that many Igbo people still perform *okwukwu* at present if not for its Igbo traditional religious value and purpose, at least for psychological imperatives.[129]

Godson Ahortor notes that among the Tongu Mafi people of Ghana cremation serves as means of expiation for the souls of those who are denied salvation through rejection into the ancestral bliss. This includes those who for no fault of theirs could not meet the requirements for ancestorhood and even those who committed grievous offenses when they were on earth. According to Ahortor, homicide and abortion are considered so grievous among the Tongu Mafi people "that the perpetrators are cremated as a form of expiation for their souls."[130] Those who died without meeting the requirements for ancestorhood are "not only a threat to the living, particularly the family members, but they are not even accepted or welcomed by the ancestors to their part of the world without expiation by cremation."[131] Ahortor observes that "These disembodied spirits or 'wandering spirits' especially of victims of accidental deaths pose harm to the living until the rituals to expiate their souls are performed."[132] Referencing Ametewee and Christensen's article, "HoMattodzoe: Expiation by Cremation among Some Tongu Ewe in Ghana," he maintains that "There have been instances where corpses were exhumed from the cemeteries for cremation by members of the deceased's family in order to expiate the souls of the dead and avoid the wrath of the ancestors through the haunting of the dead person."[133] Based on this concept of salvation among the Tongu Mafi people which he claims is similar to many other African communities, Ahortor avers that "The notion of soteriology in African thought is therefore seen as individual and communal efforts to find place with the ancestors after death."[134] Such salvation is holistic in nature as it begins here in this life.

Seeing salvation in this manner according to David Tonghou Ngong[135] has brought about the emphasis on the miraculous in African pneumatology and soteriology. He argues that such emphasis blocks other ways by which

128. Nwankwo and Okechkwu, "Igbu-Efi," 63.
129. Ogbonna, *Okwukwu*.
130. Ahortor, "Salvation and Morality," 221.
131. Ahortor, "Salvation and Morality," 221.
132. Ahortor, "Salvation and Morality," 223.
133. Ahortor, "Salvation and Morality," 221.
134. Ahortor, "Salvation and Morality," 222.
135. Ngong, *Holy Spirit*, 2010.

the Holy Spirit might be understood in African soteriological discourse. He proposes that the Holy Spirit be seen as enabling critical philosophical rationality and the development of science and technology in Africa, features he claims are vital to improving the well-being of the continent and its peoples. Ngong's proposal is in order and does not in any way discredit or diminish the African concept of soteriology. As noted earlier and will be seen below, Africans do not believe or pretend that their concept of salvation is only miraculously attainable. Therefore, they do everything spiritually and humanly possible to achieve it. In other words, Africans will not hesitate to embrace critical philosophical rationality and the development of science and technology if they make for *ubandu*, *dagbe*, wholeness of life or abundant life and enhance it. The God from whose hands this kind of holistic salvation is achieved is worshiped in Africa. Most of the time he receives worship through his intermediary spirits. The next section explores the style of worship in African traditional religious cosmology.

Nigerian Mode of Traditional Religious Worship

This section examines the style of worship in African traditional religious worldview with the aim of laying the foundation for the reader to judge by himself or herself to what extent the Nigerian charismatic and Pentecostal style of worship is influenced by the Nigerian traditional religious style of worship. Hence, the section does not intend to get into details of Nigerian traditional religious worship but focuses only on what is relevant in achieving the goal of the section.

Nigerian traditional religious worship, whether directed to the Supreme Being directly or to him indirectly via his intermediary spiritual beings, is experiential and praxis-oriented as worshipers expect to encounter their God through his intermediary spiritual beings for the realization of abundant life here on earth. The experiential and praxis-oriented nature of Nigerian traditional religious worship is evident in Nigerian traditional religious prayer and music. It is to these that attention is turned respectively.

Nigerian Traditional Religious Prayer

Prayer as an act of African traditional religious worship establishes communion between God the Supreme Being and the worshipers through God's intermediary spiritual beings. Aylward Shorter is right when he observes that "Prayer is a dimension of life in Africa, the disposition of one who believes himself to be in communion with divine reality, and it is expressed typically in symbolic action, dance and ritual."[136]

Prayer is so central and common in Nigerian traditional religious worship that Tokunboh Adeyemo describes it as "the commonest act of worship" in Africa.[137] Laurenti Magesa agrees with Adeyemo on this and maintains that it is hard for any important moment to "pass during each day of an adult's life without a verbal or mental recollection of the power of God and/or the ancestors. An accidental bruise or a gift received evokes a prayer. Sickness or good health in the morning, a feast or a funeral, good or bad news—all are recognized by appropriate prayers."[138] Africans expect to encounter God in worship through the intermediary spiritual beings for abundant life, *ubandu*, *dagbe*, wholeness of life, and for the removal of all that can hinder it. Hence, Magesa notes that for Africans, prayer as an act of worship "is a means of restoring wholeness and balance in life. In African Religion, prayer is comprehensive, requesting the removal of all that is bad and anti-life in society, and demanding restoration of all that is good. Nothing less satisfies the African religious mind."[139] While remaining humble before God and his intermediary spiritual beings in prayer, African traditional religious worshipers pray with confidence, boldness, and trust. This according to Magesa is because "the powers addressed in prayer are God and the ancestors, who have obligations towards their 'children,' the living. It is perfectly legitimate for the living to express their deepest emotions of frustration, confusion, and anger in prayer to these invisible, mystical powers when things are not going well in this world."[140]

In worship, African traditional worshipers expect to encounter and experience through his intermediary spiritual beings, the God who can save them from dying without reaching a relatively ripe old age, that is, dying an unnatural death, and from not having offspring who will immortalize him here on earth. They expect to encounter and experience God who can save them from all that can debar them from entering the ancestral bliss. Hence, African traditional religious prayer as an act of worship is experiential, spontaneous, emotional, and praxis-oriented.

Shorter corroborates the spontaneity of African traditional religious prayer when he notes that "The texts that have been collected by missionaries and ethnographers are merely the verbal aspect of a whole ritual action,

---

136. Shorter, "Divine Call I," 65.
137. Adeyemo, *Salvation*, 35.
138. Magesa, *African Traditional Religion*, 195.
139. Magesa, *African Traditional Religion*, 195.
140. Magesa, *African Traditional Religion*, 196.

and, although tradition may dictate a certain literary form and a conventional turn of phrase, they are otherwise wholly spontaneous."[141] In fact, Magesa is correct when he observes that "African prayer expressions are not standardized; rather, every prayer is uttered to fit the occasion and the current frame of mind of the one who utters it. This is what determines whether it is angry or joyful, hopeful or despairing."[142] He agrees with John Mbiti that "Despite the tone, 'the items mentioned in these prayers have a personal dimension, a community orientation and a universal application.' They hinge upon feeling and experience."[143] He maintains that prayer in African traditional religious worship

> is the time to express oneself in an uninhibited way; it is the time to let go of one's whole being, to be more forthright and honest than usual. Africans realize that prayer is a time to communicate and commune with the spiritual beings that are most intimate with, and most caring for, humanity. Not to open oneself up completely to the mystical powers in prayer can do nothing but bring more harm. Without honesty, they might not appreciate the extent of suffering or take action. Not to express oneself completely in prayer is dangerous, moreover, because it implies a further breach of trust between the visible and the invisible worlds. The consequences for the living are invariably disastrous.[144]

In African traditional religious worship, prayer becomes a means of encounter between God and the worshipers. For in prayer, human agents or experts are sometimes possessed by intermediary spiritual beings who use them to deliver messages, provide protection, and healing to worshipers. It is no surprise, Aylward Shorter maintains, "one of the most prayerful instances of [A]frican religion that I have personally witnessed was a dialogue between worshippers and a medium who, when speaking in complete sincerity of heart, was held to be under the influence of a divinity."[145]

Indeed, petition, one of the commonest characteristics of African traditional religious prayer, portrays Africans as being pragmatic in their traditional religious worship. As Magesa notes,

> They ask for practical needs that comply with their religious perception of a full life. Protection from all affliction, or removal

141. Shorter, "Divine Call I," 65.
142. Magesa, *African Traditional Religion*, 196.
143. Magesa, *African Traditional Religion*, 196.
144. Magesa, *African Traditional Religion*, 196–97.
145. Shorter, "Divine Call I," 66.

of it, is a primary concern. They also desire to be protected from all sources of badness. . . . These include evil spirits and witches and all ill-wishers. As a corollary, they pray for longevity, abundance of food and drink, animals, and above all offspring. If a final reward is expected from God and the ancestors, it is that they provide the means to affirm life in the world.[146]

In other words, Africans, while they thank God and praise God for God's greatness, goodness, compassion, and love, they do not forget the core of life and prayer, which is, to continue to ask for *dagbe, ụbandụ*, wholeness or abundant life, and for the removal of all that can hinder it in this life knowing that salvation is holistic and that it begins here on earth. At this point, citation of some recorded prayers that highlight this characteristic of African traditional religious prayer will be very useful. The prayers will be taken from Aylward Shorter's *Divine Call and Human Response: Prayer in the Religious Traditions of Africa*, and John Mbiti's *The Prayers of African Religion*, respectively.

The following prayer from the Meru of Kenya addresses God the Supreme Being on Mount Kenya via his intermediary spiritual being, Kirinyaga, the mountain of brightness. The petitioner prays for life and health and all other necessary things for the achievement of salvation, abundant life here on earth. The petitioner also prays for the removal of the troubles of the other lands around him or her knowing that the disruption of the vital force in other lands can certainly affect his or her wellbeing, thereby hindering him or her from achieving wholeness of life due to the interconnectedness of vital forces in African traditional religious cosmological worldview. The prayer reads:

> Kirinyaga, owner of all things,
> I pray thee, give me what I need,
> Because I am suffering,
> And also my children (are suffering)
> And all things that are in this country of mine.
> I beg thee for life,
> The good one, with things,
> Healthy people with no disease,
> May they bear healthy children.
> And also to women who suffer because they are barren,
> Open the way by which they may see children.

---

146. Magesa, *African Traditional Religion*, 197.

(Give) goats, cattle, food, honey.
And also the troubles of the other lands
That I do not know, remove.[147]

In African traditional religious worship, prayer and sacrifice sometimes go together in asking for abundant life. This is evident in the following prayer from the Chagga of Tanzania made on behalf of a sick man. The prayer shows Ruwa, God, being anthropomorphically addressed as "Chief," "Preserver" and even as "Elephant," the most inspiring and enigmatic animal in the forest. It also reveals that what traditional Africans offer to God in sacrifice is itself a gift from God. The prayer states:

We know you, Ruwa, Chief, Preserver,
He united the bush and the plain,
You, Ruwa, Chief, the Elephant indeed,
He who burst forth men that they lived.
We praise you and pray to you and fall before you.
You have sent us this animal which is of your own fashioning,
For you share with no man and none is given thereof.
Chief, receive this bull of your name.
Heal him to whom you gave it and his children.
Sow the seed of offspring with us,
That we may beget like bees.
May our clan hold together
That it be not cleft in the land.
May strangers not come to possess our groves.
Now Chief, Preserver, bless all that is ours.[148]

African traditional religious worship is often colored with entertainment, song and clapping of hands. And these sometimes go with prayer. The following supplication prayer for good health from the Dinka of Sudan attests to this. It says:

You Divinity, we shall kill your ox.
And better that you should be pleased with us.
You will let us walk in health,
And we have made a feast so that there should be no fever,
And that no other illness should seize people,

147. Shorter, "Divine Call II," 231.
148. Shorter, "Divine Call II," 232–33.

> That they may all be well.
> And if my clansman travels,
> Then let him complete his journey without sickness,
> And let no evil befall him or anybody.
> And you, Divinity, do not bring evil upon us,
> And I shall be pleased.
> You women, clap your hands and sing.
> And *wuu* away the fever, that nothing may be wrong with us.
> You tribe of my father, walk in health,
> Nothing shall harm us,
> And Divinity will be pleased with us,
> And we will pray to Divinity that there be no bad things,
> And sing.[149]

The impact of music on African traditional religious worship will be examined in the next subheading. For now, we give few more citations of recorded African traditional style of prayer. The Igbo of Nigeria customarily and ritually break kola nuts and eat with God, God's intermediary spiritual beings, and with their human visitors. They use kola nuts to pray for *ụbandụ*, wholeness of life, as they pray for long life, offspring, good health, wealth, and peace. The following prayer that asks God and his intermediaries to eat kola nut and in turn protect the people from unnatural death, destruction, sickness, and torments, exemplifies this:

> God, eat kola-nut,
> Spirits, eat kola-nut,
> Sky, eat kola-nut,
> Agbala, eat kola-nut.
> May we not die,
> May we not perish,
> May we not be sick,
> May we not be tormented with maladies.[150]

In fact, the style, especially the tone and content of African traditional religious prayer as an act of worship, is determined by the circumstance, emotional, physical, and spiritual dispositions of the worshipers. This is

---

149. Shorter, "Divine Call II," 233–34.
150. Shorter, "Divine Call II," 234.

evident in the following prayer from the Nyakyusa of Tanzania addressed to an ancestor on the case of a child's illness, presumed to be a reprimand for sin:

> Why are you angry, father?
> Since you left me,
> I have nourished the children.
> How have I wronged you?
> Even though I have wronged you,
> Forgive me father.
> May the child recover.
> Stand by me.[151]

The above is further corroborated by the following prayer from the Tumbuka of Malawi addressed to the "great ones," the ancestors, on occasion of an influenza epidemic. The prayer reads:

> Let the great ones gather!
> What have we done to suffer so?
> We do not say, Let so-and-so come;
> We say, all.
> Here your children are in distress.
> There is not one able to give a drink of water to another.
> Wherein have we erred?
> Here is food; we give to you.
> Aid us, your children![152]

African traditional religious worshipers pray for protection, blessings and favors from God before embarking on a specific event. In doing so, they do not hesitate sometimes to remind God of the sacrifices they made for the success of the undertaking. The following prayer from the Ngombo of Zaire on an occasion of a journey attests to this:

> Akongo (God) of my father,
> Akongo of my mother,
> Akongo of my mother's people,
> Akongo of my sisters,
> I killed a male wild-pig for you, my uncle,

---

151. Shorter, "Divine Call II," 241–42.
152. Shorter, "Divine Call II," 242.

> I killed an otter as well;
> I caught fish for you;
> One day I caught twenty for you.
> I killed a *katukatu* as well...
> When I go (on my journey),
> Let there be no obstacle;
> May I meet with nobody on the way,
> May I arrive at the town where I am going;
> Hard things may I avoid;
> May I come back safely.[153]

The above is corroborated by the following prayer from the Ga of Ghana asking for universal blessings without reminding God of their sacrifices:

> Hail, hail, hail! Let happiness come!
> Our stools and our brooms...
> If we dig a well, may it be at a spot where water is.
> If we take water to wash our shoulders, may we be refreshed.
> Nyongmo, give us blessing!
> Mawu (God), give us blessing!
> May the town be blest!
> May the religious officials be blest!
> May the priests be blest!
> May the mouthpieces of the divinities be blest!
> May we be filled going and coming.
> May we not drop our head-pads except at the big pot.
> May our fruitful women be like gourds
> And may they bring forth and sit down.
> May misfortunes jump over us.
> If today anyone takes up a stick or a stone
> against this our blessing, do we bless him?
> May Wednesday and Sunday kill him.
> May we flog him.
> Hail, let happiness come!
> Is our voice one? Hail, let happiness come![154]

---

153. Mbiti, *Prayers of African Religion*, 158.
154. Mbiti, *Prayers of African Religion*, 160–61.

African traditional religious worship is experiential and praxis-oriented aimed at an encounter between God and the worshipers. Prayer is one of the ritual or liturgical acts that facilitate this encounter. As Laurenti Magesa observes, alluding to Anthony Ephirim-Donkor's *African Spirituality: On Becoming Ancestors*, "It is part of every prayer to implore the invisible powers to be present at the worship service and to bless the elders and give protection and happiness to the community.... The words of the prayer and the gestures are formulated spontaneously to capture the occasion and to be transformed by it into the reality desired."[155] Music is another liturgical act that facilitates the encounter between God and worshipers in African traditional religious worship. The role of music in African traditional religious worship is the focus of the next subheading.

Nigerian Traditional Religious Music

Like African traditional religious prayer, African traditional religious music as an act of worship facilitates an encounter between God and worshipers. Music in African traditional religious worldview attracts the descending intermediary spiritual beings "to take possession, enter or 'mount' the head of the devotee" or human agents or experts and through them encounter the worshipers, giving them messages and providing them according to the circumstance that they need to attain wholeness of life.

As observed earlier, music in African traditional religious worship

> links deities, initiates and the whole assembly into healthy merriment. Through diligent training the initiated woman or man internalizes the rhythm of the talking drum, leaves herself open to be entered or 'mounted' by the spirit, and thereby to double as the spirit. Whether the initiate is male or female she becomes *vodhunsi* or *iyawo*—'wife' of the possessing *orisa* or *vodhun*.[156]

Magesa corroborates the impact of music and dance in facilitating possession in African traditional religious worship. He observes that among the Punu people of Congo-Brazzaville "dance, especially the trance-dance of possession, is evocative of life in its source, a symbol of life and vitality. The dance that induces possession 'opens one to energetic, vital resources beyond the individual level. In trance the possessed . . . is in immediate contact with the source of life embodied by the *bayisi* (water spirits).'"[157]

---

155. Magesa, *What Is Not Sacred?*, 65.
156. Uzukwu, *God, Spirit and Human Wholeness*, 202.
157. Magesa, *What Is Not Sacred?*, 77.

In African traditional religious worship, worshipers use music to communicate with God and God's intermediary spiritual beings. It is no surprise that Georges Niangoran-Bouah argues that "Because the drum is more eloquent and loquacious, and because it is sacred, it is used in communication with God, with local deities, with cosmic deities (sun, earth, moon, Venus), with the ancestors, and with the spirits during important events."[158] In African traditional religious worship music acts as a catalyst that makes the transcendent God to become immanent, and uplifts the worshipers to encounter him.

In fact, among the Igbo people of Nigeria "there is a strong belief that songs are used in achieving power control, for supplications and for spiritual upliftment. . . . Religious music in Igbo is, sacred and is regarded as having extraordinary power."[159] Nnamani Sunday Nnamani is correct when alluding to Meki Nzewi's work, *Women in Igbo Musical Culture in the Nigerian Filed*, he notes that "worship finds its most respectful and satisfying mode of address in music."[160]

African traditional religious worshipers know when to employ music and the kind of music to employ to attain the desired goal, which is an experiential encounter with God through God's intermediary spiritual beings. In this encounter, God is addressed according to the spiritual, emotional, physical, etc., disposition of the worshipers who expect to receive salvation, *ubandụ*, *dagbe* or wholeness of life from God. Nnamani rightly observes, referencing Dan C. C. Agu's "The Primacy in Igbo Traditional Religion," that "The high priest(s) and the diviners (are) known for their usual practice of communicating with the deities through songs which are intermittently accompanied with rhythm instruments as they invoke or consult with the deities. Most of these songs are praise songs designed to glorify or praise the deities and consequently prepare grounds for easy communication with and favourable replies from them."[161] It is not surprising, Celestine Chukwuemeka Mbaegbu argues, that African traditional religious "music inspires the worshippers to express their loyalty to the deity."[162]

When worshipers feel the need to confess an offense against God, God's intermediary spiritual beings, and humanity and be relieved of the emotional trauma and guilt that are consequences of such offenses, they employ appropriate music to that effect as music of such category enables confession of

158. Niangoran-Bouah, "Talking Drum," 87.
159. Nnamani, "Role of Folk Music," 308.
160. Nnamani, "Role of Folk Music," 308.
161. Nnamani, "Role of Folk Music," 308.
162. Mbaegbu, "Effective Power of Music," 180.

sins. Charles O. Aluede, citing J. O. Mume's *Traditional Medicine in Nigeria*, rightly observes that "In the practice of religious Igbeuku, patients are persuaded to confess their sins which torture them, and once this is done, such patients feel emotionally relieved after the priest has pronounced them clean and subjected them to rigorous dancing exercise."[163]

In African traditional religious worship, music plays a vital role in the healing of patients or worshipers tormented by evil or malevolent spirits. This is evident in the faith healing practice found, for example, in the Bori cult of Northern Nigeria, the Igbeuku and Iyayi cults of Southern Nigeria. These traditional religious groups "'base their strength on religious prayer and confession of sins to release the mentally sick people from their low dejected emotional spirits which are responsible for their physical ailments.' The faith healing has serious reliance on music which is a major vehicle in the healing processes."[164]

The vibrant, lively, emotional, and spontaneous style of worship in African traditional religious cosmology facilitate an experiential encounter between God through God's intermediary spiritual beings and African traditional religious worshipers. During such encounter, worshipers spontaneously, emotionally, and ritually address God in prayer, song, and sacrifice whom they expect to listen to them and save them through his intermediary spiritual beings from all that can hinder them from attaining wholeness of life in this life and consequently debar them from entering the ancestral bliss.

The experiential encounter and praxis-oriented nature of the charismatic and Pentecostal theology and praxis as exemplified in their pneumatology, ecclesiology, and liturgy and which resonate well with African traditional religious worldview has spurred some African scholars to view Nigerian charismatic renewal and Pentecostalism as a discontinuity and continuity of African traditional religious practices.

Nigerian Charismatic Renewal and Pentecostalism and Nigerian Traditional Religious Experiences of God, Divinities, and Spirits

It has been observed at the beginning of this chapter that charismatic renewal and Pentecostalism are interpreted within the context of the African worldview as an African religion that flows from African roots and

163. Aluede, "Music Therapy," 34.
164. Aluede, "Music Therapy," 34–35.

addresses African issues and realities. It was noted that Ogbu Kalu, for example, maintains that African Pentecostalism is rooted in the image of encounters Africans had with the Holy Spirit in an African universe that is filled with many spirits; and in Africans' "expressions of conversions that enabled the Holy Spirit to perform in better ways the roles that the indigenous spirits played in the individual and communal lives."[165] While there is a discontinuity as far as Nigerian charismatic renewal and Pentecostalism are concerned with the deities, spirits, and ancestors performing their roles as they do with and for worshipers in Nigerian traditional religion, Nigerian charismatics and Pentecostals have successfully transferred these roles to the Holy Spirit. While one might not find any reflection of continuity with the Nigerian traditional religion in Nigerian charismatic renewal and Pentecostalism as preached, there are features of Nigerian traditional religion one finds in them as lived. Devaka Premawardhana holds the same view about Makhuwa's Pentecostalism and the traditional worldview of the Makhuwa people. In fact, he is right when he avers that "It is not *despite* change but *through* change that continuity abides."[166]

This section focuses on how Nigerian charismatic renewal and Pentecostalism reflect a continuity with Nigerian traditional religious belief and praxis. It is discussed under the following subheadings:

- Nigerian Charismatic and Pentecostal Pneumatology: A Reflection of Continuity with Nigerian Traditional Experience of God, Divinities, and Spirits
- Nigerian Charismatic and Pentecostal Concept of Soteriology: A Reflection of Continuity with the Nigerian Traditional Concept of Salvation
- Nigerian Charismatic and Pentecostal Style of Worship: A Reflection of Continuity with Nigerian Traditional Mode of Worship
- Criticisms of Nigerian Charismatic Renewal and Pentecostalism by some Nigerian Scholars

The section does not pretend to get into details as most of the themes have earlier been discussed in one form or another. It rather focuses on what is relevant to the section. Nigerian charismatic renewal refers here to charismatic movements within the mainline churches in Nigeria, whose members like the members of Pentecostalism lay much emphasis on the Holy Spirit and on the experiential encounter of the Holy Spirit despite the

---

165. Kalu, *African Pentecostalism*, 17.
166. Premawardhana, *Faith in Flux*, 142.

differences between them as indicated in the introduction. For instance, Catholic charismatic renewal of Nigeria, Pilgrimage Center of Eucharistic Adoration Elele, Adoration Ministry Enugu Nigeria, Upper Room Ministries, Enugu, Holy Ghost Adoration Ministry Uke, Canaanland Adoration Ministry (E-Dey Work) Mbaise, Lumen Christi Family Adoration Ministry Issele-uku, and many others. On the other hand, Nigerian Pentecostalism refers here to Nigerian Pentecostal churches like Benson Idahosa's Church of God Mission, William F. Kumuyi's Deeper Christian Life Ministry, David Oyedepo's Living Faith Church (Winners Chapel), The Redeemed Christian Church of God under Pastor Enoch Adeboye, Dr. Daniel Olukoya's Mountain of Fire and Miracles, Chris Oyakhilome's Christ Embassy, Joseph Ayo Babalola's Christ Apostolic Church, Paul C. Nwachukwu's Grace of God Mission, Assemblies of God under Pastor Chidi Okoroafor, Tunde Bakare's The Latter Rain Assembly, and many others. Despite the differences between charismatic renewal and Pentecostalism as indicated earlier in the introduction, the pneumatology of these Nigerian Pentecostal churches and their counterparts in the mainline churches reflect continuity with the Nigerian traditional religious experience of God, divinities, and spirits. Their soteriology and style of worship also reflect continuity with the Nigerian traditional religious concept of salvation and mode of worship respectively.

Nigerian Charismatic and Pentecostal Pneumatology: A Reflection of Continuity with Nigerian Traditional Experience of God, Divinities, and Spirits

Nigerian traditional religious worshipers look up to God, the Supreme Being as the one who saves them through his intermediary spiritual beings from malevolent spirits and from all that dehumanizes them in this life, consequently debarring them from entering the ancestral bliss. Nigerian charismatics and Pentecostals no doubt look up to the Triune God for salvation from all that dehumanizes them and all that can prevent them from having a foretaste, the down payment, and the firstfruit of the kingdom here on earth while waiting for its fullness in the eschaton. However, the intermediary role has been transferred by Nigerian charismatics and Pentecostals from the deities, spirits, and ancestors to God's empowering presence, the Holy Spirit. For the Akan as well as for the Nigerian charismatics and Pentecostals for example, Jesus, through the power of the Holy Spirit, becomes the agyenkwa, "the one who rescues, redeems, and delivers us from danger." It was noted above that Elochukwu E. Uzukwu avers that Pentecostalism and charismatic movements in West Africa are experiencing God-Spirit's liberating and healing hand for communal and individual wholeness. They do this, according to him, by expanding and reinventing their indigenous religious experience of God, deities, spirits, and ancestors into their Christian life.[167] Uzukwu defends this expansion and reinvention as being in harmony not just with Hebrew insight into the One and only Yahweh that assumed other dimensions in the Hebrew Bible but also with the teachings of the Catholic Church about the values in other religions.[168]

It was also noted earlier that the dualism that characterizes the Christian Greco-Roman world is alien to the Nigerian traditional religious worldview. As Uzukwu rightly pointed out, it was missionary Christianity that "laid the foundation for the dualism which bedevils Christian life and practice" in Africa.[169] This according to him "reaches paroxysm in the excesses and alienation of neo-Pentecostalism."[170] Despite this negative role of neo-Pentecostalism, this section of this work maintains that Nigerian charismatic renewal and Pentecostalism are continuing the Nigerian traditional religious practices in helping their worshipers to continue to experience "the liberating, healing or therapeutic hand of God" through the power of God's indwelling presence, the Holy Spirit.[171] For the Nigerian charismatics and Pentecostals have transferred the intermediary roles of the deities, spirits, and ancestors to God's empowering presence, the Holy Spirit.

The Nigerian charismatic and Pentecostal claim of being filled with or possessed by the Holy Spirit defers from the mainline churches, particularly the Nigerian Catholic Church's concept of mysticism, which involves the ascent of the spirit of the mystic. Instead of the worshipers' spirits to ascend and encounter and experience the Triune God, members of the Pilgrimage Center of Eucharistic Adoration Elele, like members of other Nigerian charismatic renewal groups, as well as members of Nigerian Pentecostal churches, believe and demonstrate in praxis that the Holy Spirit descends and occasionally possesses some individual members using them to establish communication or experiential encounter between God and worshipers. In this way, these Nigerian charismatic renewal groups and Pentecostal churches reflect a continuity with Nigerian traditional religious practice where individual worshipers and human experts are occasionally possessed by benevolent spirits and deities and used them to give messages and healings that benefit worshipers.

167. Uzukwu, *God, Spirit and Human Wholeness*, 151–79.
168. Uzukwu, *God, Spirit and Human Wholeness*, 151–79.
169. Uzukwu, *God, Spirit and Human Wholeness*, 134.
170. Uzukwu, *God, Spirit and Human Wholeness*, 134–35.
171. Uzukwu, *God, Spirit and Human Wholeness*, 135.

Peter Ropo Awoniyi observes that the Nigerian worldview acknowledges the existence of spirits and recognizes that "occasionally an individual may express the upliftment of a type of spirit, most importantly during worship sessions in shrines or festivals. So worshippers feel the move of the 'spirit' in indigenous spirituality, so it is in the charismatic movement, though it is the 'Holy Spirit' in their own context."[172]

Ezekiel A. Bamigboye notes that Sunday Aigbe in his article "Pentecostal Missions and Tribal Groups" identified some major mission strategies employed by Nigerian Pentecostals to meet the concerns of Nigerian traditional religious worshipers. These strategies in fact corroborate the interpretation that Nigerian charismatic renewal and Pentecostalism reflect continuity with Nigerian traditional religious worldview. For instance, to address the concern of Nigerian traditional religious worshipers with spirits and with a continual hunger for power, Nigerian charismatics and Pentecostals respond "by proclaiming and demonstrating the presence and power of the Holy Spirit who also satisfies this inner hunger and provides power for living."[173] Another aspect of continuity is in the activities of these Nigerian Pentecostal churches like The Redeemed Christian Church of God, Deeper Christian Life Ministry, etc., and charismatic renewal groups such as Catholic charismatic renewal of Nigeria, Pilgrimage Center of Eucharistic Adoration Elele, Upper Room Ministries, Enugu, where "drumming, dancing, vision, trances, sporadic interjections and prophecies" are incorporated into their worship as in the case of Nigerian traditional religious practice "where mediums speak in tongues and even prophesy."[174] Awoniyi avers that

> indigenous spirituality engages in singing and dancing that work some worshippers, priests or priestesses into frenzy, so it happens with the Charismatic movement where variety of spiritual songs and choruses are sung to lift up the spirit of the people who sometimes begin in prophecy, demonstrate the indwelling of the Holy Spirit, see visions or go into trance.[175]

For Kelvin Onongha, a religion scholar who has written extensively on Pentecostalism in Africa, members of these Nigerian charismatic renewal groups and their counterparts in Pentecostal churches reflect continuity with African Traditional Religion in their emphasis on pragmatism, that is, what works, rather than orthodoxy. They also reflect continuity with African Traditional Religion in their "belief that the world is populated with

---

172. Awoniyi, "Charismatic Movements Appropriation," 131.
173. Bamigboye, "Pentecostalism and Cross-Cultural Mission," 173.
174. Awoniyi, "Charismatic Movements Appropriation," 131.
175. Awoniyi, "Charismatic Movements Appropriation," 131.

a myriad of malevolent spirits from which people need protection."¹⁷⁶ The same is true with the aspect of their dynamism in which they emphasize "the inherent power certain objects possess, and power that is available for control over every phenomenon or condition."¹⁷⁷ The "ability to discern the future, answer questions of causation, and provide guidance for decisions in life"¹⁷⁸ which take place through the power of God's indwelling presence, the Holy Spirit, is another aspect in which they reflect continuity with African Traditional Religion.

Pilgrimage Center of Eucharistic Adoration Elele like other Nigerian charismatic renewal groups as well as many Nigerian Pentecostal churches has successfully reinterpreted and expanded its experiences of God, divinities, spirits, and ancestors into its Christian life. This is evident in its emphasis on the power of God's indwelling presence, the Holy Spirit which manifests itself in the many healings and deliverances going on in this adoration center. It is no surprise that Christopher Ejizu believes that Pilgrimage Center of Eucharistic Adoration Elele "appears to have topped all the others in fame and healing successes."¹⁷⁹

As noted in chapter 1, these Nigerian charismatic renewal groups and Pentecostal churches, according to Christopher Ejizu, emphasize the "need for the empowerment by the Holy Spirit to enable a person to overcome malevolent spiritual forces."¹⁸⁰ He maintains that "the fundamental outlook and response of most of their Charismatic leaders and exorcists to sickness, other forms of suffering and existential problems hardly deny their indigenous cosmological roots."¹⁸¹ Ejizu reinforces this view when he observes that "a closer examination of the goings-on in some of the numerous prayer-healing houses in the country and the attitude of many of the clients shows that even though the outlook may be Christian, a lot of traditional religious superstitious beliefs, practices and methods are retained."¹⁸² He notes that there are, for instance, "certain performances that look like divination techniques, hunting and beating out of witches, ritual propitiations of malevolent spirits, and the use of a medley of concoctions."¹⁸³ This, no doubt, is an indication that these Nigerian charismatic renewal groups and

176. Onongha, "African Pentecostalism," 49.
177. Onongha, "African Pentecostalism," 49.
178. Onongha, "African Pentecostalism," 49.
179. Ejizu, "Liminality in the Contemporary," 7.
180. Ejizu, "Cosmological Perspectives," 170.
181. Ejizu, "Cosmological Perspectives," 171.
182. Ejizu, "Liminality in the Contemporary," 7.
183. Ejizu, "Liminality in the Contemporary," 7.

Pentecostalism reflect a continuity with the Nigerian traditional religious experiences of God, divinities, and spirits.

The demonstration in praxis by The Redeemed Christian Church of God and many other Nigerian Pentecostal churches as well as their counterparts in the mainline churches that the Holy Spirit is indeed the animator of the church and the life of individual members of the church is no longer in doubt at least among its members. This is evident in the healing and deliverance ministries going on in this church. Ayuk sees this as "one thing the Pentecostals brought back to life in the Nigerian Churches."[184] According to him, "Many persons used to flock to faith healers or witch doctors to get healing, but today they go to churches because the power of the Holy Spirit has been restored in full force."[185] Ayuk, as indicated in chapter 1, believes that "People go to churches where they see the power of God moving. A spiritually dead church does not allow the spirit of God to manifest itself. It believes in God but does not believe in His power to move mountains if there is a need to do so."[186] To him, "Every spirit filled person is accompanied with signs and wonders and there is nothing as convincing as the manifestation of God's power in the lives of people. When people are healed or set free from demon possession, others are made to see the reality of God in their lives."[187]

By demonstrating to be spirit-filled churches, The Redeemed Christian Church of God, Christ Embassy, Mountain of Fire and Miracles, Deeper Christian Life Ministry, and many other Nigerian Pentecostal churches and their counterparts in the mainline churches reflect a continuity with the Nigerian traditional religious beliefs and experiences of God, divinities, and spirits. As groups and churches that believe in experiential encounter with God, the Nigerian charismatic renewal groups and Pentecostal churches believe there is no real power other than the power of Jesus through the indwelling Spirit. As noted in chapter 2, they believe and exemplify in praxis that "this power encounters the hollow powers of demons, spirits, witches or sorcerers, and likewise the powers of sickness, poverty, and death, that is: the powers of evil in all its individual and structural manifestations."[188] This resonates well with the Nigerian people and the Nigerian worldview where "evil refers to anything limiting, besetting or destroying life—including

---

184. Ayuk, "Portrait of a Nigerian Pentecostal," 130.
185. Ayuk, "Portrait of a Nigerian Pentecostal," 130.
186. Ayuk, "Portrait of a Nigerian Pentecostal," 129.
187. Ayuk, "Portrait of a Nigerian Pentecostal," 129.
188. Hock, "'Jesus Power-Super-Power!,'" 62.

infertility, sickness and death as well as droughts and famines, but likewise jealousy, envy or everyday life misfortunes."[189]

In this sense, one could aver without fear of contradiction that these Nigerian charismatic renewal groups and Pentecostal churches reflect a continuity with the Nigerian traditional religious experiences of God, divinities, and spirits. It is no surprise that Klaus Hock as noted in chapter 2, maintains that the breathtaking success story of movements like William Kumuyi's Deeper Christian Life Ministry or Benson Idahosa's Church of God Mission "is at least partly linked to the fact that African ideas of power and power encounter are to a much higher degree a constitutive element of their message than is the case in other denominations."[190] These Nigerian charismatic renewal groups and Pentecostal churches do not reflect continuity with the Nigerian traditional religious experiences of God, divinities, and spirits only. They also reflect continuity with the Nigerian traditional religious concept of salvation.

Nigerian Charismatic and Pentecostal Concept of Soteriology: A Reflection of Continuity with the Nigerian Traditional Concept of Salvation

Nigerian charismatic and Pentecostal theology and praxis represent a continuity of Nigerian concept of salvation where salvation is seen as abundant life, wholeness of life that begins here on earth. Their theology and praxis resonate with Nigerian worldview where healing is understood to be integral signifying wholeness of life or salvation. Ogbu Kalu is right when he notes that "The Pentecostal theology of health and healing recognizes that coping-healing practices are mediated by the surrounding culture, worldview, symbolic system, and healing myths."[191] Healing in this sense becomes "liberation from all that dehumanizes; it is the restoration of life."[192] In fact, "Pentecostal theology is constructed on the ground that is the sign and witness of the presence of God's reign among God's people; that God's healing power is as easily available to believers as the parental obligation to put bread on the children's table."[193]

---

189. Hock, "'Jesus Power-Super-Power!,'" 64.
190. Hock, "'Jesus Power-Super-Power!,'" 65.
191. Kalu, *African Pentecostalism*, 264.
192. Kalu, *African Pentecostalism*, 265.
193. Kalu, *African Pentecostalism*, 265–66.

In the same vein, Nimi Wariboko links the origin of Nigerian Pentecostalism to indigenous worldview of Nigerians.[194] In harmony with the traditional religious worldview that shaped and nurtured Nigerian charismatic renewal and Pentecostalism, Nigerian charismatics and Pentecostals "are seeking a full life, knowledge of what makes for a full life, an understanding of the requisite spiritual support for a full life, which realization is always in the not-yet (Phil 3:12–14)."[195] The charismatic and Pentecostal concept of soteriology flows from the Nigerian traditional religious concept of salvation. For Wariboko rightly observes that "Nigerian Pentecostals consider salvation as a complete package. It is a gift, an empowerment that touches the body, soul, and spirit in the here and now and in the afterlife. Salvation is a promise of flourishing life, *eudaimonia*. For God rescues his worshippers from threat to existence, offering them power and aid to resist nonbeing."[196]

Nigerian charismatic renewal and Pentecostalism reflect continuity with Nigerian traditional religious concept of soteriology which is holistic in nature and which begins in this life. Awoniyi corroborates this when he notes that "Salvation in indigenous spirituality is not limited to the security of the soul in life after, but includes all other material needs; this belief also influences the practice in charismatic movement that insists on the 'new birth.'"[197] Awoniyi is not alone on this. Matthews A. Ojo, alluding to the Deeper Christian Life Ministry in Nigeria, notes that one major doctrinal emphasis of this Pentecostal church "is the teaching on the new birth. Relying much on John 3:1–36 and 1 Peter 1:23, Deeper Life has presented this emphasis as the core of its message."[198]

In line with the Nigerian traditional religious beliefs and practices, the Deeper Christian Life Ministry believes and demonstrates in praxis that God's salvific work in Jesus through the power of God's indwelling presence, the Holy Spirit is holistic in nature. This Nigerian Pentecostal church, just as many other Nigerian Pentecostal churches as well as their counterparts in the mainline churches, portray this belief through its emphasis on healing and deliverance. Ojo observes that "Kumuyi's public image is now that of a miracle worker, and Deeper Life is 'a place where God answers great prayers.'"[199] According to Ojo the basic premise of Kumuyi "for the teaching on healing is that Christ's death on the cross not only saves mankind from

---

194. Wariboko, *Nigerian Pentecostalism*, 18.
195. Wariboko, *Nigerian Pentecostalism*, 7.
196. Wariboko, *Nigerian Pentecostalism*, 10.
197. Awoniyi, "Charismatic Movements Appropriation," 131.
198. Ojo, "Deeper Christian Life Ministry," 153.
199. Ojo, "Deeper Christian Life Ministry," 156.

sins but also heals and guarantees good health for every Christian. Deeper Life in its doctrinal statements says that 'healing of sickness and diseases as well as continued health are provided for all people through the sacrificial death of Jesus Christ,' and 'healing is the mercy of God in action.'"[200] In Deeper Christian Life Ministry, as in many other Nigerian Pentecostal churches, "healing is regarded as a miracle and it is accepted as the single means of confirming God's revelation and of conforming to Jesus Christ who himself raised the dead, healed the sick and cast out demons. Healing is also regarded as an integral part of the evangelistic work of the Church and a form of Christian witness."[201]

The practices of Mountain of Fire and Miracles, one of the influential Nigerian Pentecostal churches, corroborate this view. Like many other Nigerian Pentecostal churches and their counterparts in the mainline churches Mountain of Fire and Miracles believes in the holistic nature of God's salvation in the Crucified and Risen Jesus through the power of God's indwelling presence, the Holy Spirit. This church demonstrates this in praxis through its emphasis on healing and deliverance. It is no surprise that Paul Gifford, after his study of Mountain of Fire and Miracles, maintains that African Pentecostalism is built on African traditional religious imagination or worldview. For him, with African Pentecostalism, "No longer is there a need for the phenomenon of 'dual allegiance,' in which one goes to a mainline Christian service on Sundays and secretly resorts to a healer-diviner on a weeknight. One no longer needs a healer-diviner to identify and counter the spiritual forces causing one's misfortunes, for this can be done on Sunday during the Pentecostal service."[202] Gifford sees this as "the biggest single reason for the success of Pentecostalism in Africa."[203]

There is no doubt, this belief and praxis of these Nigerian Pentecostal churches and their counterparts in the mainline churches reflects a continuity with the Nigerian traditional religious belief and practices in which worshipers see salvation as *ubandu, dagbe*, abundant life, or wholeness of life and go for everything that enhances it while fighting against everything that can debar it, be it human or spiritual. Peter Ropo Awoniyi is of the view that members of these Nigerian Pentecostal churches, their counterparts in the mainline churches as well as Nigerian traditional religious worshipers practice holistic healing which covers all aspects of life and make use of sacred materials in their healing practices. In his words, "Wholistic healing

---

200. Ojo, "Deeper Christian Life Ministry," 156.
201. Ojo, "Deeper Christian Life Ministry," 157.
202. Gifford, "Evil, Witchcraft, and Deliverance," 123.
203. Gifford, "Evil, Witchcraft, and Deliverance," 123.

is the practice in charismatic movement as is observed in indigenous spirituality: that is healing that affects all dimensions of human life. Healing covers all aspects of life including physical, spiritual, material, economic, emotion(nal,) and social. Likewise in indigenous spirituality, healing is done with the use of sacred materials like oil, water and mantles, though it may not be of the same quality or intent."[204]

Another aspect in which charismatic movement reflects continuity with Nigerian traditional religious practices according to Awoniyi, is in the charismatic movement members' warfare against visible and invisible enemies, be it humans or malevolent spirits. He says, "'Warfare or radical prayers in Charismatic movement whereby much time is devoted to allegedly combating enemies in spiritual battles.' It is a revival of African indigenous religious practices of cursing the enemy"[205] which, of course, is biblical.

Their emphasis on deliverance, that is, "freedom from evil spirit possession, demonic harassment, and from witchcraft" as well as their emphasis on "the promise of a better life" which must begin here in this life is another reflection of their continuity with African Traditional Religion.[206] Referencing Kwabena Asamoah-Gyadu's "Pentecostalism in Africa," Onongha observes that deliverance services are established practices among African Pentecostal churches "because of a synthesis between traditional African beliefs and their understanding of Jesus' role as healer and exorcist."[207] Awoniyi is right when he observes that "Deliverance sessions that are held to chase out and attack demonic spirits in indigenous spirituality is experienced in Charismatic movement. The belief in the existence of evil forces who are agents of Satan, that causes sickness, untimely death, spiritual attack exists in the Charismatic movement."[208] In fact, he maintains that "deliverance services or healing process are sometimes recommended through prophecies in Charismatic movement, as diviners perform the same duty in indigenous spirituality."[209] All these happen because in line with the Nigerian traditional beliefs and practices these Nigerian charismatic renewal groups and Pentecostal churches believe and show in practice a concept of salvation that is holistic, this-worldly.

It was indicated in chapter 2 that these Nigerian charismatic rrenewal groups and Pentecostal churches believe that God does not only work in

---

204. Awoniyi, "Charismatic Movements Appropriation," 130–31.
205. Awoniyi, "Charismatic Movements Appropriation," 131.
206. Onongha, "African Pentecostalism," 49.
207. Onongha, "African Pentecostalism," 50.
208. Awoniyi, "Charismatic Movements Appropriation," 131.
209. Awoniyi, "Charismatic Movements Appropriation," 131.

extraordinary or supernatural ways but also in ordinary and natural ways. It is evident in the fact that the founders of Pilgrimage Center of Eucharistic Adoration Elele, The Redeemed Christian Church of God, for instance, and many other founders of these Pentecostal churches and charismatic renewal groups in Nigeria "own banks, business companies and operate NGOs, health-care facilities and universities."[210] This approach is a reflection of continuity with the Nigerian traditional religious beliefs and practices in which worshipers believe in the concept of soteriology that is holistic in nature and do everything spiritually and humanly possible to attain it.

This reflection of continuity is the reason some African scholars as noted earlier have interpreted charismatic renewal and Pentecostalism in Africa as an African religion that flows from African roots and addresses African issues and realities. Whatever be the case, this work insists that the Nigerian indigenous religious worldview makes it paramount that the Holy Spirit, the empowering presence of God be placed at the vanguard of Nigerian Christianity. It also maintains that the Nigerian charismatic renewal and Pentecostalism are forces that must not be ignored as far as the realization of the potentials of a Spirit-animated church is concerned.

The emphasis of the Nigerian charismatic renewal groups and Pentecostal churches on the experiential encounter of the Holy Spirit, and their concept of soteriology, make them flexible in their style of worship, which no doubt, reflects a continuity with the Nigerian traditional mode of worship.

Nigerian Charismatic and Pentecostal Style of Worship: A Reflection of Continuity with Nigerian Mode of Worship

In chapter 3, it was noted that the uniqueness of the charismatic and Pentecostal worship is centered on the fact that charismatics and Pentecostals understand worship as a profound and touched experience of the presence of God which is made possible by the Holy Spirit.[211] This understanding of worship is evident in their style of prayer, preaching, healing, and lively and joyous expressive ways of worship.

There is no doubt, the style of worship of Catholic charismatic renewal of Nigeria, Pilgrimage Center of Eucharistic Adoration Elele, Adoration Ministry Enugu Nigeria, Upper Room Ministries, Enugu, Holy Ghost Adoration Ministry Uke, and many other Nigerian charismatic renewal groups as well as Nigerian Pentecostal churches like Church of God Mission, Deeper Christian Life Ministry, The Redeemed Christian Church of God,

---

210. Kalu, "Pentecostal and Charismatic Reshaping," 94.
211. Archer, "Worship," 115.

etc., reflects continuity with Nigerian traditional religious mode of worship. In fact, Nigerian charismatics and Pentecostals respond to the "rituals of dance, celebration, intensity *catioris* and transformation" of Nigerian traditional religious worshipers "with vibrant and spontaneous spiritual worship."[212] To address the Nigerian traditional religious worshipers' "philosophical concepts, cyclical history, and supernatural causality," Nigerian charismatics and Pentecostals offer what Aigbe in his article "Pentecostal Missions and Tribal Groups" according to Bamigboye tagged "pneumatological-eschatological pragmatism."[213] Indeed, Bamigboye is correct when alluding to Matthews A. Ojo's "The Contextual Significance of the Charismatic Movements in Independent Nigeria" he notes that "The Charismatic movements have offered more avenues for expressing Christian faith in a manner which is meaningful to the Nigerians."[214]

The Nigerian charismatic renewal and Pentecostalism's dynamism which reflects a continuity with Nigerian traditional religious practices extends to their style of worship as evident in their spontaneous and vibrant style of worship. Some Nigerian charismatic and Pentecostal music reflect continuity with Nigerian traditional religious music. For example, Atinuke Adenike Idamoyibo avers that Christian èsà reflects continuity with Yoruba traditional èsà. "Èsà is a musical practice of the worshippers of the masquerade cult in Yoruba land in South West Nigeria. This is a chant/song that focuses on praises and adoration of the spirit behind the cult in the traditional settings."[215] Idamoyibo observes that Pentecostal churches in Yoruba land "have adopted and adapted the performance of the genres that were once predominantly restricted to the worship of the gods (Sango and Masquerade Spirit)."[216] He maintains that "During the last decade èsà artists have collectively negotiated their loss of status in the indigenous settings, due to the dwindling practices of the spirits' cult, by refashioning their performance in the context of the Pentecostal Christian worship."[217] According to him, "there is a significant correlation between èsà performance in the church and its performance in the traditional settings; both function as a persistent source of elevated praise."[218]

---

212. Bamigboye, "Pentecostalism and Cross-Cultural Mission," 173.
213. Bamigboye, "Pentecostalism and Cross-Cultural Mission," 174.
214. Bamigboye, "Pentecostalism and Cross-Cultural Mission," 170.
215. Idamoyibo, "Indigenous Music," 329.
216. Idamoyibo, "Indigenous Music," 329.
217. Idamoyibo, "Indigenous Music," 331.
218. Idamoyibo, "Indigenous Music," 331.

Idamoyibo corroborates the claim that Nigerian charismatic renewal and Pentecostalism are interpreted within the Nigerian context as reflecting continuity with Nigerian traditional religious practices. This is evident in his claim that "This incorporation of indigenous music type into Christian worship exists within the circle of the Pentecostal churches, as not even a single example has been recorded amongst orthodox churches who however query the suitability of the adoption of the èsà genre in its new context."[219]

For The Redeemed Christian Church of God, one of the Nigerian Pentecostal churches, as well as many other Nigerian Pentecostal churches, it is the dynamism that is seen in their worship services as noted earlier rather than the preaching of doctrine that makes the church and life itself meaningful for the people. They believe that the styles of music, preaching, and prayer that characterize their worships facilitate an experiential encounter with the Triune God through the power of the Holy Spirit in which worshipers experience the redeeming, sanctifying, and healing power of God. Ayuk Ayuk attests to this when alluding to Leiblich and McCann's work *Africans Now Missionaries to US*. He observes that The Redeemed Christian Church of God and many other Nigerian Pentecostal churches "are characterized by their use of music and dance in the liturgy, their belief that prayer will solve problems, and their attempts to adapt Christian values to African beliefs and ways of life."[220] In this way, no doubt, The Redeemed Christian Church of God's joyous and vibrant style of worship characterized with emotions, ecstasies, and prophecies like those of other Nigerian Pentecostal churches and their counterparts in the mainline churches reflect a continuity with the Nigerian traditional religious mode of worship. Peter Ropo Awoniyi observes that "Worship in indigenous religion which is characterized with much emotionalism has influence on Charismatic movements."[221] When these Nigerian charismatic renewal groups and Pentecostal churches pray, they pray with emotions and ask for abundant life and for all that will enhance it and against all that will debar it. They reflect in this way a continuity with the Nigerian traditional religious mode of prayer in which worshipers ask for ụbandụ, dagbe, or wholeness of life and for all that will enhance it and against all that can debar it, be it spiritual or physical.

In Nigerian traditional religious worship, music facilitates possession of devotees by deities and spirits who get into communication with worshipers through them. For the Nigerian charismatic renewal groups and Pentecostal churches music, as indicated in chapter 3, facilitates experiential

---

219. Idamoyibo, "Indigenous Music," 331.
220. Ayuk, "Portrait of a Nigerian Pentecostal," 123.
221. Awoniyi, "Charismatic Movements Appropriation," 131.

encounter between worshipers and God through God's indwelling presence, the Holy Spirit. This is another way in which these Nigerian charismatic renewal groups and Pentecostal churches reflect continuity with the Nigerian traditional religious beliefs and practices.

The above analysis shows why an erudite scholar like Uzukwu would maintain that West African charismatics and Pentecostals as noted above are expanding and reinventing their indigenous religious experience of God, deities, spirits, and ancestors into their Christian life. It also shows why Ogbu Kalu interpreted African Pentecostalism as an African religion that flows from African roots and addresses African issues and realities as indicated earlier. This section of this work maintains that these scholars are right in their claims and interpretations. However, there are some scholars who for the same reason have seen charismatic renewal and Pentecostalism especially within the Nigerian context as a phenomenal disorder; Christianity without memory dressed in borrowed robes. Before presenting these criticisms, it is important to note that neither charismatics, nor Pentecostals, nor mainline Catholicism will accept the permeation of spirits of the ancestral world as dimensions of the Holy Spirit. In other words, charismatics and Pentecostals will hardly, if at all, accept the theological interpretations made here which portrays their theology and praxis as reflecting continuity with the Nigerian Traditional Religion.

Elochukwu E. Uzukwu is right when he averred that missionary Christianity not only repudiated West African deities, spirits, and ancestors but also diabolized them. This approach, according to him, laid the footing for the dualism that bedevils Christian life and practice in West Africa even though dualism is alien in West African worldview. The dualism reaches its paranoid height in the excesses and exclusiveness of neo-Pentecostalism.[222]

Having been demonized, charismatics and Pentecostals see African deities, spirits, and ancestors as the main adversaries in the spiritual warfare they embark on.[223] Amanze validates this when he avowed: "With one voice missionaries from all the mission churches as well as Pentecostal Churches attacked firmly and decisively what appeared to them as the rearing of the ugly head of Satan whom they came to fight under the banner of Christ"[224] This, further, corroborates the fact that the Nigerian charismatics and Pentecostals do not and will not accept the permeation of spirits of the ancestral world as dimensions of the Holy Spirit despite the theological interpretations that

---

222. Uzukwu, *God, Spirit and Human Wholeness*, 134–35.
223. Lindhardt, "Pentecostalism," 35.
224. Amanze, *African Christianity in Botswana*, 59.

depict their experiential and praxis-oriented theology as reflecting continuity with the Nigerian Traditional Religion.

While repudiating and demonizing Nigerian deities, spirits, and ancestors and waging war against them, the Nigerian charismatics and Pentecostals often unconsciously tap into deep-seated religious and cultural beliefs of Nigeria through their experience of the Holy Spirit as Allan H. Anderson would say referring to Pentecostalism in general in a paper "Pentecostalism and the Pre-Christian African Spirit World" read at the European Research Network on Global Pentecostalism conference University of Uppsala, Sweden, 10–11 June 2016.

Even though neither charismatics, nor Pentecostals, nor mainline churches, particularly Catholicism, will accept the permeation of spirits of the ancestral world as dimensions of the Holy Spirit, the theological interpretations that depict the experiential and praxis-oriented theology of the Nigerian charismatics and Pentecostals as reflecting continuity with the Nigerian Traditional Religion remain theologically valid. For, the Jewish-Christian Religion from its inception has been characterized by such theological interpretations.[225]

Let me now explore some of the criticisms against Nigerian charismatic renewal and Pentecostalism by some Nigerian scholars.

Criticisms of Nigerian Charismatic Renewal and Pentecostalism by some Nigerian Scholars

It was noted above that Nigerian charismatic renewal and Pentecostalism reflect continuity with Nigerian traditional religious beliefs and practices in their pneumatology, soteriology, and style of worship which contributed immensely to their rapid growth in this part of the world. It was also seen to be the reason they are interpreted to be an African religion that flows from African roots and addresses African issues and realities. Their members were said to be expanding and reinventing their indigenous religious experience of God, deities, spirits, and ancestors into their Christian life. However, for the same reason, the Movements have been heavily criticized negatively by some Nigerian scholars. For instance, Maurice Izunwa sees these movements as highly eclectic; arguing that they pick and choose their "ideas and principles from different philosophical schools and religious

---

225. Uzukwu, *God, Spirit and Human Wholeness*, 105–35.

systems" and merging them into Christianity.²²⁶ In fact, he tags it as syncretism and a "contamination of the Christian Pentecost."²²⁷

Sola Adewale on his own part conceives the movements as suffering from the problem of the theology of immediacy as far as the protest against magisterial discernment and the search for quick and immediate solutions to problems are concerned.²²⁸ He cites "the mad rush by Nigerian Christians to any form of gathering where all sorts of miracles are advertised" as evidence to this problem of the theology of immediacy.²²⁹ For Adewale, members of these Movements protest against magisterial discernment by their "claims of divine visitation or inspiration as regards religious issues without any recourse to the constituted authority of the Church."²³⁰ His argument is that the power of discernment of true spirit from false spirit reposes on the constituted authority of the church and by that he means "the papacy and the Catholic hierarchy."²³¹ He accuses the Movements of having superficial knowledge and lacking theological rigor as well as having shallow understanding of the Christian faith.²³² Adewale goes on to accuse the Movements of preaching cross-less Christianity based on their approach to wholeness of life.²³³ Deji Ayegboyin accuses Neo-Pentecostalism of Nigeria and by extension charismatic renewal and Pentecostalism of Nigeria as being dressed in borrowed robes. His contention is that New Pentecostal Churches (NPCs) in Nigeria are influenced by the beliefs and practices of African Indigenous Churches (AICs).²³⁴ According to him the "AICs are products of the various Charismatic movements in Yorubaland" that sprang up to tackle specific needs of the time and to serve "as veritable vehicles for the realisation of the practical needs of religion."²³⁵ He identifies the following as some of the apparent influences of AICs on NPCs: dynamism in pneumatic emphasis, fundamental place and contextualization of prayer, and centrality of life and healing.²³⁶ Others are: trepidation about the enemy and externalization of

---

226. Izunwa, "Inspired by 'Arithmetic,'" 170.
227. Izunwa, "Inspired by 'Arithmetic,'" 170.
228. Adewale, "Charismatic Movement and Pentacostalism," 50.
229. Adewale, "Charismatic Movement and Pentacostalism," 52.
230. Adewale, "Charismatic Movement and Pentacostalism," 52.
231. Adewale, "Charismatic Movement and Pentacostalism," 53.
232. Adewale, "Charismatic Movement and Pentacostalism," 54
233. Adewale, "Charismatic Movement and Pentacostalism," 55.
234. Ayegboyin, "Dressed in Borrowed Robes," 70.
235. Ayegboyin, "Dressed in Borrowed Robes," 72.
236. Ayegboyin, "Dressed in Borrowed Robes," 74–80.

evil, contextualized worship, contextual forms of leadership, mission and evangelism, and dignified place of women.[237]

Emeka Nwosuh takes up the task of discerning in the spirit of the Second Vatican Council the spirit of Pentecostalism in order to discern what the Spirit is saying to the church in Nigeria through this Movement.[238] Nwosuh identifies Spirit Baptism as the theological root upon which Pentecostalism is established.[239] Following Pentecostal theology, he maintains that one might aver that Spirit Baptism is a necessary factor in the completion of "the fullness of Christian experience which begins with conversion or regeneration."[240] Nwosuh argues that Pentecostalism portrays an aspect of spirituality that has little or no regard to "institution, structure, hierarchy or authority."[241] With the exception of some Pentecostal churches (e.g., the Deeper Life Ministries), he accuses the Movement of fostering gospel prosperity preaching, a preaching which he argues does not pay sufficient attention to deep implications of the Christian lived experience of the mystery of the Cross.[242] According to Nwosuh "Pentecostal spirituality is considerably disconnected from the integral Christian spirituality."[243] He blames this disconnection on Pentecostal pneumatology, which he says is disassociated from other branches of Christian theology like ecclesiology, Christology, soteriology etc.[244] In spite of these shortcomings, Nwosuh maintains that "rather than stand in opposition to them, Pentecostal spirituality in some of its aspects complements other forms of spirituality."[245] He sees it as a new face of Christianity and insists that what is needed is a filtering of its ideas and presuppositions instead of dismissing the Movement.[246]

Anthony Akinwole is more intolerant to Pentecostalism than Nwosuh. For him Pentecostalism is Christianity without memory.[247] Due to what he perceives as a discontinuity of Pentecostalism in general with the apostolic origins of Christianity, Akinwole insists that it cannot be seen as the new face of Christianity.[248] He avers "that Pentecostalism neither preserves a valid Epis-

---

237. Ayegboyin, "Dressed in Borrowed Robes," 80–88.
238. Nwosuh, "Pentecostalism," 90.
239. Nwosuh, "Pentecostalism," 101.
240. Nwosuh, "Pentecostalism," 101.
241. Nwosuh, "Pentecostalism," 104.
242. Nwosuh, "Pentecostalism," 105.
243. Nwosuh, "Pentecostalism," 106.
244. Nwosuh, "Pentecostalism," 107.
245. Nwosuh, "Pentecostalism," 106.
246. Nwosuh, "Pentecostalism," 106.
247. Akinwole, "Christianity without Memory," 111.
248. Akinwole, "Christianity without Memory," 112.

copate nor the genuine and integral substance of the Eucharistic mystery."[249] Akinwole accuses Pentecostalism of opening a way for a misreading of the Gospel due to what he claims to be Pentecostalism's lack in valid Episcopate and consequently, authentic Eucharist. A situation he tags a disconnection from apostolic origins.[250] He sees valid Episcopate and authentic Eucharist as "the two defining moments in the history of Christianity."[251] Since according to him Pentecostalism loses touch with these two moments, he considers it "an adulterated product" that serves no good.[252]

Celestina Omoso Isiramen presents neo-Pentecostals' activities in Nigeria as both a therapy and a delusion. In an era where the living conditions of most Nigerians are seen to be considerably deteriorated, and where wicked spirits are believed to be thwarting the well-being of people, Isiramen avers that neo-Pentecostal preachers appear as therapists who offer people hope and possible means of overcoming the challenges.[253] According to her, they emphasize in their teachings "their therapeutic competence in delivering people from the manifold 'demons' responsible for their unsuccessful ventures through spiritual warfare."[254] She claims that revivals, crusades, miracle exhibitions, and electronic media are means through which they advertise their therapeutic competence.[255] Despite this seemingly therapeutic nature of Pentecostalism in Nigeria, Isiramen sees it as an impetus for delusion. Her claim stems from the fact that the actual socioeconomic, and spiritual conditions of most of the adherents of Pentecostal churches in Nigeria run contrary to what their pastors preach particularly when they say that "God is not a poor God . . . all His followers must, therefore, be prosperous materially, physically and spiritually."[256] No doubt, Isiramen's view here corroborates Devaka Premawardhana's submission based on his study of Pentecostalism among the Makhuwa people of northern Mozambique which he averred is characterized by circular mobility. He submitted that no matter how "explosive" or flourishing Pentecostalism may be, it can never fully capture the daily complexities of real lives as evident in the case of Makhuwan Pentecostalism. He, therefore, maintained that triumphalist accounts of Pentecostalism's "explosion" be tempered.[257] This is true. However, it doesn't in any way diminish

---

249. Akinwole, "Christianity without Memory," 114.
250. Akinwole, "Christianity without Memory," 114.
251. Akinwole, "Christianity without Memory," 115.
252. Akinwole, "Christianity without Memory," 121.
253. Isiramen, "Pentecostalism," 285.
254. Isiramen, "Pentecostalism," 285.
255. Isiramen, "Pentecostalism," 285.
256. Isiramen, "Pentecostalism," 287.
257. Premawardhana, *Faith in Flux*, 159–71.

the importance of Pentecostalism when dealing with the realization of the potentials of a Spirit-animated church.

Emmanuel Onuh sees Pentecostal and Catholic charismatic style of prayer, preaching, and worship as nothing but "selling Jesus at a discount."[258] He avers that this style of prayer, preaching, and worship must be put to an end as it poses serious danger to the orthodoxy of the Catholic Church in its deviation from the church's traditional mode of prayer, preaching, and worship.[259] He avers that "Pentecostalism is poles apart from Catholicism" and identifies it with paganism except that it calls the name of Jesus.[260]

Fidelis U. Okafor[261] frowns at how the charismatic and Pentecostal theology and praxes are influencing the practices of many Catholic clergy and laity in Nigeria to the point he believes it vitiates Christian belief and Catholic doctrine. He warns against imitating Pentecostals especially in their style of prayer, worship, and preaching. To him, such imitation can destroy the Catholic identity and orthodoxy and can give rise to a new and delusional sense of Christian unity. Following in the same line of thought as Fidelis U. Okafor, Fabian C. Okafor[262] avers that some innovations in the Eucharistic liturgy among some Nigerian Catholic clergy are the effects of Pentecostal influences. He maintains that these innovations distort the authentic meaning of the Catholic liturgy.

The next chapter, which is the final chapter of this work argues differently. It maintains that the theology and praxis of the charismatic renewal and Pentecostalism particularly within the Nigerian context resonate with the Nigerian traditional religious worldview as evident in their style of prayer, preaching, healing, and lively and joyous and expressive ways of worship. Their religious expressions are culture-rooted and homegrown. The chapter, therefore, argues that more than anything else, the theology and praxis of the charismatic renewal and Pentecostalism as Spirit-animated groups and churches are inspiring and enabling the Catholic Church in Nigeria to realize the potentials of a Spirit-filled church. This is happening because the charismatic renewal within the Nigerian Catholic Church is a vital part of the changing face of the Catholic Church in Nigeria. Through it, the Nigerian Catholic Church has wittingly or unwittingly initiated the renewal of her pneumatology, ecclesiology, and liturgy in line with those of a truly Spirit-directed church.

258. Onuh, *Pentecostalism*, 66–77.
259. Onuh, *Pentecostalism* 66–77
260. Onuh, *Pentecostalism*, viii.
261. Okafor, "New Trends," 16–26.
262. Okafor, "Some Innovations," 77–89.

— CHAPTER 5 —

Charismatic Renewal and Pentecostalism: The Renewal of the Nigerian Catholic Church

IT WAS NOTED IN the previous chapters that charismatics and Pentecostals, in their theology, pay less attention to the speculative interpretations of their doctrinal beliefs. Instead of spending time thinking theologically, they prefer to live out their theology practically unlike their non-charismatic and Pentecostal counterparts in mainline churches. In other words, while charismatics and Pentecostals might not neglect the detailing of charismatic and Pentecostal beliefs and doctrines, they emphasize more the discovering of these beliefs and doctrines within the context of praxis. Charismatic and Pentecostal theology is therefore a theology of encounter where charismatics and Pentecostals encounter God, the Bible, and the community in a lively and experiential manner. It was shown that what is fundamental and at the heart of charismatic renewal and Pentecostalism is not a set of doctrines or rules to be proved and defended against all odds, but the desire to have a personal, experiential encounter of the Spirit of God. Charismatics and Pentecostals constantly expect a deep-seated experience of the Holy Spirit in their dealings with God, particularly as it relates to their identity as children of God, their perception and understanding of God, their liturgical services, their missiological and evangelical activities, their scriptural readings and applications, and their relationships with other believers. In fact, it was observed that the experiential knowledge of God either through a rational recognition of his being or via an emotional or expressive appreciation of his character, is the goal of charismatics and Pentecostals which practically sets them apart from other Christian traditions. It was noted that while other Christian faith traditions might perceive revelation as something meant to affect only the mind, charismatics and Pentecostals see it as something intended to affect the mind as well as the emotions. They therefore explore theology, not only in a rationalistic context, but also with a desire and willingness to encounter and experience the divine and to allow themselves to be impacted by their discoveries in a manner that will edify their minds and transform their lives. They believe and aver that these kinds of encounters are seen in the Bible. Hence, where creedal confession and formal ceremony have sometimes appeared to be absent in charismatic and Pentecostal spirituality, there is often the presence of experiential, spontaneous, emotional, honest, deeply personal, and life-transforming encounter. This form of charismatic and Pentecostal theology and praxis truly makes them Spirit-filled groups and churches as evident in their pneumatology, and pneumatocentric ecclesiology and liturgy presented in the first three chapters.

Chapter 4 demonstrated that this charismatic and Pentecostal experiential and praxis-oriented theology resonates with the Nigerian worldview and traditional religious practices. It presented Nigerian charismatic renewal and Pentecostalism as reflecting continuity with the Nigerian traditional religious practices despite the radical discontinuity they make with Nigerian deities, spirits, and ancestors as they do not accept the permeation of spirits of the ancestral world as dimensions of the Holy Spirit. This reflecting of continuity with the Nigerian Traditional Religion was the reason some scholars have interpreted charismatic renewal and Pentecostalism, especially within the Nigerian context, as an African religion that flows from African roots and addresses African issues and realities. It is also the reason some of them maintain that African charismatics and Pentecostals are expanding and reinventing their indigenous religious experience of God, deities, spirits, and ancestors into their Christian life. The theology and praxis that gave birth to this interpretation and claim was noted to be the reason behind the rapid growth of the charismatic renewal and Pentecostalism in Nigeria. Ironically, it was noted to be the same reason some Nigerian scholars have seen the charismatic renewal and Pentecostalism within the Nigerian context as Christianity without memory dressed in borrowed robes, a distorter of authentic Catholic liturgy, a delusion, and a way of selling Jesus at a discount. Despite this criticism, as observed earlier, charismatic renewal and Pentecostalism in Nigeria have continued to be attractive to the Nigerian people. Could this attraction be for the fact that at least in praxis these movements do not displace but coexist with the pragmatic worldview of the Nigerian people, as is the case with Pentecostalism and the Makhuwa people's pragmatic approach to life as Devaka Premawardhana noted?[1] Or is the attraction a misperception of the circular mobility that characterizes such pragmatic approach in search for wellbeing? Whatever the case is, the primary focus and argument of this work has been and continues to be that the Christian church is a Spirit-filled, Spirit-directed, and Spirit-animated church. The Nigerian traditional religious worldview that is filled with multiple and constant activities of spirits makes the Holy Spirit a *sine qua non* in Nigerian Christianity. It necessitates that the Holy Spirit be placed at the vanguard of Nigerian Christianity if the Christian church in Nigeria should truly comprehend and savor the salvific work of God in Jesus Christ made manifest in the Spirit. Finally, the work maintains that whatever the excesses and abuses of the Nigerian charismatic renewal and Pentecostalism, or the effect of the circular mobility that characterizes their pragmatic approach, they cannot be neglected when dealing with a Spirit-animated church. It recognizes the charismatic renewal within the Catholic Church in Nigeria as an essential part of the changing face of the Nigerian Catholic Church. Through it, the Nigerian Catholic Church has consciously or unconsciously initiated the renewal of her pneumatology, ecclesiology, and liturgy in line with those of a truly Spirit-led church.

This chapter, therefore, argues that charismatic renewal and Pentecostalism within the Nigerian context are enabling the Catholic Church in Nigeria to realize the potentials of a Spirit-driven church through their emphasis on the Holy Spirit and their pneumatocentric ecclesiology and liturgy. As Spirit-driven groups and churches, they are the home of renewal for the Nigerian Catholic Church's pneumatology, ecclesiology, and liturgy. It uses Wolfgang Vondey's work, *Beyond Pentecostalism: The Crisis of Global Christianity and the Renewal of the Theological Agenda* as a template to lay out the argument that charismatic renewal and Pentecostalism belong to the borders of Christianity, the home of renewal. It then draws out some conclusions on the implication of this on the Nigerian Catholic Church. The implication, the chapter avers, is that as groups and churches that have practically demonstrated to be Spirit-animated, charismatic renewal and Pentecostalism within the Nigerian context are enabling the Catholic Church in Nigeria to realize the potentials of a Spirit-directed church. This, eventually, implies the renewal of her pneumatology, ecclesiology, and liturgy in harmony with those of a Spirit-driven church. Although the chapter avers that the charismatic and Pentecostal experiential encounter and praxis-oriented theology, particularly within the Nigerian context, is enabling the Nigerian Catholic Church to realize the potentials of a Spirit-directed church, it does

---

1. Premawardhana, *Faith in Flux*, 149.

not mean that their theology and praxis are perfect and beyond renewal. This will be discussed later in the chapter. The chapter is treated under the following subheadings:

- The Margins of Christianity as the Home of Renewal
- Charismatic Renewal and Pentecostalism as the Home of Renewal
- The Charismatic and Pentecostal Theology and Praxis in Need of Some Renewal
- Conclusion

The Margins of Christianity as the Home of Renewal

Based on Vondey's perception that the institutional structures of Christendom have collapsed, he discerns a "crisis of Christendom." For him the collapse of Christendom denotes the dissolution of those structures that supported and maintained a Christian empire vested in the culture, customs, beliefs, and concepts of the Western world.[2] With the collapse, Christianity now struggles to express itself in a meaningful and coherent way in a world that is no longer dominated by the structures of Christendom. Despite this collapse, modern ecclesiology has conceivably remained within those structures.[3] The ecclesiology of the Nigerian Catholic Church is not exempt. Her ecclesiology in practice has remained within the structures of the ecclesiology of Christendom even though the Catholic Church in principle has embraced an ecclesiology in which the church is seen as the people of God through the ecclesiological reforms of Vatican II Council.

Although Vatican II identifies the church as the people of God, its ecclesiology is Christocentric and speaks very little about the Holy Spirit. It is, therefore, not surprising that Nigerian Catholic Church's ecclesiology has remained stocked in the structures of the ecclesiology of Christendom despite the ecclesiological reforms of Vatican II Council. One of the limitations of the ecclesiology of Christendom is its Christocentric character. Vondey decries this situation because a definition of ecclesiality and continuous understanding of the church in the obsolete terms of an abstract, universal institution has immobilized and restrained the theological agenda.[4]

He presents four limitations of an ecclesiology of Christendom:

---

2. Vondey, *Beyond Pentecostalism*, 145.
3. Vondey, *Beyond Pentecostalism*, 142.
4. Vondey, *Beyond Pentecostalism*, 142.

- The concept "church" of Christendom is completely a Western concept which marks the boundaries of a "Christian" world in contrast to the "global" world because the "church" in this world was not in agreement with the emerging of Christianity in other cultures, particularly the East and the Southern Hemisphere. Its catholicity, therefore, neglected the implications and demands of the multicultural diversity and religious pluralism that characterized the "global" world. In the same vein, its apostolicity hinges solely on the idea of unbroken succession of the apostles through episcopal ordination instead of on the idea that the church is characterized by heroic faith and daily experience of God's miraculous power which characterized the apostolic and early Christian churches. In other words, its concept of apostolicity is devoid of the fact that the apostolic church is a church where spiritual gifts are not the exclusive reserve of the hierarchy but meant for all believers as was the case in the time of the apostles. As a Western concept, the liturgy of the "church" of Christendom is adapted to Western medieval ideas of performance instead of the multicultural contexts of the globalized world.[5]

- The profile of the Western notion of "church" is rooted on an institutional concept of ecclesiality. This concept makes it inclined to suppress the importance of the faith of an individual, women's role in ministry, the exercise of spiritual gifts, the importance of ecumenical communion, and interreligious dialogue. This concept also led to the domination and marginalization of all forms of movement in the church by the established institutional "culture."

- The justification of this Western notion of the "church" by a Christology that presents "church" as the mystical body of Christ. A concept that promotes a Christology "from above" and suppresses a more dynamic approach "from below." The neglect of pneumatology and a static view of history and humanity in the ecclesiology of Christendom drastically demean the true concept and nature of the church. This attitude makes the church's mission a mere performative presentation and enactment of the already established and traditional universal church in particular and specific cultural settings rather than an extension and transformation of the origin of the church across cultural borders and margins.[6]

---

5. Vondey, *Beyond Pentecostalism*, 146–47.
6. Vondey, *Beyond Pentecostalism*, 148.

- The ecclesiology of Christendom is ecumenically deficient because its concept of "church" hampers the acceptance of the authority of the separated churches, making ecumenical dialogue difficult if not impossible. The true character and concept of the church are, therefore, not found in the ecclesiology of Christendom. Rather, they are found in global Pentecostalism characterized by the idea of renewal.

Vondey avers that Pentecostals, just as the apostles and the early Christians, saw themselves as "men and women moved by the Holy Spirit." Global Pentecostalism is, therefore, a movement not in the ordinary sense of the word but in the sense that the Holy Spirit is mightily moving in anew upon men, women, and children. It is not an organization but Spirit-filled people whose lives are yielded to God's will for the need of the world. As a movement, global Pentecostalism rejects the structures of Christendom. The ecclesiology of Christendom sees church and culture as two distinct realms. When dealing with the two, Vondey decries the fact that ecclesiology is always the subject and not the object of consideration while culture is often seen as an ambiguous thing in need of purification and redemption.

The neglect of the concept of culture in the definition of the nature and purpose of the church by the ecclesiology of Christendom and later by classical Pentecostals led Vondey to propose an ecclesiology that is based on the play of the imagination. In this ecclesiology, the church is seen as a playground of cultures. Base ecclesial communities can be meaningful and valuable only if they function as cultural agents that are open to imagination, creativity, improvisation, and change. Vondey alludes to Jean-Jacques Suurmond's description of the church as a liberated community in which the world is invited into play with the Word and Spirit to drive home his argument of the ecclesiology of the play of imagination. He argues that global Pentecostalism advocates that ecclesiality is practiced and experienced most concretely in a variety of liturgical rhythms where church and culture meet and interact in a mutual movement that shapes and forms the ecclesial community in that particular setting.[7] When viewed through the lens of global Pentecostalism, the notion of "movement" seems to be the ecclesiological equivalent of the cultural term "play" which does not only apply to Pentecostalism but also, in principle, to all churches.[8]

Seeing the church as the playground of living cultures can help to overcome the usual separation of church and culture, charism and institution, and community and individual. In fact, seeing the church as playground requires an ecclesiology that truly makes the church everyday

---

7. Vondey, *Beyond Pentecostalism*, 170.
8. Vondey, *Beyond Pentecostalism*, 170.

"places" and "situations" of transformation, which open up the world for an encounter with God and humanity in ways and manners that traditional ecclesiology has not done.[9]

Those who reject play as a proper metaphor for the theological enterprise see it as something childish, and not serious, a vague and even frivolous behavior that contradicts and opposes orthodox theological sensibility.[10] However, the dynamic, imaginative play of global Pentecostalism is seen as a source for renewal not only in liturgy, catechesis, worship, preaching, ecumenical relations, and theological parlance but also in religious life, institutions, and structures.[11] In fact, the playfulness of global Pentecostalism is captured in the idea of revival, a concept that articulates the movement's self-understanding in various ways. Revival describes the understanding that global Pentecostalism is in its crux alleged as bringing to life again or reviving the biblical event of Pentecost.[12] However, Pentecostal revivals were not only seen as immoral, immature, deluded, frivolous, insane, and stupid, but also as demonic.

The controversial physical manifestations which often accompanied the revivals earned global Pentecostals the derogatory nickname "holy rollers" a label that was often used indiscriminately to describe the unorthodox style of worship of global Pentecostals marked by jumping, shaking, falling, and rolling on the floor that defiled and contradicted the established social and religious norms and expectations. This label, however, did not capture the density and complexity of Pentecostal beliefs and practices, and all that accompanied the revivals. For instance, global Pentecostals see glossolalia, one of the descriptors of global Pentecostal revivals, as an exuberant and cheerful manifestation of the "play" of the Holy Spirit.[13] Pentecostal revivals became institutionalized when glossolalia and the doctrine of Spirit baptism were enshrined. Revival became inimical to play when it was institutionalized. With this, the global Pentecostal emphasis on renewal offers the resources to overcome the limitations of revivalism.[14] What is fundamental, therefore, is the renewal of the orthodox theological agenda, not its revival.

The phenomenon of Pentecostal revivals is not limited to a particular form of Christianity. Hence, renewal exemplifies the struggle to integrate the phenomenon beyond its origins. In fact, renewal exceeds the functional and

9. Vondey, *Beyond Pentecostalism*, 170.
10. Vondey, *Beyond Pentecostalism*, 179.
11. Vondey, *Beyond Pentecostalism*, 193.
12. Vondey, *Beyond Pentecostalism*, 185.
13. Vondey, *Beyond Pentecostalism*, 187.
14. Vondey, *Beyond Pentecostalism*, 191.

practical aspects, scope, and theological emphasis of revival in the sense that it aligns more to the character and self-understanding of charismatic renewal and Pentecostalism as religious movements.[15] It focuses on the outpouring of God's Spirit on all flesh, which indeed is the most fundamental and essential thing for the worldwide effectiveness of the gospel.[16]

Renewal's emphasis on the outpouring of the Holy Spirit assures that it cannot be reduced to particular phenomena and methods. It, therefore, qualifies to be a theological representative of the notion of play. As an imagination of play, renewal guides play away from a purely inherent and intrinsic motivation to the demands and resources of particular contexts and moments.[17] Global Pentecostalism's idea of renewal, which focuses on the advent or outpouring of the Holy Spirit, God's indwelling presence, on all flesh makes renewal inimical to the institutionalization of religious experiences. It also constricted global Pentecostals from making their patterns of observation and interpretation to become orthodox practices.[18] Global Pentecostalism's resistance to institutionalization of religious experiences is exemplified in many global Pentecostal practices that give room for religious experiences that are "patterned after scriptural practices, on the one hand, and the indigenous, spiritual beliefs and practices that seem to border on syncretism, on the other hand."[19]

The ecclesiology of Christendom affected the church's liturgy as well. What happens in liturgy today could be tagged as "crisis of the liturgy." The crisis is because many in the late modern world have viewed liturgy as meaningless for liturgy has typically been understood as performance rather than play. The creation and development of performative structures of the liturgy in the Middle Ages gave rise to this crisis.[20] Seeing liturgy in this manner, where the playfulness of liturgical action is neglected in preference to "dramatic" performance, paved the way for the clericalization and sacramentalization of liturgical action. While the former addresses the problem of liturgical actions being performed on behalf of, rather than together with, the people, the latter refers to attention being paid to sacramental rituals in liturgical celebrations instead of the overall action.[21]

---

15. Vondey, *Beyond Pentecostalism*, 193.
16. Vondey, *Beyond Pentecostalism*, 193.
17. Vondey, *Beyond Pentecostalism*, 194.
18. Vondey, *Beyond Pentecostalism*, 195.
19. Vondey, *Beyond Pentecostalism*, 195.
20. Vondey, *Beyond Pentecostalism*, 110–11.
21. Vondey, *Beyond Pentecostalism*, 115.

The dominant place of the clergy at liturgy since the Middle Ages brings to the fore the hierarchical character liturgy assumed during this eon. This character is of course in accord with the concept of Christendom which the church assumed during the epoch. However, in modern times? Christendom has collapsed, giving rise to the crisis of the liturgy. The crisis is a good one since it simply entails resistance to liturgy being merely a reenactment of medieval performative structures.[22] The performance of the liturgy as a reenactment of medieval structures suppresses the playfulness of the liturgy. Vatican II liturgical reform seems to comprehend this. However, the ecclesiological and liturgical reforms of Vatican II Council are not pneumatocentric, which makes it difficult if not impossible to realize the full potentials of a Spirit-directed church and Spirit-oriented liturgy under the reform. Global Pentecostal liturgical imagination, therefore, discloses an effort to transform and convert the orthodox elements of the Christian liturgy into a Spirit-oriented dynamic of play.[23]

Instead of being a liturgy "performed," the camp meeting of African slaves in North America who secretly met to worship their God was a liturgy where the whole event "played" out as the situations allowed and as the Spirit of God directed.[24] The origin of global Pentecostal liturgy is traced to these camp meetings of African slaves in North America. It is no surprise, therefore, that global Pentecostal liturgy developed as a destructuralizing, flexible, verbal, participation-centered, and Spirit-oriented "open arrangement" of worship, prayer, and praise. This is in divergence with the structural Anglo-European liturgy with its abstractly static, written, priest-centered, and performance-oriented outline of sacramental celebration. In this way, rather than being a structure provided for the possibility of an experiential encounter with the Triune God, global Pentecostal liturgical theology and praxis present liturgy as an unrestricted response to an encounter with God.

This contrast in liturgical praxes and theology between the established ecclesiastical traditions and Pentecostalism is the brain behind the erroneous interpretation that Pentecostalism has no liturgy at all.[25] Global Pentecostal view of liturgy, which is Spirit-oriented and experiential in character, portrays liturgy as "the people of God at play" freely responding to God. The Spirit-oriented ecclesiology and liturgy of global Pentecostalism contrast with those of the established ecclesiastical traditions. This makes global Pentecostalism

---

22. Vondey, *Beyond Pentecostalism*, 117.
23. Vondey, *Beyond Pentecostalism*, 110.
24. Vondey, *Beyond Pentecostalism*, 123.
25. Vondey, *Beyond Pentecostalism*, 128–29.

with its ecclesiology and liturgy to be outside of what is considered central to the dominant worldview, pushing it to the margins of Christianity.

Global Christianity as well as its liturgical expressions, by the virtue of its mission is always geared towards the margins of the world. Theology itself would want to extend the witness to the gospel beyond Jerusalem to other parts of the world. The renewal of the crucial inequities of existence in the world is the focus of the margins because the margins fight and resist complexity of structures that make accommodation, systematization, and institutionalization possible.[26] Hence, the margins of Christianity or those considered to be outside the established ecclesiastical traditions are the homeland of renewal. This requires that global theology should depend on the voices that come from the margins in order to remain grounded in the realities of life as a whole.[27] In fact, the renewal of theological agenda from the margins is a goal and not a state of being because it is ruled by the desire to bring a balance between what is considered central and what appears marginal to the dominant worldview.

Talking about the renewal of the theological agenda from the margins recalls Walter D. Mignolo's "subaltern knowledges" and "border thinking" in his effort to decolonize the colonial mentality in his Latin American people.[28] He reveals how global designs, including those of Christianity "were conceived and enacted" for over five hundred years now "from a particular local history" thereby putting the rest of the world at the margins, portraying them as people without history, knowledge, and culture. He articulates the part which "colonial difference" plays in present-day conceptions of modernity and the endorsement of "subaltern knowledges" operating on the borders of the "current world system." To overcome this subjugation or suppression, the "abstract universalism" of contemporary epistemology and world history or what is measured as fundamental to the dominant worldview must give way to local histories and multiple local hegemonies.[29] Subaltern knowledges and "border thinking" resist and reject the "abstract universalism" of modern epistemology and world history. In fact, "border thinking" refers to the moments in which the invented and unrealistic modern world system cracks.[30] It is like Vondey's collapse of the structures of Christendom or crisis of Christendom. Global theology, therefore, depends

---

26. Vondey, *Beyond Pentecostalism*, 196.
27. Vondey, *Beyond Pentecostalism*, 196.
28. Mignolo, *Local Histories*.
29. Mignolo, *Local Histories*, 22.
30. Mignolo, *Local Histories*, 23.

on knowledge and thinking from the borders and the voices from the margins to remain grounded in the realities of life.

Are charismatic renewal and Pentecostalism within the Nigerian context among Vondey's global Pentecostalism and, therefore, the home of renewal? As Spirit-filled and Spirit-driven groups and churches, what are the pneumatology, ecclesiology, and worship of the Nigerian charismatics and Pentecostals saying to the Nigerian Catholic Church? The following section tries to address these questions.

Charismatic Renewal and Pentecostalism as the Home of Renewal

This segment uses Vondey's argument above to demonstrate that charismatic renewal and Pentecostalism particularly within the Nigerian context are Spirit-filled movements and churches that are enabling the Catholic Church in Nigeria to realize the potentials of a Spirit-driven church through their pneumatology and pneumatocentric ecclesiology and liturgy. As Spirit-filled movements and churches characterized by the idea of renewal as evident in the previous chapters, they are seen as belonging to the margins of Christianity, those outside the established ecclesiastical traditions, hence, the home of renewal. The section also avers that although the Catholic Church has rejected and moved away from the structures of Christendom through the ecclesiological and liturgical reforms of Vatican II Council, the ecclesiology and liturgy of Vatican II remain essentially Christocentric in character. The section, therefore, maintains that the emphasis of the charismatic renewal and Pentecostalism on the Holy Spirit and their pneumatocentric ecclesiology and liturgy are inspiring the Nigerian Catholic Church to realize the potentials of a Spirit-animated church in order to remain grounded in the realities of life in Nigerian Christianity as a whole. This is in line with Vondey's submission that the rejection and resistance of the structures of Christendom by global Pentecostalism requires global theology to be contingent on the voices that come from the margins or border in order to remain grounded in the realities of life as a whole. The rest of the section is dedicated to arguing this out and to drawing out the implications of this, which in fact is the renewal of the Nigerian Catholic Church's pneumatology, ecclesiology, and liturgy.

According to Vondey's argument above, the ecclesiology of Christendom, which presented the church as "an abstract, universal institution" in which Christianity is globally expressed in Western cultural religious categories, has collapsed, giving rise to "crisis of Christendom." Although he agreed that Christendom has collapsed, he maintained that modern ecclesiology has abstractly remained within those structures. However, he found solace in the fact that the ecclesiology and liturgy of global Pentecostalism are Spirit-driven and Spirit-oriented, which truly makes them resist the structures of Christendom. This is evident in the fact that global Pentecostals, just as the apostles and the early Christians, see themselves as "men and women moved by the Holy Spirit." In other words, they see themselves as Spirit-filled people whose lives are yielded to God's will for the need of the world. Global Pentecostalism's rejection of the structures of Christendom through its emphasis on renewal gave rise to Vondey's ecclesiology that is based on the play of the imagination in which the church is seen as a playground of cultures. It also gave rise to a liturgical concept in which liturgy is seen as a play of God's children with God their Father. In fact, global Pentecostalism's pneumatocentric ecclesiology and liturgy, and its emphasis on the renewal of the orthodox theological agenda place it at the borders of Christianity, the home of renewal. In the same vein, the pneumatocentric ecclesiology and liturgy of the charismatic renewal and Pentecostalism contrast with those of the established ecclesiastical traditions. The contrast places charismatic renewal and Pentecostalism especially within the Nigerian context outside the circle of what is considered central by the dominant worldview. They belong, therefore, to the margins or borders of Christianity and, consequently, the home of renewal. As part of the margins of Christianity and the home of renewal, the voices of charismatic renewal and Pentecostalism within the Nigerian context must not be neglected by the Nigerian Catholic Church if she is to remain grounded in the realities of life in Nigerian Christianity.

The pneumatocentric ecclesiology of charismatics and Pentecostals sees the church as a playground of cultures. Their pneumatocentric ecclesiology recognizes and upholds the importance of the faith of an individual, women's role in ministry, and the exercise of spiritual gifts by all believers. The pneumatocentric ecclesiology of charismatics and Pentecostals makes their mission as churches to be truly an expansion and transformation of the origin of the church across cultural boundaries instead of a mere performative enactment of the already established universal church in particular cultural contexts. As base ecclesial communities, charismatic renewal and Pentecostalism function as cultural agents that are open to imagination, creativity, improvisation, and change. This, no doubt, is evident in their ecclesiology and worship discussed in chapters 2 and 3 respectively, and in the Nigerian charismatic renewal and Pentecostalism's reflection of continuity with the Nigerian traditional religious worldview as demonstrated in chapter 4. This places charismatic renewal and Pentecostalism especially within the

Nigerian context in the category of global Pentecostalism. As any Movement within this category would do, charismatic renewal and Pentecostalism within the Nigerian context have shown that ecclesiality is experienced most concretely in a diversity of liturgical rhythms where church and Nigerian culture meet in a mutual movement that has shaped the charismatic and Pentecostal ecclesial communities in Nigeria.

The Catholic Church in general recognizes the collapse of the structures of Christendom which led to the ecclesiological and liturgical reforms that came with Vatican II Council, as evident in many documents of the Council. For instance, the Council in *Lumen Gentium* no. 9 describes the church as the new people of God not according to the flesh, but in the Spirit. In other words, it is the Holy Spirit that makes the church the new people of God; and the church is made up of all believers and not only the segment of the hierarchy. The Council in chapter V of *Lumen Gentium* also emphasizes the universal call to holiness of all believers and the fact that this holiness is cultivated by all who are moved by God's indwelling presence, the Holy Spirit. The Council Fathers in *Sacrosanctum Concilium* no. 14 stress the full and active participation of all people of God in liturgical celebrations and encourage whatever could make it realizable. All these demonstrate that the Catholic Church in general through Vatican II Council has rejected the structures of Christendom. However, despite the reform, the ecclesiology and liturgy of Vatican II Council have essentially remained Christocentric in character, making it difficult if not impossible for the Catholic Church in general to realize the potentials of a Spirit-driven church and Spirit-oriented liturgy.

The foundation for the success of the global Pentecostalism's rejection of the structures of Christendom, and its emphasis on the renewal of the orthodox theological agenda is rooted on global Pentecostals' emphasis on the Holy Spirit, which makes them see themselves as Spirit-filled people or "men and women moved by the Holy Spirit." This, no doubt, synchronizes with the pneumatology of the charismatic renewal and Pentecostalism studied in chapter 1. The study revealed that charismatics and Pentecostals see themselves as Spirit-filled and Spirit-animated people. It showed that their pneumatology is experiential and praxis-oriented as believers allow themselves to be led and animated by God's indwelling presence, the Holy Spirit. As Spirit-filled people who follow the directions of the Holy Spirit, there is always room for flexibility and spontaneity in their pneumatology. This pneumatology of the charismatic renewal and Pentecostalism greatly influences their ecclesiology and worship, as evident in chapters 2 and 3 respectively. Their ecclesiology becomes pneumatocentric, contrary to the ecclesiologies of Christendom and Vatican II Council that are Christocentric.

A lot of transformation and experiential encounter with the Triune God is going on in most Catholic charismatic centers and Pentecostal churches in Nigeria as demonstrated in some sections of the previous chapters. This shows that charismatic renewal and Pentecostalism within the Nigerian context, like global Pentecostalism, are indeed presenting the church through their pneumatology, ecclesiology, and worship as everyday home and circumstances of transformation. This is evident in the fact that their pneumatology, ecclesiology, and worship have turned the charismatic and Pentecostals churches in Nigeria into places and circumstances where an encounter between God and humanity takes place in ways traditional ecclesiological genres and orderings have never done.[31] The idea of renewal which characterizes charismatic renewal and Pentecostalism makes them to focus primarily on the advent or outpouring of God's Spirit on all flesh, which indeed is the essential and fundamental thing needed for the effectiveness of the gospel in Nigeria and the world in general. Characterized by the idea of renewal, Nigerian charismatic renewal and Pentecostalism resist any temptation to institutionalize their religious experiences, patterns of worship and interpretation, as conventional or orthodox praxes. This is evident in their religious practices that are patterned after biblical practices, on the one hand, and the Nigerian indigenous or homegrown religious beliefs and practices that seem to edge and border on syncretism, on the other hand.[32]

Charismatic renewal and Pentecostalism particularly within the Nigerian context are, therefore, Spirit-filled movements and churches that are enabling the Catholic Church in Nigeria to realize the potentials of a Spirit-driven church through their pneumatocentric ecclesiology and liturgy. To realize her potentials as Spirit-led church, it is necessary that the Nigerian Catholic Church listens to the voices of the charismatic renewal and Pentecostalism within the Nigerian context. This would enable her to remain grounded in the realities of life as a whole in Nigerian Christianity. Their emphasis on the Holy Spirit and their pneumatocentric ecclesiology and liturgy indeed make them Spirit-animated groups and churches, and voices from the margins. As Spirit-driven churches and voices from the margins, they are inspiring and enabling the Nigerian Catholic Church to realize the potentials of a Spirit-filled church. To realize the potentials of a Spirit-filled church through the pneumatocentric ecclesiology of charismatic renewal and Pentecostalism is like using Walter D. Mignolo's "subaltern knowledges"

---

31. Vondey, *Beyond Pentecostalism*, 170.
32. Vondey, *Beyond Pentecostalism*, 195.

and "border thinking" to resist and reject the colonial mentality of the West that puts the rest of the world at the margins.

For the Nigerian Catholic Church to realize the potentials of a Spirit-animated church, she must renew her pneumatology, ecclesiology, and liturgy to reflect those of a Spirit-animated church. In fact, the renewal has already started wittingly or unwittingly through the charismatic renewal within the Nigerian Catholic Church which, no doubt, is a vital part of the changing face of the Catholic Church in Nigeria. The rest of this section is dedicated to fleshing this out.

The Renewal of the Nigerian Catholic Church's Pneumatology

The pneumatology of charismatic renewal and Pentecostalism resists and rejects institutionalization of religious experiences even though their pneumatology is experiential and praxis-oriented. In other words, although charismatics and Pentecostals in their pneumatology pay more attention to experiential encounters with the Holy Spirit than to doctrinal definitions and explanations about the Holy Spirit, as observed in chapter 1, the experiences vary based on circumstances and contexts. Chapter 4 portrayed the Nigerian charismatic renewal and Pentecostalism as placing the Holy Spirit at the driving seat of their theology, to use Uzukwu's words, by successfully transferring the roles of deities, spirits, and ancestors to God's indwelling presence, the Holy Spirit. They successfully demonstrated that the best way to experience the liberating, saving, healing, and therapeutic hand of God in Nigerian Christianity is through God's empowering presence, the Holy Spirit. As Spirit-filled people whose pneumatocentric ecclesiology and liturgy contrast in praxis with those of the established ecclesiastical traditions, they belong to the margins or borders of Christianity, the home of renewal. The fact that they are not within the established ecclesiastical traditions that are considered central by the dominant worldview makes their position and location marginal. From the margins, therefore, they speak out not necessarily in words but in action. Considering the importance and functions of deities, spirits, and ancestors in Nigerian religious worldview, the Holy Spirit is a *sine qua non* in Nigerian Christianity. The Catholic Church in Nigeria willingly or unwillingly is realizing the potentials of a Spirit-driven church, has placed the Holy Spirit at the forefront of her theology, and has transferred the functions of the deities, spirits, and ancestors to God's empowering presence, the Holy Spirit, through the experiential encounter and praxis-oriented pneumatology of the charismatic renewal in the Nigerian Catholic Church. The Catholic Church in Nigeria is consciously or unconsciously recognizing the Holy Spirit as the all in all or "the Oga kwatakwata" in Nigerian parlance through the charismatics in her midst.

Conversion to Christianity does not make a Nigerian Christian repudiate Nigerian philosophy and religious worldview. Rather, the latter enhances the former, which is in line with the reform of Vatican II Council. In Nigerian traditional religious worldview, the role of the deities, spirits, and ancestors is indispensable in the religious experience and encounter of God, the Supreme Being. In Nigerian Christianity, therefore, the salvific work of God in the Crucified and Risen Jesus is naturally best experienced through God's indwelling presence, the Holy Spirit. This does not contradict the teachings of the church about the Holy Spirit who is seen as the author, sustainer, and finisher of our Christian life in the Bible and down the centuries.

In the Scriptures and down the centuries, the Holy Spirit has been the absolute key to the comprehension of the entire Christian life and was experienced by believers in concrete and palpable ways. It is no surprise that Gordon Fee maintains that when Paul uses the language of "both signs and wonders and deeds of power," he uses it "to cover the broad range of miracles that attended his ministry through the power of the Holy Spirit."[33] The teachings on the Holy Spirit in the Scriptures and through the centuries show that it is the Holy Spirit who perfects and finalizes the work of the Risen Lord and renders it to us. It is the same Holy Spirit of God who makes the Risen Lord himself truly present among his people not only in a sacramental manner but also in profound and tangible ways. In fact, the teachings on the Holy Spirit that were studied in chapter 1 reveal that the Holy Spirit empowers believers not only to believe in God as the Savior but more importantly, to experience and encounter God as the Savior and to be witnesses of God's saving act.

Despite a radical reorganization of African cosmology by the new African Pentecostalism, as evident in its dualistic pessimism and its unfair demonization of all spirits in the ancestral religious world, the emphasis of charismatics and Pentecostals on the Holy Spirit is an indication that the Holy Spirit is for them "the Oga kwatakwata" and is indeed at the vanguard of their theology and praxis. They do not only believe that the Holy Spirit should be at the frontline of their theology, they live it out in practice. They rightly do so. For, as Uzukwu noted, any theology that does not focus on the directing and abiding Holy Spirit does not qualify to be a Christian theology. More so, it is the Holy Spirit who empowers believers to experience and encounter "the God who loves and cares for the daily needs of his

---

33. Fee, *God's Empowering Presence*, 356.

people."³⁴ Through their pneumatology, therefore, charismatic renewal and Pentecostalism within the Nigerian context is simply enabling the Nigerian Catholic Church to realize the potentials of a Spirit-filled church in Nigerian Christianity. Elochukwu E. Uzukwu would agree that by doing so, the Nigerian Catholic Church would be expanding and reinventing her indigenous religious experience of God, deities, spirits, and ancestors into her Christian life. She would be presenting the Holy Spirit as the natural entry point to explore the Triune God in Nigerian Catholicism. And she would be doing so rightly. The experiences of the Nigerian charismatics and Pentecostals who have successfully attributed to the Holy Spirit the energies and powers attributed to the deities, spirits, and ancestors attest to this.

In Nigerian charismatic groups and Pentecostal churches, God's indwelling and empowering presence, the Holy Spirit, has totally taken over the life of the Christian for complete and holistic community and individual growth and healing as evident in the previous chapters.³⁵ For them, the Holy Spirit is truly the animator and enabler of Christian communities. She makes it possible for Christians to experience and encounter the power of the Triune God in the Crucified and Risen Jesus. This is an experiential encounter that brings holistic healing and transformation not only to themselves but also to those they encounter while witnessing to the Crucified and Risen Jesus.

The presence of God's empowering presence, the Holy Spirit in Nigerian Christianity, is indispensable due to the importance of the role of the Holy Spirit in the church and in the lives of individual members of the church as the teachings on the Holy Spirit in the Scriptures and through the centuries indicated. However, the role of deities, spirits, and ancestors in Nigerian traditional religious philosophy and worldview makes it even more indispensable. For believers in Nigerian Christianity to silence the powers of evil, gratify various types of life-needs, and be delivered and in turn deliver people from all kinds of afflictions, they must live as Spirit-filled people and lay a special claim to the charism of the Holy Spirit. Nigerian Christianity should, therefore, live out the implications and potentials of being a Spirit-animated church. Charismatic renewal and Pentecostalism within the Nigerian context are living this out as evident in the previous chapters and are, therefore, enabling the Nigerian Catholic Church to realize her potentials as a Spirit-driven church. For, in Nigerian Christianity, if the most powerful and loving God cannot heal a person and bring wholeness of life, he is not

---

34. Ma, "'When the Poor,'" 31.
35. Uzukwu, *God, Spirit and Human Wholeness*, 217.

as useful and beneficial as the deities, benevolent spirits, and ancestors many Nigerians have been relying on for such needs.[36]

Conversion to Christianity is not an automatic immunity from the attacks of malevolent spirits and from all that dehumanizes one and could debar one from attaining *ụbandụ*, abundant life in this life, while waiting for its fullness in the eschaton. Nigerian Christians, however, expect better protection, love, and care from the God of their new religion than they were receiving in their former religion. The traditional religious philosophy or worldview of Nigerians indicates that in Nigerian Christianity, therefore, the protective and delivering power of the Triune God from diabolic forces and from all that dehumanizes one is naturally best experienced through God's indwelling presence, the Holy Spirit. The role of the Holy Spirit in the church and in the life of individual members of the church corroborates this. The emphasis on the Holy Spirit by charismatics and Pentecostals within the Nigerian context as well as their pneumatology in general is, therefore, aiding the Nigerian Catholic Church to realize the latent power of a Spirit-led church. This has knowingly or unknowingly lessened the scope of tension and conflict or double allegiance—one to Catholic beliefs and practices and the other to charismatic and Pentecostal as well as indigenous religious beliefs and practices—in the religious experience of the members of the Nigerian Catholic Church, as the charismatic renewal in the Nigerian Catholic Church is a vital part of the changing face of the Catholic Church in Nigeria. Moreover, there would be no more reason for the likes of Bishop A. K. Obiefuna to lament and confess that their Catholic members are worshiping "idols" and false gods by going to take oaths before the chief priests and priestesses of their indigenous traditional religion, by secretly erecting shrines in their homes and in their compounds, and by seeking for means of protection through the help of these human and spiritual agents of their indigenous traditional religion.[37]

The Catholic Church in Nigeria is not only realizing the potentials of a Spirit-driven church through the charismatic renewal in the Nigerian Catholic Church, an essential part of her changing face, she has also initiated intentionally or unintentionally through the same movement, the renewal of her ecclesiology and liturgy in accord with those of a Spirit-oriented church. This is the focus of the next two subheadings respectively.

---

36. Ma, "'When the Poor,'" 31.
37. Obiefuna, *Idolatry*, 11.

The Renewal of the Nigerian Catholic Church's Ecclesiology

It was observed in chapter 2 that Pentecostals and charismatics, no doubt, would agree that all that concerns Christ and the church is God's doing. However, they would maintain that it is God's doing through God's empowering presence, the Holy Spirit. Hence, for them, while the church is the body of Christ and Christ himself is her head; and while the church is betrothed to Christ as his bride, the crucial role of the Holy Spirit in the church and in the lives of the individual members of the church makes them prefer a pneumatological to christological ecclesiology.

The ecclesiology of charismatics and Pentecostals, like their theology in general, is an ecclesiology of an encounter that is praxis-oriented and experiential. The previous chapters demonstrated that Pentecostals and charismatics do not simply believe in the Holy Spirit and in the role of the Holy Spirit in the church and in the lives of individual members of the church—they experience the Holy Spirit in very tangible and visible ways. How the Trinity operates amid charismatics and Pentecostals, and how the Triune God enters their experiences of life, inform what they believe the church is and should be. The centrality of the Holy Spirit in their lives and the role of the Holy Spirit in the church, therefore, make them to see the church as the sacrament of God's presence and power among his people; and the medium of the redemptive and salvific acts of the Triune God. Put differently, charismatics and Pentecostals espouse an ecclesiology where the church is seen as a people of God touched and transformed by God's indwelling presence, the Holy Spirit, who are in turn being used by the same Spirit to touch and transform the world. Their pneumatocentric ecclesiology makes them see themselves as Spirit-filled people called by God to witness and testify to the character and power of his reign and kingdom, and to serve as a medium or instrument through which God will express and manifest himself to his people and to the world[38] through the power of his indwelling presence, the Holy Spirit.

The people of God ecclesiology of Vatican II Council is essentially Christocentric as it gives little position to the Holy Spirit. This contrasts it with the ecclesiology of the charismatic renewal and Pentecostalism, which is fundamentally Spirit-centered. The charismatic and Pentecostal pneumatocentric ecclesiology is, therefore, assisting the Nigerian Catholic Church to realize the potentials of a Spirit-animated church as she demonstrates in praxis to be a community or church that is called and chosen to be, on the finite and determinate level, the kind of reality that God is

---

38. Pinnock, "Church in the Power," 152.

in eternity.[39] Their ecclesiology is enabling the Catholic Church in Nigeria to truly become a medium of God's mission on earth. Actualizing the potentials of a Spirit-filled church indeed makes the church a fellowship in the Spirit, and a gathering of God's people who gather to experience and encounter the presence of the living God through God's empowering presence, the Holy Spirit. It makes emphasis to be not so much on a theory of church as it is on an experience of the church that is animated and led by God's empowering presence, the Holy Spirit.

Living out the potentials of a Spirit-driven church makes manifestations or indices of God's indwelling presence, the Holy Spirit who is the animator and guide of the church and individual members of the church the outstanding "mark" of the church. It makes the Triune God truly cease to be a distant or detached figure but a reality that is encountered and experienced. Reclaiming the dormant power of a Spirit-animated church makes believers and participants to speak of Jesus and God not just as someone who is very real but as someone who can be trusted and counted on to help in daily struggles for life. There is no room for triumphalism in a Spirit-driven church as believers believe there are situations the Spirit does not physically take them out of but sustains and fortifies them in the situations and provides meaning to what could otherwise be destructive and damaging experiences. A Spirit-driven church becomes a church in the manner of the apostolic church where spiritual gifts are not the exclusive reserve of the hierarchy but meant for all believers for the Spirit has been poured on all flesh. In a Spirit-animated church, spiritual gifts are held in high esteem, as they are the specific and exact means by which the church becomes a graced community or people of God, the bride of Christ ever more faithful and dedicated to her ministry and mission as she becomes ever more faithful and devoted to Christ[40] through the power of God's indwelling presence, the Holy Spirit. In a Spirit-led church, believers realize the implication of their baptism for Christian baptism is an incorporation into a Spirit-filled, Spirit-empowered entity or community.[41]

Charismatics and Pentecostals within the Nigerian context have demonstrated through their emphasis on the Holy Spirit and through their pneumatocentric ecclesiology that they are indeed Spirit-filled people and Spirit-empowered entity. If there is any reason many Nigerians run to Catholic charismatic renewal of Nigeria, Pilgrimage Center of Eucharistic Adoration Elele, Adoration Ministry Enugu Nigeria, Upper Room Ministries,

---

39. Pinnock, "Church in the Power," 154.
40. Macchia, "Pinnock's Pneumatology," 172.
41. Chan, "Mother Church," 180.

Enugu, Holy Ghost Adoration Ministry Uke, Canaanland Adoration Ministry (E-Dey Work) Mbaise, Lumen Christi Family Adoration Ministry Issele-uku, and The Redeemed Christian Church of God, Deeper Christian Life Ministry, etc., it is because these charismatic groups and churches have truly demonstrated that they are Spirit-driven groups and churches. People see in them the restoration of the apostolic signs of healing, miracles, prophecy, and so on. They are, therefore, enabling the Nigerian Catholic Church to realize the potentials of a Spirit-driven church. They are aiding them to show in practice that "the Spirit constitutes the church, giving the church its unique identity as a Spirit-filled body," and "that the church thus constituted gives the Spirit's distinctive character and role in the world as the church-located and church-shaped Spirit."[42]

To realize the potential of a Spirit-filled church naturally makes the church apostolic in character, not necessarily in the sense of apostolic succession, but in the restoration of the apostolic signs of healing, miracles, prophecy, and other charismatic gifts of the Holy Spirit. It makes the church truly become the redeeming, sanctifying, and healing presence of God among his people through the power of the Holy Spirit.

In the economy of salvation, it is not only the chosen, redeemed, and sanctified people of God who desire to experience and encounter their loving, redeeming, and sanctifying God through his indwelling presence, the Holy Spirit. The Triune God himself desires to be present with his chosen, redeemed, and sanctified people. He does this through his indwelling presence, the Holy Spirit. In fact, Gordon Fee might be right when he observed as noted earlier that "whatever else the Spirit meant in Paul's understanding, it meant at least that the desire for God's presence had been fulfilled by the coming of the Spirit."[43] It might not be wrong, therefore, for one to aver that the salvific work of God in the Crucified and Risen Christ begins, continues, and is sustained by God's empowering presence, the Holy Spirit, at every stage of Christian life. A Spirit-filled church, therefore, is a group of chosen, sanctified, and redeemed people who gather together to pray and to wait for the coming of the Holy Spirit of God. No doubt, this is what the early church was after the ascension.

Following in the footsteps of the early church, a Spirit-driven church truly becomes the sacrament of God's presence, who comes to give people back their life by healing the sick, enriching the poor, liberating the oppressed and the marginalized, setting sinners free, and liberating people from whatever dehumanizes them. This seems to be what the Council

---

42. Chan, "Mother Church," 189.
43. Fee, *God's Empowering Presence*, 868.

Fathers of Vatican II mean when they affirm in *Sacrosanctum Concilium*, the Constitution on the Liturgy no. 7, that "Christ is always present in his Church." Through their emphasis on the Holy Spirit and their pneumatocentric ecclesiology, charismatics and Pentecostals within the Nigerian context replicate the early church in being a Spirit-animated church. Hence, they are enabling the Nigerian Catholic Church to realize the potentials of a Spirit-filled church.

Although the ecclesiology of Vatican II Council is essentially Christocentric and gives little position to the Holy Spirit, the teachings on the Holy Spirit in the Scripture and through the centuries examined in chapter 1, indicate that the Holy Spirit is the animator of the church and individual members of the church. It is doubtful if Vatican II would object to this. However, while the Catholic Church might have succeeded at least in theory to see the church as a playground of cultures through Vatican II ecclesiological reforms, the reality on ground shows that she has not fully realized the potentials of a Spirit-animated church. A Spirit-driven church enables Christian faith to be freely and genuinely expressed in cultural values of the particular chosen, redeemed, and sanctified people of God. For God chooses his own people from different cultures of the world. In this way, a Spirit-animated church truly becomes a playground of cultures. However, a Spirit-animated church does much more than this. Global Pentecostalism exemplifies this through its emphasis on the Holy Spirit and its pneumatocentric ecclesiology which is characterized by the idea of renewal. The charismatic and Pentecostal pneumatocentric ecclesiology within the Nigerian context, therefore, inspires the Nigerian Catholic Church to realize the potentials of a Spirit-driven church. This is so, because the charismatic renewal in the Nigerian Catholic is an indispensable part of the changing face of the Catholic Church in Nigeria. Through it, the Nigerian Catholic Church has already initiated deliberately or non-deliberately the renewal of her ecclesiology in line with that of a Spirit-led church.

A Spirit-animated church is culture-rooted and salvation in Nigerian traditional cultural religious worldview is holistic, which includes liberation from all that could hinder people from realizing their potentials both as a community and as individuals. In Nigerian Christianity, salvation in a Spirit-led church would naturally include deliverance from spiritual, physical, and emotional sicknesses, poverty, injustices, oppression, and all that dehumanizes the human person. That includes liberation from whatever that hinders any Christian church in Nigeria from realizing the potentials of a Spirit-driven church.

Salvation in a Spirit-animated church naturally would become *ụbandụ, dagbe,* abundant life, or wholeness of life, which begins in this life. In other words, wholeness of life would logically become part of the fruits of the Holy Spirit. Jesus would become indeed the *agyenkwa*, the one who saves, rescues, redeems, heals, and delivers us from danger through the power of God's indwelling presence, the Holy Spirit. A "bowl of rice and healing of terminal diseases in a poverty-stricken society" like Nigeria would be "as important as the matter of sin and salvation."[44] In fact, a bowl of rice and healing of terminal diseases in a Spirit-driven church are all attainable spiritually and physically through supernatural and natural means by the power of God's indwelling presence, the Holy Spirit, who possesses and animates the church and individual members of the church saving them and using them as instruments of salvation that must begin here on earth. This is so, since in Nigerian Christianity, salvation includes deliverance from one's enemies and whatever threatens one's wellbeing in this life, which include but are not limited to sickness, witchcraft, sorcery, magic, barrenness, failure, troublesome spirits, danger, misfortune, calamity, poverty, and unnatural death.

It is good, no doubt, for the leaders of the Nigerian Catholic Church to encourage their members to be Christlike. However, in situations where bad governance, nepotism and so on have combined to create insecurity and hopelessness at all levels in the Nigerian society, a Spirit-animated church understands that the first task of Christianity is to liberate people from hopelessness and frustration by generating and creating new empowering and assuring tools of hope, optimism, and courage instead of remaining with the old practices that have never helped.[45]

A Spirit-filled church, no doubt, would worry about the excesses and abuses of prosperity gospel preachers. However, she knows that the idiom of prosperity preaching extends beyond material wealth to include such issues as renewal of individuals' and communities' spiritual relationship with God in Christ through the power of the Holy Spirit, the renewal of all forms of brokenness, the establishment of health, the reversal of economic misery, and individuals' and communities' political and social well-being.[46]

In fact, activities of Nigerian charismatics and Pentecostals as Spirit-animated groups and churches have led to the reinterpretation of health and prosperity preaching in Nigeria. For instance, preachers who indulge in health and prosperity preaching in a poverty-stricken society like Nigeria are seen to be crafting a theology of hope to deal with the existential

---

44. Ma, "'When the Poor,'" 31.
45. Kalu, *African Pentecostalism*, 213.
46. Kalu, *African Pentecostalism*, 213.

problems of the people.⁴⁷ While not believing in and promoting crossless Christianity, a Spirit-led church refuses to idolize suffering. She sees signs and wonders or miracles as divine-human agent's interceding activity and as a way of creating specific and particular goods for the wellbeing of the people as there is no dichotomy between the invisible and visible realms.⁴⁸ She recognizes that in Nigerian Christianity, salvation "encompasses the body, soul, and spirit and is simultaneously about the well-being in the here and now and in the afterlife."⁴⁹ She knows that a believer is saved as many times as possible in this earthly existence before he or she is finally saved in the eschaton by gaining entrance into the heavenly bliss. This, no doubt, is biblical as well. For, Jesus went about as recorded in the Scriptures doing good, healing the sick, saving the captives, redeeming those possessed by evil spirits, liberating the oppressed and the marginalized, feeding the hungry and the poor, and liberating humanity from all that dehumanizes it. Such a church testifies in praxis that Jesus came that they may have life and have it abundantly (John 10:10).

Charismatic renewal and Pentecostalism within the Nigerian context have exemplified themselves through their emphasis on the Holy Spirit and their pneumatocentric ecclesiology to be truly Spirit-filled groups and churches. They are, therefore, enabling the Nigerian Catholic Church to realize the potentials of a Spirit-driven church. For the charismatic renewal in the Nigerian Catholic Church is indeed an important part of the changing face of the Catholic Church in Nigeria. Like the ecclesiology of a Spirit-animated church, the liturgy of a Spirit-driven church is not rooted on the structures of liturgy of Christendom and is essentially pneumatocentric.

The Renewal of the Nigerian Catholic Church's Liturgy

The uniqueness of the charismatic and Pentecostal worship as observed in previous chapters is centered on the fact that charismatics and Pentecostals understand worship to be an experiential encounter of being in the presence of God made possible by God's indwelling presence, the Holy Spirit. Their pneumatology, which is experiential and praxis-oriented, makes not only their ecclesiology but also their worship, experiential, and praxis-oriented. Worship for them is centered on the need to feel and experience the presence of the Triune God through the power of God's indwelling presence, the Holy Spirit. What matters to them in worship, as noted, is to

---

47. Wariboko, *Nigerian Pentecostalism*, 35.
48. Wariboko, *Nigerian Pentecostalism*, 196.
49. Wariboko, *Nigerian Pentecostalism*, 196.

be led by the Holy Spirit whom they believe animates worship, the church, and the individual members of the church, into the "throne room" where they encounter God whose salvific works in the Crucified and Risen Jesus through God's empowering presence, the Holy Spirit, give them *ụbandụ, dagbe*, wholeness of life or abundant life.

Their belief that the Holy Spirit animates worship makes their worship to be characterized by spontaneity in which worshipers, despite plans and previous rehearsals, allow themselves to be led by the Holy Spirit. Chapter 4 above showed that the style of worship of the Catholic charismatic renewal of Nigeria, Pilgrimage Center of Eucharistic Adoration Elele, Adoration Ministry Enugu Nigeria, Upper Room Ministries, Enugu, Holy Ghost Adoration Ministry Uke, etc., and Deeper Christian Life Ministry, Living Faith Church (Winners Chapel), The Redeemed Christian Church of God, Mountain of Fire and Miracles, etc., reflects continuity with Nigerian traditional religious mode of worship. By reflecting continuity with Nigerian traditional religious style of worship, the charismatic and Pentecostal liturgy or worship, particularly within the Nigerian context, resonates with Elochukwu Uzukwu, who avers that the gestures with which humans express their relationship with the God of Jesus Christ must always be homegrown.[50]

Although Romano Guardini's German liturgical movement did not exclude liturgical texts, his understanding of liturgical actions as a play of God's people before God their Father harmonizes with the concept of worship in a Spirit-filled church. He is perhaps right when in the bid to resolve the tension between the playfulness and purposefulness of the liturgy he suggests that worshipers should avoid "continually yearning to do something, to attack something, to accomplish something useful, but to play the divinely ordered game of the liturgy in liberty and beauty and holy joy before God."[51]

A theology of worship that does not give room for liturgy to be truly a play of God's children with God their Father is disconnected from the liturgy of a Spirit-driven church. Godwin K. Obiorah probably is right when he reminds the Nigerian Catholic Church that singing, clapping, and dancing are natural to Nigerians and should, therefore, consider reviewing her "worship with a view to making it lively, dynamic, captivating[,] involving, experiential and a true celebration."[52] According to him, this indeed is what Psalm 150 is all about.

---

50. Uzukwu, *Worship as Body Language*, ix.
51. Guardini, *Spirit of the Liturgy*, 71–72.
52. Obiorah, "Challenges Posed by Pentecostalism," 35.

For a Spirit-led church, as for Nigerians and Africans in general God is not abstract and static but concrete and dynamic. Hence, during worship, "expectancy" and "experience" can instantly elicit passionate or enthusiastic responses both from worshipers and from God. Maybe Elochukwu E. Uzukwu is right to maintain that limiting the sense of liturgical rite to outward rituals is part of the consequences that medieval depravity brought into liturgical life in the West.[53] Unfortunately, that decadence spread into liturgical life of other cultures necessitating the liturgical reforms of Vatican II Council.

The liturgy of the Nigerian charismatic renewal and Pentecostalism is in line with the concept of liturgy of the Pentecostal scholar Wolfgang Vondey who sees liturgy as "play," that is, the play of the children of God before God their Father. It also resonates with the concept of liturgy of the Council Fathers of Vatican II in their liturgical reform. For instance, it sounds to be the true meaning of the statement of the Second Vatican Council in its decree and guidelines for the missionary activities of the church *Ad Gentes*, when it states in no. 22 that the Christian life will be adapted to the mentality and character of each culture and local traditions. Hence, the local churches should "borrow from the customs, traditions, wisdom, teaching, arts and sciences of their people everything, which could be used to praise the glory of the creator, manifest the grace of the saviour, or contribute to the right ordering of Christian life." It seems, also, to be the true significance of the statement of Pope Paul VI when he maintains in *Africae Terrarum* no. 7 that "The expression, that is, the language and mode of manifesting this one faith may be manifold. Hence it may be original, suited in the language, the style, the character, the genius, and the culture of the one who professes this one faith." The same is true of the statement of Pope John Paul II in his Address to the Italian National Congress of the Ecclesial Movement for Cultural Commitment on January 16, 1982 when he insists that "the synthesis between culture and faith is not only a demand of culture but also of faith," because "a faith that does not become culture is not fully accepted, not entirely thought out, not faithfully lived." This, most probably, is the real meaning of the declaration of the bishops of Africa and Madagascar during the 1974 Synod when they declare that "Theology must be open to the aspiration of the people of Africa if it is to help Christianity to become incarnate in the life of the peoples of the African continent."[54] No doubt, it seems to be the true import of the admonition of

---

53. Uzukwu, *Liturgy*, 4.

54. Association of Member Episcopal Conferences in Eastern Africa AMECEA, Documentation Service, November 2, 1974, 2–3

Francis Libermann to his missionaries and consequently to all missionaries to Africa, when he says, "Strip yourselves of Europe, its customs and its mentality. Become black with the blacks.... Leave them in their own way of being. Adapt yourselves to the customs, mentality and habits of (the black to make of them) a people of God."[55]

It has not been long that, influenced by the charismatic and Pentecostal style of worship, especially within the Nigerian culture, and of course in response to Vatican II liturgical reforms, some Catholic Church dioceses in Nigeria allowed some indigenous cultural liturgical gestures like dancing and playing of traditional musical instruments in their liturgy. Yet, this has been seen by some Nigerian Catholic theologians as a distortion of authentic Catholic liturgy and a way of selling Jesus at a discount. The use of Western or European cultural gestures in liturgy seems to be what makes Catholic liturgy authentic and orthodox for them. However, as indicated by Vatican II liturgical reforms, Christian liturgy is best expressed in the language, the style, the character, the genius, and the culture of the one who professes this one Christian faith.

Joyful shouting, swaying, and singing; waving and clapping of hands; dancing and moving around in the place of worship and pouring out of emotions before God in worship is not only natural but also cultural to Nigerians. Just as any religion that is not culture-rooted cannot be lived, in the same way, any liturgical expression or gesture that is not culture-specific cannot produce the desired effect, which is the opening of the door for an experiential encounter between worshipers and God. For the apostles and early Christians, Christianity was a sect of Judaism, not a different religion. Christian liturgy during this epoch was, therefore, dominantly a modification of the Jewish traditional religious ritual structures.[56]

Vatican II liturgical reforms, no doubt, permit liturgical expressions that are culture-rooted and homegrown, and encourage full and active participation of all believers in liturgy. However, its liturgy, like its ecclesiology, is fundamentally Christocentric and priest-oriented in nature. It practically allows the Holy Spirit little or no role in liturgy, which essentially hampers the Catholic Church from truly realizing the potentials of a Spirit-animated church. Liturgy in a Spirit-driven church goes beyond ritual expressions being culture-rooted and homegrown.

In a Spirit-driven church, the fear of syncretism is conquered through a theology of worship that in practice accords the Spirit her rightful place in worship. In a Spirit-driven church, liturgical gestures are culture-rooted

---

55. Koren, *Essay on the Spiritan Charism*, 22.
56. McGowan, *Ancient Christian Worship*, 2014; Bradshaw, *Search for the Origins*.

and homegrown, and worshipers are led by the Holy Spirit into the "throne room" where they encounter God. It is true that wherever the encounter with God takes place in worship that place can be emotional, but there is nothing wrong with that as emotions are a genuine part of worship. For when the people of God gather at worship, the totality of the human person is involved. However, emotional expressions arising during worship must be subjected to a test using biblical teachings, reason, and prayer. In this way, there would be a balance between intellectual and emotional activities during worship, consequently avoiding always associating one's own emotions with the power of the Holy Spirit. Worship itself would become trinitarian in character, in the sense that worship or liturgy demonstrates in praxis a "doxological encounter, in *ecstatic immediacy*, with God the Father; mediated by Christ risen and embodied in him, and carried by the Spirit."[57] In a Spirit-led church, God becomes truly present in worship through the Holy Spirit. Liturgy becomes indeed what it truly is, an encounter and a communion with the Spirit and with God's people through which the worshipers are led into God's presence where they experience *dagbe, ubandu,* or abundant life, the fullness of which is to be realized eschatologically.

In a Spirit-animated church where church is truly the redeeming, sanctifying, and healing presence of God, liturgical services or worship are meant to provide the scenario, the ambient through which worshipers encounter and experience the redeeming, sanctifying, and healing presence of the Triune God through the power of God's indwelling presence, the Holy Spirit. Liturgy in a Spirit-driven church becomes truly apostolic in nature in the sense that it is characterized by heroic faith and daily experience of God's miraculous power, which characterized the worship of the apostles and the early Christians as evident in the Acts of the Apostles.

In fact, liturgy in a Spirit-filled church is characterized by spontaneity in which worshipers, despite plans and previous rehearsals, allow themselves to be led by the Holy Spirit. Led by the Holy Spirit, worshipers expect to encounter and experience the Triune God during liturgical celebrations. However, when they expect and desire to experience and encounter God in worship, they are not just expecting a mere cognitive awareness of God's presence or being but rather a tangible and palpable encounter with the redeeming God whom they trust and expect to deliver them through the power of his indwelling presence, the Holy Spirit, from all that deprives them from having *ubandu*, abundant life, in the here and now, until when its fullness is realized eschatologically.

---

57. Beeck, *God Encountered*, 218.

Liturgical directors and celebrants in a Spirit-filled church are always paying attention to the varying scenes of human interjections and responses to be able to lead worshipers into an appropriate and fitting manner of worship as the Spirit gives the lead. Hence, for a transforming encounter to take place during worship in a Spirit-driven church, worshipers allow worship and consequently themselves to be transformed by the power of the Holy Spirit, who is the true agent of transformation. They know that while liturgical rituals are essential to worship, it is God's indwelling presence, the Holy Spirit, who is the true agent of transformation. Human agents of worship or liturgical ministers in such a church always allow themselves to be led, possessed and used in liturgical celebrations by God's empowering presence, the Holy Spirit, to positively touch the lives of the worshipers who gather to encounter, experience, and worship their loving and redeeming God in the Crucified and Risen Jesus. Indeed, in a Spirit-animated church, all believers are human agents of worship, for all believers are gifted in one way or another by the Holy Spirit to make essential contributions to all façades of the church's worship. The use of their gifts in worship helps to facilitate the experiential encounter they expect with their loving and redeeming God through God's indwelling presence, the Holy Spirit. Hence, flexibility in worship is necessary in a Spirit-driven church which shift attention more to oral rather than written communication. Such flexibility gives room for spontaneity and allows a wider range of participation in liturgy or what the Council Fathers of Vatican II call full and active participation of all people of God. It ensures that God's empowering presence, the Holy Spirit, is always integrally involved in worship. Although the Holy Spirit, the Spirit of Jesus, the indwelling presence of God comes every time and anywhere two or three gathers in the name of Jesus as Jesus promised, yet, the attitudes and sensibilities of human agents of worship make a difference in how God's presence is manifested, experienced, and encountered by worshipers.[58] Hence, in a Spirit-animated church, worshipers in liturgical worship show more radical accessibility, openness, vulnerability, and docility to God's indwelling presence, the Holy Spirit. They become deliberately present to God—even as God's presence is anticipated to become very tangible and real in worship.[59] The point here is that even though the Spirit blows where the Spirit wills, worshipers in a Spirit-driven church deliberately seek God's presence with an open spirit to experience the close presence of the Holy Spirit in their worship.

---

58. Albrecht, "Worshiping and the Spirit," 239.
59. Albrecht, "Worshiping and the Spirit," 239.

Seeking God's presence with an open spirit is an integral part of Christian worship experience. For, despite worshipers' liturgical services and works during worship, genuine worship remains the work of the Holy Spirit through whom the Triune God manifests his presence among worshipers. Any theology of worship that muffles the sensitivity and openness of worshipers to the directions and desires of the Holy Spirit during worship and blocks their spontaneous response to such directions and desires does a great disservice to authentic Christian liturgy. For flexibility born out of openness to the direction and desire of the Holy Spirit makes an encounter with God in worship palpable. Moreover, worshipers in a Spirit-led church believe that "having the room" to freely express their worship without being "boxed in" by restraining human structures would greatly aid them to really encounter God in worship. In fact, "freedom in worship means that God by the Holy Spirit is free to move in the ways that the Holy Spirit wishes. God is sovereign, yet worshipers can inhibit God's desire for and movements in the service."[60]

Decency and order during worship are necessary and encouraged. However, a Spirit-filled church maintains that the order should synchronize with the work and direction of the Holy Spirit; and that it should accommodate spiritual worship, not impede it.[61] In a Spirit-driven church, worshipers believe that "Jesus is the same yesterday, today, forever, and everywhere; that Jesus still saves, heals, speaks by his Spirit; that by the Spirit he meets men and women wherever they seek him."[62] Hence, preaching, singing, and prayers are expected to be rendered in a manner that they become vehicles to open the worshipers up for the indwelling Spirit of God. For, just as a dynamic faith was provided for people centuries ago during the apostolic and early Christian times through the hearing of the message of God's forgiveness, a redeeming, sanctifying, and healing experience of the presence of the Spirit of God in power are expected to be provided for the people today.

In fact, in a Spirit-animated church where the Holy Spirit is the principal agent of transformation in liturgy, God is not an ambiguous, vague, detached and distant figure but a reality that can be experienced and encountered[63] through the power of God's indwelling presence, the Holy Spirit. When worshipers in a Spirit-filled church read the Bible, they read it with the expectation to encounter God's words speaking directly to their life's situations. Scriptural passages read during liturgical celebrations

60. Albrecht, "Worshiping and the Spirit," 242.
61. Albrecht, "Worshiping and the Spirit," 242.
62. Albrecht, "Worshiping and the Spirit," 244.
63. Pinnock, "Church in the Power," 158.

are, therefore, primarily more of a place of encounter with the divine author than a resource for the identification and embellishment of various doctrines. In fact, these biblical passages are expected not simply to serve the purpose of teaching the readers and audience intellectually but also emotionally. They are anticipated to result into an experiential encounter with God, not just better exegesis; to enable and facilitate an exposure of truth as well as of God.[64] Hence, while the ordo and the lectionary might be helpful in their own way, worshipers in a Spirit-driven church would be careful and flexible not to allow themselves to be boxed in by any fixed readings and prayers that don't speak to the life situations of the worshipers at the moment. The same flexibility allows worshipers to freely and comfortably express various emotions provoked by biblical narratives that speak to their context during worship.

When it comes to the interpretation of the Scripture during liturgy, a Spirit-filled church permits a flexibility that ensures that the human mind does not affect or hinder the work of the Holy Spirit who has been given to animate the church and lead believers into truth.[65] Consequently, various contexts of the worshipers are taken into consideration when interpreting scriptural passages, bearing in mind that such contexts are as significant to the hermeneutical procedure as any exegetical or theological technique.[66] Human agents of worship in a Spirit-animated church, therefore, combine both human preparation and reliance on the empowerment of the Holy Spirit in their preaching or homilies. For the Holy Spirit works both in the study and in the lectern or pulpit.[67] In a Spirit-driven church, emotions in preaching or homily are valued while emotionalism is eschewed. For, while emotion is a sincere and fervent expression of powerful feeling in response to significant truth, emotionalism is virtual or simulated feeling fleetingly indulged as an end in itself, or unnatural, false sentimentalism attracting attention to itself and serving its own goals and ends.[68]

Like preaching or homily, music is a medium through which God invites worshipers during worship to an experiential encounter of him. In a Spirit-motivated church, human agents of worship are, therefore, flexible in their choice and style of liturgical music. While making all necessary human preparations, music directors are challenged at the same time to create room for spontaneity as the Holy Spirit gives the lead. In a Spirit-driven church,

---

64. Warrington, *Pentecostal Theology*, 189.
65. Warrington, *Pentecostal Theology*, 195.
66. Warrington, *Pentecostal Theology*, 199.
67. Leoh, "Pentecostal Preacher," 42.
68. Leoh, "Pentecostal Preacher," 45.

music is the medium through which worshipers express various forms of emotions to God ranging from praise, worship, adoration, thanksgiving, to lamentation, confession of sins, asking for pardon, for protection, deliverance, healing, blessings of all kinds, and so on. Liturgical music is, therefore, more experientially and emotionally oriented than doctrinally based.

Like preaching and music, prayer is another means through which worshipers encounter the Triune God in worship. But it is the Holy Spirit who assists in our prayer because, as Paul says, "in our present weakness we don't know for what to pray, the Spirit himself makes intercession for us with 'inarticulate groanings' (Rom 8:26–27)."[69] Therefore, a Spirit-directed church, is always flexible in her liturgical prayers. Human agents of liturgy in such churches are more spontaneous in the direction of the Holy Spirit who assists us in our prayers. In a Spirit-led church, Mass and set prayers are "prayed" not "said." In other words, the gift of the Holy Spirit in prayer enables worshipers to go in more profoundly, expressively, and deliberately into the spirit and content of the prayers of the Mass and the breviary.[70]

A theology of worship that is not pneumatocentric, and in praxis hinders the role of the Holy Spirit in worship, hampers the playfulness of liturgy and prevents liturgical prayers from becoming a vehicle through which worshipers encounter the redeeming, sanctifying, and healing love of God the Father made manifest in his Son Jesus Christ through the power of the Holy Spirit. In fact, when the Holy Spirit is at the forefront of liturgy enabling experiential encounter with the Triune God, liturgy truly becomes a play of God's people with their God; and liturgical actions would transform the orthodox elements of the Christian liturgy into a Spirit-oriented dynamic of play.

Liturgy in a Spirit-animated church truly paves the way for the "de-clericalization" of liturgical actions and brings about the implementation of the liturgical reforms of Vatican II Council. For liturgical actions in a Spirit-directed church are truly performed together with the people rather than on behalf of them. In a Spirit-driven church, emphasis is not so much on the sacramental rituals as on the overall action that can facilitate an experiential encounter with the Triune God in worship through God's empowering presence, the Holy Spirit. In such churches, liturgy is not "performed"; rather, the whole event "plays" out according to the circumstances of the moment and according to the directions of God's indwelling presence, the Holy Spirit, who animates liturgy and makes encounter between worshipers and the Triune God in worship possible and palpable.

---

69. Fee, *God's Empowering Presence*, 867.

70. Steven, "Spirit in Contemporary Charismatic Worship," 251.

With a Spirit-filled liturgy in a Spirit-driven church, liturgy truly becomes a destructuralizing, flexible, verbal, participation-centered, and Spirit-oriented "open arrangement" of worship, prayer, and praise that contrast with the structures of Anglo-European liturgy.

Liturgy in a Spirit-animated church is more of a free and spontaneous response to a palpable encounter with God rather than a structure made available for the possibility of that encounter.[71] The style of worship of the charismatic renewal and Pentecostalism within the Nigerian context, no doubt, shows that they are indeed groups and churches animated and driven by the Spirit. Hence, more than anything else, the pneumatocentric ecclesiology and liturgy of charismatics and Pentecostals within the Nigerian context is enabling the Catholic Church in Nigeria to realize the potentials of a Spirit-animated church. Being an essential part of the changing face of the Nigerian Catholic Church, the charismatic renewal in the Catholic Church in Nigeria is enabling her to realize the potentials of a Spirit-animated church by its pneumatocentric liturgy. Through the charismatic renewal in her midst, the Nigerian Catholic Church has intentionally or unintentionally commenced the renewal of her liturgy to be truly a liturgy of a Spirit-animated church. She has started to respond to the spirit-filled ritual, fête, passion *catioris*, and transformation of Nigerian traditional religious worshipers with lively, Spirit-animated and spontaneous spiritual worship.[72]

With the Catholic charismatic renewal as a crucial part of the changing face of the Nigerian Catholic Church, the Catholic Church in Nigeria has begun wittingly or unwittingly to listen to the voice from the margins of Christianity, the home of renewal, inspiring and enabling her to realize the potentials of a Spirit-filled church by the renewal of her pneumatology, ecclesiology, and liturgy, which has significantly reduced the rate of losing her members to Pentecostal churches. It has also, considerably, minimized the paying of double allegiance by her members, one to their Catholic faith and the other to their traditional religious beliefs and practices and or to Pentecostal faith and praxis.

There is no doubt that the charismatic and Pentecostal experiential encounter and praxis-oriented theology, particularly within the Nigerian context, is enabling the Nigerian Catholic Church to realize the potentials of a Spirit-directed church through the renewal of her pneumatology, ecclesiology, and liturgy as argued in this chapter. That, however, does not mean that the Nigerian charismatic and Pentecostal theology and praxis

---

71. Vondey, *Beyond Pentecostalism*, 128.
72. Bamigboye, "Pentecostalism and Cross-Cultural Mission," 173.

are in no need of renewal. The next section points out some of the areas where renewal is needed.

The Charismatic and Pentecostal Theology and Praxis in Need of Some Renewal

It is the contention of this writer that no institution or organization where human beings are involved is so perfect that it does not need constant renewal. Charismatic renewal and Pentecostalism are no exceptions. Based on this, the work acknowledges that charismatic renewal and Pentecostalism, especially within the Nigerian context, need to renew some aspects of their theologies and praxes. This section briefly focuses on that.

No doubt, the ecclesiology and liturgy of charismatics and Pentecostals are rightly pneumatocentric. However, the prayer and devotion of charismatic renewal and Pentecostalism should not center only on one person of the Trinity but should rather reflect the trinitarian framework of every experience of the Holy Spirit.[73]

Love is one of the fruits of the Holy Spirit. The conspicuous segregation and discrimination against those who do not belong to their groups and churches by most charismatic groups and Pentecostal churches is a negation of true Christian love. Charismatics and Pentecostals should, therefore, be sensitive to others and share with "the other" in solidarity which resonates with "Paul's theme that the fruit of the Spirit is love."[74]

Members of charismatic renewal and Pentecostalism, particularly within the Nigerian culture, need to complement emotions or feelings with intellectual content, teaching, and concern in their dealings with the Holy Spirit and the appeal to "present experience" and "new things."[75] Indeed, "to become *mired in the past without willingness to change can on occasion* be a traditionalist failure" just as to always "look *for what is new and 'exciting' can on occasion* become the Renewal Movement's mistake of *denigrating the past.*"[76]

No doubt, it is the Holy Spirit that gives a gift of healing, but not with a divided dualism of "natural" and "supernatural." Unfortunately, in Nigerian charismatic renewal and Pentecostalism, this divided dualism has led many charismatics and Pentecostals to often neglect the importance of taking a sick person first to the hospital while praying for him or her

---

73. Thiselton, *Holy Spirit*, 483.
74. Thiselton, *Holy Spirit*, 484.
75. Thiselton, *Holy Spirit*, 484–86.
76. Thiselton, *Holy Spirit*, 484–86.

at the same time. Instead, they take the person to a prayer house and only go to the hospital when often it is too late. It is necessary therefore, to renew "*the 'heightened dualism,' the frequent exaggerated claims, and the 'paranoid' preoccupation with demonic forces* which too often arises within the Renewal Movement."[77]

Health and prosperity preaching in a poverty-stricken society, no doubt, could be a theology of hope as indeed it has been reinterpreted that those who indulge in this are crafting a theology of hope to deal with the existential problems of the people. However, the exaggerated flamboyant lifestyle of some of these preachers which greatly contrast with the real life experiences of their members is of great concern. Some of them have private jets; they and their family members go to the best and most expensive hospitals in the world and their children go to the best and most affluent schools while most of their members could barely afford a decent meal a day and could not afford basic education and healthcare. When sick, some of them resort only to prayer and use of oil and other materials blessed by their pastors. Consequently, some of them die of illnesses that could have been taken care of in the hospital while still praying and using their blessed materials. This must be urgently corrected.

Pentecostals and exponents of charismatic renewal need to check on exaggerated dependency on prophecy as God is believed to also work through processes of training, reflection, and thought, and not only by "spontaneous" intuition and feeling.[78] In fact, the popularization of demonology—the Devil, particularly by the Nigerian charismatics and Pentecostals is of great concern; and the practice needs urgent renewal especially, as it has wrongly led to the demonization of West African deities and ancestors.[79] Painfully, this demonization is unfortunately being promoted by most Nigerian and indeed African movie industries. Some traditionalists rightly decry this and warn movie industries to desist from this as reported by Nwafor Sunday.[80]

The exaggerated beating of people alleged to be witches and or those alleged to be possessed by evil spirits during deliverance, and the rate of cutting down trees and destroying places and things suspected to be anchorages of evil forces, are of immense concern. These people, things, and places can simply be exorcized if need be without such exaggeration and destructions.

---

77. Thiselton, *Holy Spirit*, 488.
78. Thiselton, *Holy Spirit*, 489.
79. Meyer, *Translating the Devil*, 1999.
80. Nwafor, "Stop Demonizing," 2019.

Members of charismatic renewal and Pentecostalism should realize that all the scriptural passages that talk of baptism in the Spirit show that it is addressed to all Christians and "should never become the monopoly of an 'elite'"[81] in the same manner that many Pentecostals are no longer eager "to make tongues 'initial evidence' of baptism in the Spirit."[82] Pentecostals should listen to those Pentecostal scholars who maintain that baptism in the Spirit is not subsequent to conversion-initiation as demonstrated in chapter 1.

In a community or group where the Paraclete is the sole guide and instructor, divisions are impossible to control as each part will continue to claim to be in the truth having been instructed and guided by the Holy Spirit. Charismatics and Pentecostals should therefore learn from the Johannine community as laid down in the fourth Gospel and the Johannine epistles.[83]

They should check the heightened, exaggerated, and false prophetic visions and messages that have pitched so many family members against each other, often creating deadly, destructive, and irreparable division in the family. That said, this work maintains that charismatic renewal and Pentecostalism, especially within the Nigerian milieu, is enabling and inspiring the Catholic Church in Nigeria to realize the potentials of a Spirit-driven church. Through the Catholic charismatic renewal which, no doubt, is an important part of her altering face, she has knowingly or unknowingly initiated the renewal of her pneumatological, ecclesiological, and liturgical doctrines and practices to truly reflect a pneumatology, ecclesiology, and liturgy of a Spirit-animated church.

Conclusion

This last chapter used Wolfgang Vondey as a template to present charismatic renewal and Pentecostalism particularly within the Nigerian context as belonging to the margins of Christianity and therefore, the home of renewal. It showed that the charismatic and Pentecostal pneumatology, ecclesiology, and liturgy that are pneumatocenftric make them truly Spirit-animated, Spirit-filled, and Spirit-driven groups and churches. It maintained that, despite the ecclesiological and liturgical reforms of Vatican II Council, the ecclesiology and liturgy of the Catholic Church in general remained essentially Christocentric in character, making it difficult for the Catholic Church to fully realize the potentials of a Spirit-filled church. Hence, it averred that despite some exaggerations and abuses noted on the

---

81. Thiselton, *Holy Spirit*, 491.
82. Thiselton, *Holy Spirit*, 491.
83. Brown, *Churches the Apostles Left Behind*, 66.

part of the Nigerian charismatic renewal and Pentecostalism, the Movements are inspiring and enabling the Nigerian Catholic Church to realize the potentials of a Spirit-directed church. This is so because the charismatic renewal in the Catholic Church in Nigeria is an indispensable part of the changing face of the Nigerian Catholic Church. Through it, the Catholic Church in Nigeria has wittingly or unwittingly begun the renewal of her pneumatological, ecclesiological, and liturgical doctrines and praxes in harmony with those of a Spirit-directed church.

Conclusion and Recommendations

THIS WORK EXAMINED THE charismatic and Pentecostal experiential encounter and praxis-oriented theology especially as it played out in their pneumatological, ecclesiological, and liturgical beliefs and praxes, particularly within the Nigerian context. It showed that their theology and praxes resonate with the Nigerian worldview and, hence, reflect a continuity with the Nigerian traditional religious beliefs and practices. It maintained that the charismatic renewal in the Nigerian Catholic Church is an essential part of the changing face of the Catholic Church in Nigeria. It used Wolfgang Vondey as a template to present charismatic renewal and Pentecostalism as belonging to the margins of Christianity and therefore, the home of renewal. It also maintained that in Nigerian Christianity, it is through the Holy Spirit that God's healing, loving, and liberating hand is best experienced. Above all it showed that the charismatic and Pentecostal pneumatology, ecclesiology, and liturgy that are pneumatocentric make them truly Spirit-animated, Spirit-filled, and Spirit-driven groups and churches. Hence, it averred that charismatic renewal and Pentecostalism within the Nigerian context are inspiring and enabling the Nigerian Catholic Church to realize the potentials of a Spirit-directed church through the renewal of her pneumatological, ecclesiological, and liturgical doctrines and praxes. It observed that although Vatican II Council reformed the ecclesiology and liturgy of the Catholic Church, they remained Christocentric in theory and praxis, making it difficult if not impossible for the Catholic Church in general to realize the potentials of a Spirit-driven church.

The work recognized that the charismatic and Pentecostal theology and praxis especially within the Nigerian environment are not perfect and, therefore, need some renewal themselves. It pointed out some aspects of their theology and praxis that need renewal with emphasis on the heightened dualism and "paranoid" preoccupation with demonic forces that have led to a wrongful demonization of Nigerian and, in fact, West African deities and ancestors; and the heightened and exaggerated prophetic visions and messages that are causing irreparable hatred and division in many families in Nigeria and beyond. Despite this inadequacy, the work maintained that the pneumatology, ecclesiology, and theology of worship of the charismatic renewal and Pentecostalism, particularly within the Nigerian context, are enabling and inspiring the Catholic Church in Nigeria to realize the potentials of a Spirit-led church. It showed that this is happening because the charismatic renewal in the Nigerian Catholic Church is a vital part of the changing face of the Catholic Church in Nigeria. Through it, the Nigerian Catholic Church has consciously or unconsciously initiated the renewal of her pneumatological, ecclesiological, and liturgical beliefs and practices in accord with those of a Spirit-animated church.

Let me conclude by making the following recommendations to the Nigerian Catholic Church.

There is a saying that you don't throw away the baby with the bathwater. It is undoubtedly true that the Nigerian charismatic renewal and Pentecostalism have abused and exaggerated some of their pneumatological practices as pointed out above. However, it doesn't remove the fact that they can't be ignored when it comes to realizing the potentials of a Spirit-directed church. Moreover, it cannot be denied that the charismatic renewal within the Nigerian Catholic Church is a vibrant and essential part of the changing face of the Catholic Church in Nigeria. Through the theology and praxis of the charismatic renewal in the Nigerian Catholic Church, therefore, the Catholic Church in Nigeria has wittingly or unwittingly begun the process of renewal of her pneumatological, ecclesiological, and liturgical practices.

I, therefore, recommend that the Catholic Church in Nigeria takes time to objectively study the pneumatology, ecclesiology, and worship of the charismatic renewal and Pentecostalism in Nigeria. This will help her to know what to discard and what to take to add to her own in her bid to fully realize the potentials of a Spirit-animated church. Learning from them does not diminish or belittle her in any way. Rather, it's a sign of greatness for it takes humility and maturity to do so. She should allow the renewal which the charismatic renewal has initiated in her midst to permeate every aspect of her life and enable her to fully realize the potentials of a Spirit-animated church.

The requisite role of the deities, ancestors, and spirits in Nigerian traditional religious worldview and the indispensable role of the Holy Spirit in the church and in the life of individual members of the church indicate that the Holy Spirit is the "Oga kwatakwata" in Nigerian Christianity. Therefore, I recommend that the Catholic Church in Nigeria fully expands what an important part of her changing face is already doing and place the Holy Spirit at the vanguard of her theology not just in theory but in praxis. This should be taken seriously, especially in her seminaries and religious institutes where future clergy and religious workers are trained.

Vatican II Council has directed in its ecclesiological and liturgical reforms that the church is the people of God and that there should be full participation of all the faithful during liturgy. I recommend that the Nigerian Catholic Church establishes that while the clergy preside and lead at liturgical services, they should pay heed to meaningful and useful interjections from the congregation as the Holy Spirit can and indeed does speak and lead through anyone, for the Spirit has been poured on all flesh. The Spirit is not a spirit of confusion, hence conflicting voices coming from the congregation should not only be ignored but stopped as soon as they come up.

Both liturgical reform of Vatican II Council and the bishops of Africa and Madagascar, as noted earlier, directed and recommended that liturgical expressions and gestures should be home-rooted if they must achieve the desired goal. I, therefore, recommend that while free to borrow what is good from other cultures, the Nigerian Catholic Church should insist that the gestures, languages, and cryptograms used in liturgical celebrations are rooted in the cultures of the worshiping communities.

Unlike in Western, especially the Greco-Roman, religious worldview, there is no fight for supremacy among divine beings in Nigerian traditional religious worldview. If the Nigerian Catholic Church should truly comprehend and appreciate the relational God-Christ-Spirit in Christian trinitarian theology, I recommend that she takes seriously the relationality among the multiple divine beings in the Nigerian worldview, which rules out any fight for supremacy among these divine beings. This would help her to accord the Spirit his rightful place in her ecclesiology and liturgy and consequently enable her to significantly realize the potentials of a Spirit-animated church.

The Scripture says that Jesus came that they might have life and have it in abundance (John 10:10). Paul made it clear that through the Holy Spirit God's people enjoy the firstfruit, the down payment, and the foretaste of the kingdom here on earth while waiting for its fullness in the eschaton (Ephe 1:14; Rom 8:23). To understand the true nature and importance of salvation that Jesus came to bring and the role of the Holy Spirit in this salvific work, I recommend that the Nigerian Catholic Church takes seriously the concept of soteriology in Nigerian religious worldview.

The Nigerian Catholic Church should grant the clergy and their liturgical team permission and the freedom to replace the readings of the day with more appropriate ones that speak better to the contextual and existential situations of the congregation. While using liturgical prayer texts, they should be free to spontaneously add prayers based on the context as the Spirit gives the lead. Music directors should be free to instinctively intone songs that naturally fit into the mood of the worshipers. These would help to facilitate an experiential and palpable encounter between the worshipers and the Triune God through God's empowering presence, the Holy Spirit. Making such an encounter realizable is, indeed, what is expected of a Spirit-animated, Spirit-directed, and Spirit-filled church like the Nigerian Catholic Church.

Bibliography

Achunike, Hilary C. *The Influence of Pentecostalism on Catholic Priests and Seminarians in Nigeria*. Onitsha: Africana, 2004.

Adeboye, Olufunke. "'Arrowhead' of Nigerian Pentecostalism: The Redeemed Christian Church of God, 1952-2005." *Pneuma* 29.1 (2007) 24–58.

Adewale, Sola. "The Charismatic Movement and Pentecostalism." In *Tradition and Compromises: Essays on the Challenge of Pentecostalism*, edited by Anthony Akinwole and Joseph Kenny, 37–60. Lagos: Dominican, 2004.

Adeyemo, Tokunboh. *Salvation in African Tradition*. Nairobi: Evangel, 1979.

Ahortor, Godson. "Salvation and Morality: The Interconnections in African Thought." *European Scientific Journal* 12.26 (2016) 220–34.

Akinwole, Anthony. "Christianity without Memory: An Evaluation of Pentecostalism in Response to Emeka Nwosuh." In *Tradition and Compromises: Essays on the Challenge of Pentecostalism*, edited by Anthony Akinwole and Joseph Kenny, 111–23. Lagos: Dominican, 2004.

Albrecht, Daniel E. "An Anatomy of Worship: A Pentecostal Analysis." In *The Spirit and Spirituality: Essays in Honor of Russell P. Spittler*, edited by Wonsuk Ma and Robert P. Menzies, 70–82. London: T. & T. Clark, 2004.

———. *Rites in the Spirit: A Ritual Approach to Pentecostal/Charismatic Spirituality*. Sheffield: Sheffield Academic, 1999.

———. "Worshiping and the Spirit: Transmuting Liturgy Pentecostally." In *The Spirit in Worship, Worship in Spirit*, edited by Teresa Berger and Bryan D. Spinks, 223–44. Collegeville: Liturgical, 2009.

Alexander, Kimberly E. "The Pentecostal Healing Community." In *Toward a Pentecostal Ecclesiology: The Church and the Fivefold Gospel*, edited by John Christopher Thomas, 183–206. Cleveland: CPT, 2010.

Alexander, Kimberly E. "'Singing Heavenly Music': R. Hollis Gause's Theology of Worship and Pentecostal Experience." In *Toward a Pentecostal Theology of Worship*, edited by Lee Roy Martin. Cleveland: CPT, 2016.

Allam, Sylvester Onmoke. "Pentecostalism in Liturgical Celebration: A Phenomenal Disorder." In *Pentecostalism: Proceedings of the National Seminaries Committee Workshop Held at St. Augustine's Major Seminary, Jos, Plateau State, 4th–7th May, 2004*, edited by Charles M Hammawa, 97–109. Jos: Fab, 2005.

Althouse, Peter. "Ascension—Pentecost—Eschatology: A Theological Framework for Pentecostal Ecclesiology." In *Toward a Pentecostal Ecclesiology: The Church and the Fivefold Gospel*, edited by John Christopher Thomas, 225–47. Cleveland: CPT, 2010.

———. "Towards a Pentecostal Ecclesiology: Participation in the Missional Life of the Triune God." *Journal of Pentecostal Theology* 18.2 (2009) 230–45.

Aluede, Charles O. "Music Therapy in Traditional African Societies: Origin, Basis and Application in Nigeria." *Journal of Human Ecology* 20.1 (2006) 31–35.

Amanze, James. *African Christianity in Botswana: The Case of African Independent Churches*. Gweru: Mambo, 2000.

Anderson, Allan H. *An Introduction to Pentecostalism*. Cambridge: Cambridge University Press, 2004.

———. "Pentecostal Pneumatology and African Power Concepts: Continuity or Change?" *Missionalia* 1.19 (1990) 65–74.

Anderson, Gordon L. "Pentecostals Believe in More Than Tongues." In *Pentecostals from the Inside Out*, edited by Harold B. Smith, 53–64. Scripture, 1990.

Archer, Kenneth J. "The Fivefold Gospel and the Mission of the Church: Ecclesiastical Implications and Opportunities." In *Toward a Pentecostal Theology: The Church and the Fivefold Gospel*, edited by John Christopher Thomas, 7–43. Cleveland: CPT, 2010.

Archer, Melissa L. "Worship in the Book of Revelation." In *Toward a Pentecostal Theology of Worship*, edited by Lee Roy Martin, 113–38. Cleveland: CPT, 2016.

Asamoah-Gyadu, J. Kwabena. "An African Pentecostal on Mission in Eastern Europe: The Church of the 'Embassy of God' in the Ukraine." *Pneuma The Journal of the Society for Pentecostal Studies* 27.2 (2005) 297–21.

Asante, Emmanuel. "The Gospel in Context: An African Perspective." *Interpretation: A Journal of Bible and Theology* 55.4 (2001) 355–66.

Awoniyi, Peter Ropo. "Charismatic Movements Appropriation of Indigenous Spirituality in Nigeria." *Ogbomoso Journal of Theology* 13.2 (2008) 122–35.

Ayegboyin, Deji. "Dressed in Borrowed Robes: The Experience of New Pentecostal Movements in Nigeria." In *Tradition and Compromises: Essays on the Challenge of Pentecostalism*, edited by Anthony Akinwole and Joseph Kenny, 70–89. Lagos: Dominican, 2004.

Ayuk, Ayuk A. "Portrait of a Nigerian Pentecostal Missionary." *Asian Journal of Pentecostal Studies* 8.1 (2005) 117–41.

———. "The Pentecostal Transformation of the Nigerian Church Life." *Asian Journal of Pentecostal Studies* 5.2 (2002) 189–204.

Bamigboye, Ezekiel. "Pentecostalism and Cross-Cultural Mission in the 21st Century Nigeria." *Ogbomoso Journal of Theology* 13.1 (2008) 167–81.

Bartel, LeRoy R. "The Holy Spirit and the Teacher: False Views of the Holy Spirit's Role." In *The Holy Spirit in Christian Education*, edited by Sylvia Lee, 103–16. Springfield: Gospel, 1988.

Beeck, Frans Jozef Van. *God Encountered: A Contemporary Catholic Systematic Theology. Volume One: Understanding the Christian Faith*. Collegeville: Liturgical, 1989.

Bevans, Stephen. "Models of Contextual Theology." *Missiology: An International Review* 13.2 (1985) 185–202.

Boone, Jerome. "Worship and the Torah." In *Toward a Pentecostal Theology of Worship*, 5–26. Cleveland: CPT, 2016.

Bradshaw, Paul F. *The Search for the Origins of Christian Worship: Sources and Methods for the Study of Early Liturgy*. 2nd ed. Oxford: Oxford University Press, 2002.

Brown, Raymond. *The Churches the Apostles Left Behind*. New York: Paulist, 1984.
Burgess, Richard. "Crisis and Renewal: Civil War Revival and the New Pentecostal Churches in Nigeria's Igboland." *Pneuma The Journal of the Society for Pentecostal Studies* 24.2 (2002) 205–24.
Cartledge, Mark J. *Encountering the Spirit: The Charismatic Tradition*. New York: Orbis, 2007.
Castelo, Daniel. "The Improvisational Quality of Ecclessial Holiness." In *Toward a Pentecostal Ecclesiology: The Church and the Fivefold Gospel*, edited by John Christopher Thomas, 87–104. Cleveland: CPT, 2010.
Chan, Simon. "Evidential Glossolalia and the Doctrine of Subsequence." *Asian Journal of Pentecostal Studies* 2.2 (1999) 195–211.
———. "Mother Church: Toward a Pentecostal Ecclesielogy." *Pneuma The Journal of the Society for Pentecostal Studies* 22.2 (2000) 177–208.
Cheung, Tak-Ming. "Understanding of Spirit-Baptism." *Journal of Pentecostal Theology* 4.8 (1998) 115–28.
Congar, Yves. *I Believe in the Holy Spirit*. New York: Seabury, 1983.
Conradie, Ernst M. "Ecumenical Perspectives on Pentecostal Pneumatology." *Missionalia* 43.1 (2015) 63–81.
Cross, Terry L. "A Response to Clark Pinnock's 'Church in the Power of the Holy Spirit.'" *Journal of Pentecostal Theology* 14.2 (2006) 175–82.
———. "The Divine-Human Encounter: Towards a Pentecostal Theology of Experience." *Pneuma* 31 (2009) 3–34.
Danielson, Kelly J. Godoy de, and Robert Danielson. "Pentecostal Music in the Public Square: The Christian Songs and Music of Juan Luis Guerra." *The Asbury Theological Journal* 72.1 (2017) 60–77.
Darko, Daniel K. "What Does It Mean to Be Saved? An African Reading of Ephesians." *Journal of Pentecostal Theology* 1.24 (2015) 44–56.
De Koch, W. J. "The Church as a Redeemed, Un-Redeemed, and Redeeming Community." In *Toward a Pentecostal Ecclesiology: The Church and the Fivefold Gospel*, edited by John Christopher Thomas, 47–68. Cleveland: CPT, 2010.
Dulles, Avery. *Models of the Church*. Garden City: Doubleday, 1974.
Dunn, James D. G. "Baptism in the Spirit: A Response to Pentecostal Scholarship on Luke-Acts." *Journal of Pentecostal Theology* 1.3 (1993) 3–27.
———. *Baptism in the Holy Spirit: A Re-Examination of the New Testament Teaching on the Gift of the Spirit in Relation to Pentecostalism Today*. Philadelphia: Westminster, 1977.
Ejizu, Christopher I. "Cosmological Perspective on Exorcism and Prayer-Healing in Contemporary Nigeria." *Mission Studies* 8.2 (1991) 165–76.
———. "Liminality in the Contemporary Nigerian Christian Religious Experience." *Mission Studies* 4.2 (1987) 4–14.
Ekeke, Emeka C., and Chike A. Ekeopara. "God, Divinities and Spirits in African Traditional Religious Ontology." *American Journal of Social and Management Sciences* 1.2 (2010) 209–18.
"Ekklēsia." https://www.biblestudytools.com/lexicons/greek/nas/ekklesia.html.
Endong, Floribert Patrick Calvain. "Glossolalia in the Nigerian Gospel Music: Aesthetic Feature or Archetype of a Pentecostal Identity?" *International Journal of Art & Humanity Science* 2.2 (2015) 14–20.
Evan-Pritchard, Edward E. *Nuer Religion*. Oxford: Oxford University Press, 1956.
Fee, Gordon D. *God's Empowering Presence: The Holy Spirit in the Letters of Paul*. Grand Rapids: Baker Academic, 2011.

———. *Listening to the Spirit in the Text*. Grand Rapids: Eerdmans, 2000.
Gifford, Paul. "Evil, Witchcraft, and Deliverance in the African Pentecostal Worldview." In *Pentecostal Theology in Africa*, edited by Clifton R. Clarke, 112–31. Eugene, OR: Wipf & Stock, 2014.
Gleeson, Brian. "The Church as Sacrament Revisited: Sign and Source of Encounter with Christ." *Australian EJournal of Theology* 4.1 (2005) 1–13.
Grey, Jacqueline. "The Book of Isaiah and Pentecostal Worship." In *Toward a Pentecostal Theology of Worship*, edited by Lee Roy Martin, 27–46. Cleveland: CPT, 2016.
Griggs, Richard I. "Musical Worship as a Pentecostal Sacrament: Toward a Soteriological Liturgy." Master's thesis, Southeastern University—Lakeland, April 28, 2017. http://firescholars.seu.edu/honors/64.
Guardini, Romano. *The Spirit of the Liturgy*. New York: Herder & Herder, 1998.
Hardouin, Jean. *Acta Conciliorum et Epistolae Decretales ac Constitutiones Summorum Pontificum*. 11 vols. N.p.: Parisiis: Typographia Regia, 1715.
Hock, Klaus. "'Jesus Power—Super-Power!' On the Interface between Christian Fundamentalism and New Religious Movements in Africa." *Mission Studies* 12.1 (1995) 56–70.
Hollenweger, Walter J. "From Azusa Street to the Toronto Phenomenon: Historical Roots of the Pentecostal Movement." In *Pentecostal Movements as an Ecumenical Challenge*, edited by J. Moltmann and K.-J. Kuschel, 3–14. Concilium 3. London: SCM, 1996.
Hughes, Ray H. *Classical Pentecostal Sermon Library*. Cleveland: Pathway, 2011.
Idamoyibo, Atinuke Adenike. "Indigenous Music in a New Role." *Nordic Journal of African Studies* 25.3–4 (2016) 329–48.
Idowu, Bolaji E. *African Traditional Religion: A Definition*. London: SCM, 1973.
Ikenga-Metuh, Emefie. *Comparative Studies of African Traditional Religions*. Onitsha: IMICO, 1987.
Kelly, Aoife. "How Irish Missionaries Fought Fake News and Risked Their Lives to Save Millions from Starvation during Biafran War." *Independent*, May 21, 2018. https://www.independent.ie/entertainment/television/tv-news/how-irish-missionaries-fought-fake-news-and-risked-their-lives-to-save-millions-from-starvation-during-biafran-war-36929802.html.
Isiramen, Celestina Omoso. "Pentecostalism in the Nigerian Society: A Therapy or a Delusion?" In *The New Religious Movement: Pentecostalism in Perspective: Proceedings of the 21st Conference of the Catholic Theological Association of Nigeria*, edited by Amuluche Gre Nnamani, 282–92. Benin City: Ava, 2007.
Izunwa, Maurice. "Inspired by 'Arithmetic': Modern Pentecostalism in Eclectic and Syncretic Perspective." In *The New Religious Movement: Pentecostalism in Perspective: Proceedings of the 21st Conference of the Catholic Theological Association of Nigeria*, edited by Amuluche Greg Nnamani, 166–78. Benin City: Ava, 2007.
Jell-Bahlsen, Sabine. "The Lake Goddess, Uhammiri/Ogbuide: The Female Side of the Universe in Igbo Cosmology." In *African Spirituality: Forms, Meanings, and Expressions*, edited by Jacob Obafemi Kehinde Olupona, 38–53. World Spirituality: An Encyclopedic History of the Religious Quest 3. New York: Crossroad, 2000.
———. *The Water Goddess in Igbo Cosmology: Ogbuide of Oguta Lake*. Trenton: African World, 2008.
Kalu, Ogbu. *African Pentecostalism: An Introduction*. Oxford: Oxford University Press, 2008.

———. "Pentecostal and Charismatic Reshaping of the African Religious Landscape in the 1990s." *Mission Studies* 20.1 (2003) 84–111.
Kärkkäinen, Veli-Matti. "Church as Charismatic Fellowship: Ecclesiological Reflections from the Pentecostal-Roman Catholic Dialogue." *Journal of Pentecostal Theology* 9.1 (2001) 100–121.
———. "Pneumatologies in Systematic Theology." In *Studying Global Pentecostalism: Theories and Methods*, edited by Allan H Anderson et al., 223–43. Berkeley: University of California Press, 2010.
———. "'Truth on Fire': Pentecostal Theology of Mission and the Challenges of a New Millennium." *Asian Journal of Pentecostal Studies* 3.1 (2000) 33–60.
Kittel, Gerhard, and Gerhard Friedrich, eds. *Theological Dictionary of the New Testament*. Abridged. Grand Rapids: Eerdmans, 1985.
Koren, Henry J. *Essays on the Spiritan Charism and on Spiritan History*. Bethel Park, PA: Spiritus, 1990.
Kwenda, Chirevo V. "Affliction and Healing: Salvation in African Religion." *Journal of Theology for Southern Africa* 103 (1999) 1–12.
Land, Steven J. *Pentecostal Spirituality: A Passion for the Kingdom*. Cleveland: CPT, 2010.
Leoh, Vincent. "A Pentecostal Preacher as an Empowered Witness." *Asian Journal of Pentecostal Studies* 9.1 (2006) 35–58.
Lindhardt, Martin. "Pentecostalism and the Encounter with Traditional Religion in Tanzania: Combat, Congruence and Confusion." *PentecoStudies* 16.1 (2017) 35–58.
Ma, Wonsuk. "Pentecostal Worship in Asia: Its Theological Implications and Contributions." *Asian Journal of Pentecostal Studies* 10.1 (2007) 136–52.
———. "'When the Poor Are Fired Up': The Role of Pneumatology in Pentecostal Charismatic Mission." *Transformation* 24.1 (2007) 28–34.
Macchia, Frank D. *Baptized in the Spirit: A Global Pentecostal Theology*. Grand Rapids: Zondervan, 2006.
———. "Groans Too Deep for Words: Towards a Theology of Tongues as Initial Evidence." *Asian Journal of Pentecostal Studies* 1.2 (1998) 149–73.
———. "Pinnock's Pneumatology: A Pentecostal Appreciation." *Journal of Pentecostal Theology* 14.2 (2006) 167–73.
———. "Signs of Grace: Towards a Charismatic Theology of Worship." In *Toward a Pentecostal Theology of Worship*, edited by Lee Roy Martin, 153–64. Cleveland: CPT, 2016.
———. "The Church of the Latter Rain: The Church and Eschatology in Pentecostal Perspective." In *Toward a Pentecostal Ecclesiology: The Church and the Fivefold Gospel*, edited by John Christopher Thomas, 248–58. Cleveland: CPT, 2010.
Magesa, Laurenti. *African Traditional Religion: The Moral Raditions of Abundant Life*. Maryknoll: Orbis, 1997.
———. *Anatomy of Inculturation: Transforming the Church in Africa*. Maryknoll: Orbis, 2004.
———. *What Is Not Sacred? African Spirituality*. Maryknoll: Orbis, 2013.
Martin, Lee Roy. *Pentecostal Hermeneutics: A Reader*. Leiden: Brill, 2013.
———. "The Book of Psalms and Pentecostal Worship." In *Toward a Pentecostal Theology of Worship*, edited by Lee Roy Martin, 47–88. Cleveland: CPT, 2016.
Mbaegbu, Celestine C. "The Effective Power of Music in Africa." *Open Journal of Philosophy* 5 (2015) 176–83.
Mbiti, John S. *African Religions and Philosophy*. London: Heinemann, 1969.

———. *Concepts of God in Africa*. London: SPCK, 1975.
———. *The Prayers of African Religion*. Maryknoll: Orbis, 1975.
McGowan, Andrew B. *Ancient Christian Worship: Early Christian Practices in Social, Historical, and Theological Perspective*. Grand Rapids: Baker Academic, 2014.
Menzies, Robert P. "Acts 2.17-21: A Paradigm for Pentecostal Mission." *Journal of Pentecostal Theology* 2.17 (2008) 200–218.
———. *Empowered for Witness: The Spirit in Luke-Acts*. Sheffield: Sheffield Academic, 1994.
———. "Luke and the Spirit: A Response to James Dunn." *Journal of Pentecostal Theology* 2.4 (1994) 115–38.
———. "The Role of Glossolalia in Luke-Acts." *Asian Journal of Pentecostal Studies* 15.1 (2012) 47–72.
———. "The Spirit of Prophecy, Luke-Acts and Pentecostal Theology: A Response to Max Turner." *Journal of Pentecostal Theology* 7.15 (1999) 49–74.
Meyer, Brigit. *Translating the Devil - Religion and Modernity among the Ewe in Ghana*. Edinburgh: Edinburgh University Press, 1999.
Mignolo, Walter D. *Local Histories/Global Designs: Coloniality, Subaltern Knowledges, and Border Thinking*. Princeton: Princeton University Press, 2000.
Mills, Robert A. "Musical Prayers: Reflections on the African Roots of Pentecostal Music." *Journal of Pentecostal Theology* 6.12 (1998) 109–26.
Mosely, David J. R. S. "'Parables' and 'Polyphony': The Resonance of Music as Witness in the Theology of Karl Barth and Dietrich Bonhoeffer." In *Resonant Witness: Conversations Between Music and Theology*, edited by Jeremy S. Begbie and Steven R. Guthrie, 240–70. Grand Rapids: Eerdmans, 2011.
Mugabe, Henry J. "Salvation from an African Perspective." *Indian Journal of Theology* 36.1 (1994) 31–42.
Nadia, Lovell. *Cord of Blood: Possession and the Making of Voodoo*. London: Pluto, 2002.
Nel, Marius. "A Critical Evaluation of Theological Distinctives of Pentecostal Theology." *Studia Historiae Ecclesiasticae* 1.40 (2014) 291–309.
Ngele, Omaka K., et al. "Sōteria [Salvation] in Christianity and Ụbandu [Wholeness] in Igbo Traditional Religion: Towards a Renewed Understanding." *HTS Teologiese Studies* 73.3 (2017) 1–7.
Ngong, David Tonghou. *The Holy Spirit and Salvation in African Christian Theology : Imagining a More Hopeful Future for Africa*. New York: Lang, 2010.
Niangoran-Bouah, Georges. "The Talking Drum: A Traditional African Instrument of Liturgy and Mediation with the Sacred." In *African Traditional Religions in Contemporary Society*, edited by Jacob K. Olupona, 81–92. Minnesota: Paragon, 1991.
Nnamani, Nnamani Sunday. "The Role of Folk Music in Traditional African Society: The Igbo Experience." *Journal of Modern Education Review* 4.4 (2014) 304–10.
Nwankwo, Elochukwu A., and Anozie Okechkwu. "Igbu-Efi: Indigenous Practice and Politics of After-Death in Igbo Culture Area." *Review of Knowledge Economy* 1.2 (2014) 62–73.
Nwosuh, Emeka. "Pentecostalism: The New Face of a Christian Spirituality." In *Tradition and Compromises: Essays on the Challenge of Pentecostalism*, edited by Anthony Akinwole and Joseph Kenny, 90–110. Lagos: Dominican, 2004.
Obiefuna, Anthony K. *Idolatry in a Century-old Faith*. Enugu: Cecta, 1985.
Obiorah, Godwin K. "Challenges Posed by Pentecostalism to the Catholic Church." In *New Trends in Faith and Practice: From Crisis to Confusion*, edited by Fidelis U. Okafor, 27–52. Nsukka: Afro-Orbis, 2006.

Oduyoye, Mercy Amba. *Hearing and Knowing*. Maryknoll: Orbis, 1986.
Ogbonna, Maduawuchi S. *Okwukwu: Psychological Imperatives of Funeral Rites Among the Igbo of Nigeria*. New York: Triatlantic, 2001.
Ojo, Matthews. "Indigenous Gospel Music and Social Reconstruction in Modern Nigeria." *Missionalia* 26.2 (1988) 210–31.
Ojo, Matthews A. "Deeper Christian Life Ministry: A Case Study of The Charismatic Movements in Western Nigeria." *Journal of Religion in Africa* 18.2 (1988) 141–62.
Okafor, Fabian C. "Some Innovations in the Eucharistic Liturgy: Effect of Pentecostalism." In *New Trends in Faith and Practice: From Crisis to Confusion*, edited by Fidelis U. Okafor, 77–89. Nsukka: Afro-Orbis, 2006.
Okafor, Fidelis U. "New Trends in Faith and Practice: From Crisis to Confusion." In *New Trends in Faith and Practice: From Crisis to Confusion*, edited by Fidelis U. Okafor, 16–26. Nsukka: Afro-Orbis, 2006.
Oladeji, Moses O. "The Charismatic Movement and Church Growth in Nigeria." *Ogbomoso Journal of Theology* 13.2 (2008) 151–65.
Onongha, Kelvin. "African Pentecostalism and Its Relationship to Witchcraft Beliefs and Accusations: Biblical Responses to a Pernicious Problem Confronting the Adventist Church in Africa." *Journal of Adventist Mission Studies* 13.1 (2017) 45–54.
Onuh, Emmanuel. *Pentecostalism: Selling Jesus at a Discount*. Nsukka: Goodwill, 1999.
Onyinah, Opoku. "Pentecostal Healing Communities." In *Toward a Pentecostal Ecclesiology: The Church and the Fivefold Gospel*, edited by John Christopher Thomas, 205–22. Cleveland: CPT, 2010.
Opoku, Kofi Asare. *West African Traditional Religion*. Accra: FEP, 1978.
Paul VI, Pope. *Lumen Gentium*. https://www.vatican.va/archive/hist_councils/ii_vatican_council/documents/vat-ii_const_19641121_lumen-gentium_en.html.
Peterson, David. *Engaging with God: A Biblical Theology of Worship*. Downers Grove: InterVarsity, 1992.
Pinnock, Clark H. "Church in the Power of the Holy Spirit: The Promise of Pentecostal Ecclesiology." *Journal of Pentecostal Theology* 14.2 (2006) 147–65.
Premawardhana, Devaka. *Faith in Flux: Pentecostalism and Mobility in Rural Mosambique*. Philadelphia: University of Pennsylvania Press, 2018.
Prusak, Bernard P. *The Church Unfinished: Ecclesiology Through the Centuries*. New York: Paulist, 2004.
Raboteau, Albert Jordy. *The Invisible Institution: The Origins and Conditions of Black Religions Before Emancipation*. Ann Arbor: University Microfilms, 1975.
Ramírez, Daniel. *Migrating Faith: Pentecostalism in the United States and Mexico in the Twentieth Century*. Chapel Hill: University of North Carolina Press, 2015.
Rodriguez, Dario Andres Lopez. "The Redeeming Community: The God of Life and the Community of Life." In *Toward a Pentecostal Ecclesiology: The Church and the Fivefold Gospel*, edited by John Christopher Thomas, 69–83. Cleveland: CPT, 2010.
Segler, Franklin M., and Randall Bradley. *Christian Worship: Its Theology and Practice*. 3rd ed. Nashville: B&H, 2006.
Shelton, James B. *Mighty in Word & Deed: The Role of the Holy Spirit in Luke-Acts*. Peabody: Hendrickson, 1991.
Shorter, Aylward. *African Christian Theology*. London: Chapman, 1975.
———. "Divine Call and Human Response: Prayer in the Religious Traditions of Africa, I." *The Way* 23.1 (1983) 65–76.
———. "Divine Call and Human Response: Prayer in the Religious Traditions of Africa, II." *The Way* 23.3 (1983) 231–43.

Sommer, Benjamin D. *The Bodies of God and the World of Ancient Israel*. 1st ed. Cambridge: Cambridge University Press, 2011.

Spinks, Bryan D. *The Place of Christ in Liturgical Prayer: Trinity, Christology, and Liturgical Theology*. Collegeville: Liturgical, 2008.

Steven, James. "The Spirit in Contemporary Charismatic Worship." In *The Spirit in Worship, Worship in Spirit*, edited by Teresa Berger and Bryan D. Spinks, 245–59. Collegeville: Liturgical, 2009.

Stronstad, Roger. *The Charismatic Theology of St. Luke*. Grand Rapids: Baker Academic, 2012.

Suenens, Joseph Léon. *A New Pentecost?* New York: Seabury, 1975.

Sunday, Nwafor. "Stop Demonizing Igbo Tradition, Traditionalist Warns Movie Industries." *Vanguard*, August 31, 2019. https://www.vanguardngr.com/2019/08/stop-demonizing-igbo-tradition-traditionalist-warns-movie-industries/.

Thiselton, Anthony C. *The Holy Spirit: In Biblical Teaching, through the Centuries, and Today*. Grand Rapids: Eerdmans, 2013.

Tillich, Paul. *Systematic Theology*. Vol. 3, *Life and Spirit History and the Kingdom of God*. Chicago: The University of Chicago Press, 1963.

Turner, Max. *The Holy Spirit and Spiritual Gifts: In the New Testament Church and Today*. Rev. ed. Grand Rapids: Baker Academic, 2012.

Udok, Ekaette Clement, and Adeola Funmilayo Odunuga. "Music and Pentecostalism: The Nigerian Experience." *Review of Arts and Humanities* 5.1 (2016) 52–60.

Umeh, John A. *After God Is Dibia: Igbo Cosmology, Divination & Sacred Science in Nigeria, Vol. 1*. London: Kamak, 1997.

Uzukwu, Elochukwu Eugene. *God, Spirit, and Human Wholeness: Appropriating Faith and Culture in West African Style*. Eugene, OR: Pickwick, 2012.

———. *Worship as Body Language*. Collegeville: Liturgical, 1997.

Vondey, Wolfgang. *Beyond Pentecostalism: The Crisis of Global Christianity and the Renewal of the Theological Agenda*. Grand Rapids: Eerdmans, 2010.

Wainwright, Geoffery. "Christian Worship: Scriptural Basis and Theological Frame." In *The Oxford History of Christian Worship*, edited by Wainwright Geoffrey and Karen B. Westerfield Tucker, 1–31. Oxford: Oxford University Press, 2006.

———. *Doxology: The Praise of God in Worship, Doctrine, and Life*. Oxford: Oxford University Press, 1980.

Walsh, Vincent M. *A Key to Charismatic Renewal in the Catholic Church*. Holland: Key of David, 1974.

Wariboko, Nimi. *Nigerian Pentecostalism*. Rochester: University of Rochester Press, 2014.

Warrington, Keith. *Pentecostal Theology: A Theology of Encounter*. New York: T. & T. Clark, 2008.

Webber, Robert E. *Worship Old & New*. Rev. ed. Grand Rapids: Zondervan, 1994.

Wenk, Matthias. "The Church as Sanctified Community." In *Toward a Pentecostal Ecclesiology: The Church and the Fivefold Gospel*, edited by John Christopher Thomas, 105–35. Cleveland: CPT, 2010.

Williams, John Rodman. *Renewal Theology: Systematic Theology from a Charismatic Perspective. Three Volumes in One*. Grand Rapids: Zondervan, 1996.

www.ingramcontent.com/pod-product-compliance
Lightning Source LLC
Chambersburg PA
CBHW062017220426
43662CB00010B/1360